IMAGES
of America

CINCINNATI'S GENERAL PROTESTANT ORPHAN HOME

BEECH ACRES PARENTING CENTER

On the Cover: Every year the children visited Aglamesis Brothers, the local ice cream shop, between Christmas and New Year's Day. During this trip, the children would not only get to leave the orphanage, they would also pick out a treat of their choice. (To read more about this trip, see page 68.) (Beech Acres Parenting Center.)

IMAGES
of America

Cincinnati's General Protestant Orphan Home

Beech Acres Parenting Center

Christine Hall and Natasha Rezaian
for Beech Acres Parenting Center

ARCADIA
PUBLISHING

ISBN 978-0-7385-7801-9

Published by Arcadia Publishing
Charleston, South Carolina

Printed in the United States of America

Library of Congress Control Number: 2010928099

For all general information, please contact Arcadia Publishing:
Telephone 843-853-2070
Fax 843-853-0044
E-mail sales@arcadiapublishing.com
For customer service and orders:
Toll-Free 1-888-313-2665

Visit us on the Internet at www.arcadiapublishing.com

For the children—the reason we have and will continue to serve.

Contents

Acknowledgments

Beech Acres Parenting Center has achieved great success throughout its history because of the passion of a diverse group of people with a shared commitment to the well-being of children. Founders, board members, staff, foster parents, donors, volunteers, contractors, and community partners have each shared unique talents that, taken as a whole, have made it possible for Beech Acres to serve many thousands of children, parents, and families throughout its 161 years.

We appreciate those who participated in creating this book by sharing memories, input, records, and photographs. The long list of contributors includes veteran staff members Rick Sorg, Diane Jordan-Grizzard, Pam McKie, Karen Sandker, Chandra Mathews-Smith, and John Wallen. Retired staff members Pat Bernard and Sandi Hannig were great historians, scanners, and photograph archivists. Former board members Penny Wilkinson (1984–1991), Linda Smith (1983–1992, president 1989–1990), and Grant Hesser (1984–1996, president 1992–1993) offered their perspectives on an era of significant change in the history of Beech Acres. Thank you Pat Landen, sister, and Betty Landen, wife, of the late Jake Landen for sharing your memories and photographs of the leadership he provided as board president (1981–1984) during that critical time. Likewise, former board member Dick Whiting (1977–1990, president 1985–1988) and his sister Clair Sharpless offered details of three generations of committed service by the Townsley/Whiting family. Jim and Ellie Berghausen (board member 1993–2004, president 2001–2003) generously offered information about the Guckenberger/Berghausen family legacy, which dates to 1866. Sue and Rick Nielsen and nephew Chip shared stories and photographs of that family's three generations of service, highlighted by patriarch Simon C. Nielsen's leadership in the 1940s.

We also want to thank the group of 30 former residents of the General Protestant Orphan Home who continue to meet monthly after all these years. Without their regular reminiscing and storytelling lunches, many rich details included in the book could not have been written.

Finally, many thanks go to Jim Mason, president and CEO for the past 21 years. Jim generously contributed his passion for the mission, historic perspective, and vision for the future. He continually conveys deep respect and appreciation for each board and staff member, foster parent, donor, volunteer, contractor, and community partner who enabled Beech Acres Parenting Center to thrive in its service to children and families for over 161 years.

It is a privilege to share the incredible history of this iconic Cincinnati institution.

INTRODUCTION

Beech Acres Parenting Center enjoys a long and noble history of caring for Greater Cincinnati's children. For over 161 years, this southwest Ohio not-for-profit organization has provided help and hope for many thousands of children, parents, and families. Across numerous name changes reflecting adaptive strategies, the ultimate purpose of the organization has consistently been to help children grow to become caring, capable, contributing, and connected adults.

The photographs and narratives that follow tell of the amazing journey through three periods of its history, loosely identified as the orphan home, social services, and parenting center eras. Throughout Beech Acres' history, the organization has remained relevant to the needs of children, modifying services as society and family needs changed. Each shift has required bold vision, courage, significant community support, and perseverance. These remarkable qualities have been abundantly provided through the decades, along with tremendous passion and wisdom, from the organization's board and staff, volunteers, and community partners. These thousands of men and women, during their unique times, have been committed to continuously improving and renewing the organization's response to the ever-changing needs of children and families as society has evolved around them.

In 1849, the organization was founded in response to a mid-19th-century cholera epidemic that raced through the region, taking the lives of over 4,000 citizens and leaving many children orphaned. For the first 125 years of the organization's history, as an orphanage, it provided a safe, clean, and secure place for children to grow up who had been displaced by parental death, poverty, or other family disruptions.

Social and cultural changes in the mid-20th century began to dramatically affect children and families. Rates of divorce, child abuse, substance abuse, juvenile delinquency, and school failure rapidly climbed. Despite its secure position as an orphanage, the board of directors knew it needed a new response to a worsening situation for the community's children. For the next 25 years (1975–2000), Beech Acres vigorously shifted from restorative to preventive services in an effort to stem the tide of increasing childhood trauma. It focused on providing traditional child welfare, mental health, and other social services to children and expanded programs to serve their families as well.

Across those first 150 years, board and staff members learned a critical lesson that has shaped the organization's 21st-century response; the lesson is simple common sense: The quality of parenting a child grows up with, whether from a birth parent, adoptive parent, foster parent, grandparent, orphanage housemother, guardian, teacher, or other dedicated adult, is the critical ingredient to that child becoming a capable, contributing, caring, and connected adult.

Today, as a parenting center, the organization still serves children every day, but it does so hand in hand with their parents and other caregivers rather than in isolation. It believes that working with children, parents, and caregivers together is proactive and helps promote sustainable change. The parenting center is designed to provide parents, and other dedicated adults, with the tools they need to shift from rearing children in a typically reactive mode to one that is more intentional and builds on the strengths of each child and parent.

Each era is also notable by an adjustment in the organization's popular name. The founding name of the German General Protestant Orphan Asylum was shortened during World War I to the General Protestant Orphan Home. Most of the orphans and friends of the organization typically simplified that to the "Home" or "GPOH."

Upon purchasing 60 acres of beech trees on the line between Mount Washington and Anderson Township, previously known as the "Beeches" in 1949, the name Beech Acres—The General Protestant Orphan Home was popularized. During the social services era (1975–2000), Beech Acres became more commonly used as references to the orphanage waned.

The shift to focusing its work on the relationship between parents, or other dedicated adults, and their children, seen in the first decade of the 21st century, resulted in a change to its current name, Beech Acres Parenting Center. Throughout this book, we tried to utilize the names, or nicknames, most commonly associated with the specific era under review.

Each era also enjoyed its leaders and champions who are recognized in their proper context. Some families' contributions have transcended several generations and eras. A few will be highlighted as examples of others. The Guckenberger/Berghausen family, the Townsley/Whiting family, and the Nielsen family are icons of Beech Acres—The General Protestant Orphan Home's proud history. The stories of their involvement over generations personify the power of an enduring commitment to a common cause.

The list of leaders and contributors of talent, time, and treasure is so long it would require a book of its own to ensure proper acknowledgement. Of course, a danger of limited space and sometimes inaccurate or missing historical records is that some contributors may not be adequately recognized. While some worthy contributions may not make it to the printed page, rest assured that the children and families who have benefited from the kindness expressed by every contributor have felt gratitude.

All images in this book come from the Beech Acres Parenting Center's archives. We are pleased to share a portion of these photographs and other documents with you. When the founding members got together in 1849 to form a plan to help the community's orphaned children, photographs were still daguerreotypes and needed about 30 minutes of light exposure. It was not until 1851 that the new photographic collodion process was invented, creating the ability to take a photograph in only two or three seconds of exposure. We are proud to share several photographs from that time. The historical perspectives were compiled from the archives and from the written and verbal recollections of former residents, staff, volunteers, and friends of Beech Acres Parenting Center.

As president and CEO of this outstanding organization for over 21 years, it is difficult to communicate the privilege it has been to partner with the incredible mix of board, staff, and community members with whom I have served. Likewise, the thousands of loyal donors and supporters who have steadfastly contributed to our mission for years, many for decades, humble me. To list everyone who has inspired me, challenged me, taught me, supported me, and befriended me is impossible. You know who you are and how much you have enriched my life. More importantly, you know how you have offered help and hope to thousands of children to become capable, caring, contributing, and connected adults. After all, that's what we are all here for, isn't it?

The challenging, yet intensely rewarding, responsibility of rearing the next generation belongs to everyone in our community. We invite you to learn more and get involved.

—Jim Mason, President and CEO

One

Early Years of the Orphanage

By 1840, Cincinnati was the leading processor of pork in America and proudly adopted the nickname, "Porkopolis." Its bustling economy and rapidly growing neighborhoods came at a price. Crowded streets of pork-processing plants, houses, and churches lined man-made canals. Those canals also served as a source of water and transportation, as well as a dump for sewage and industrial waste. Not surprisingly, when a cholera epidemic raced through the region, the city paid a heavy toll. The lives of over 4,000 residents were lost.

The First German Protestant Aid Association of Cincinnati sought to relieve, as far as possible, suffering and want among its members. The care of orphans, whose number grew rapidly during the epidemic, led to an effort to provide for permanent relief. A meeting was called on July 29, 1849, in the North German Church to find a solution. The association's members decided to build an asylum for the orphaned children of their community.

The German General Protestant Orphan Society was established to raise funds for the new orphan home. The committee arranged a benefit concert with the Gesang und Bildungsverein, a literacy and music club, held five days later that raised $119, a significant amount of money at the time.

On October 28, 1849, the committee decided to purchase four acres belonging to Judge Burnet, situated between what was at the time Sycamore Street and Reading Road, in Mount Auburn. Local architect Bringemann & Geissmann drew up a plan for the new building, and construction bids were sought. Several members of the committee volunteered to assist with construction; others donated free materials.

A group of passionate women ran a fundraising fair, which took place at the Masonic Hall in 1849 from December 16 to December 26. An amazing total of $4,181.88 was raised, providing funds for land purchase and construction of the orphans' new home.

On July 21, 1850, the cornerstone was laid. Listed on the stone were names of the society's members, a copy of the articles of incorporation, and various editions of several of Cincinnati's German papers. A year later, on July 20, 1851, the first orphans were admitted to the asylum. They were brothers August and Anthony Stumpe. Louis Eichler was appointed superintendent at an annual salary of $200. By September 7, 1851, there were 10 residents: seven boys and three girls. Rules for admission were approved, primarily limited to full or half orphans (one parent having died with the other unable to care for the child) in the Cincinnati area, including Covington and Newport, Kentucky.

The official dedication of the home was held on September 2, 1851. It is said that the entire German Protestant population of Cincinnati attended the festivities. The German Protestant community had truly stepped up to care for its youngest members.

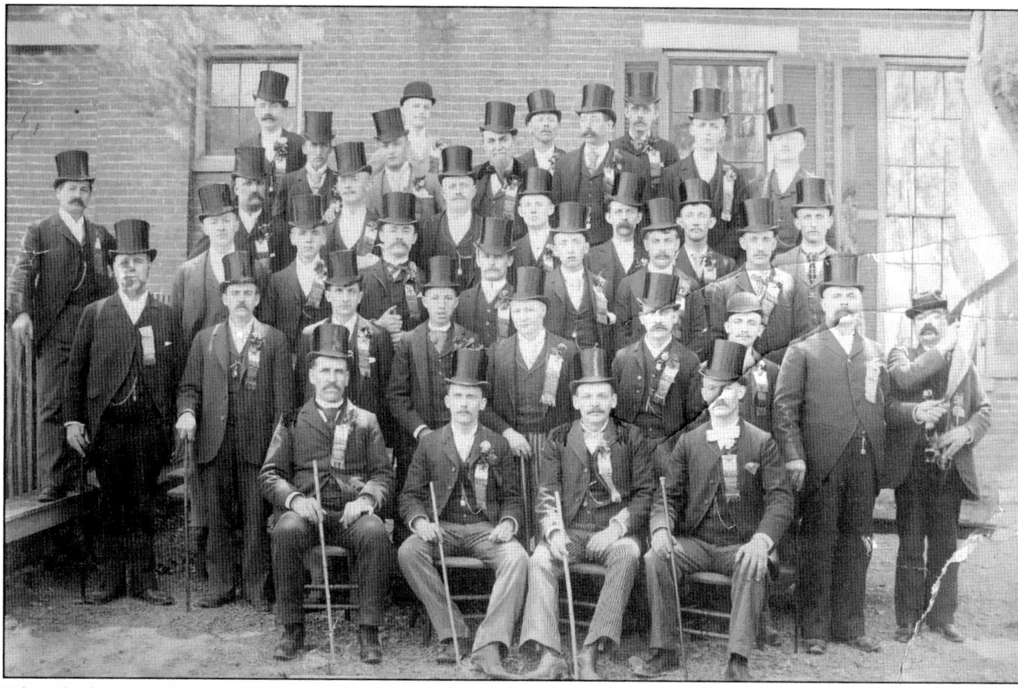

The cholera epidemic of 1849 killed 4,114 persons in Cincinnati; the largest percentage was German. The First German Protestant Aid Association of Cincinnati sought to relieve the suffering and aid the widowed and orphaned. The notion of establishing an orphan home arose upon the death of aid association member William Stumpe and his wife, who left three boys behind.

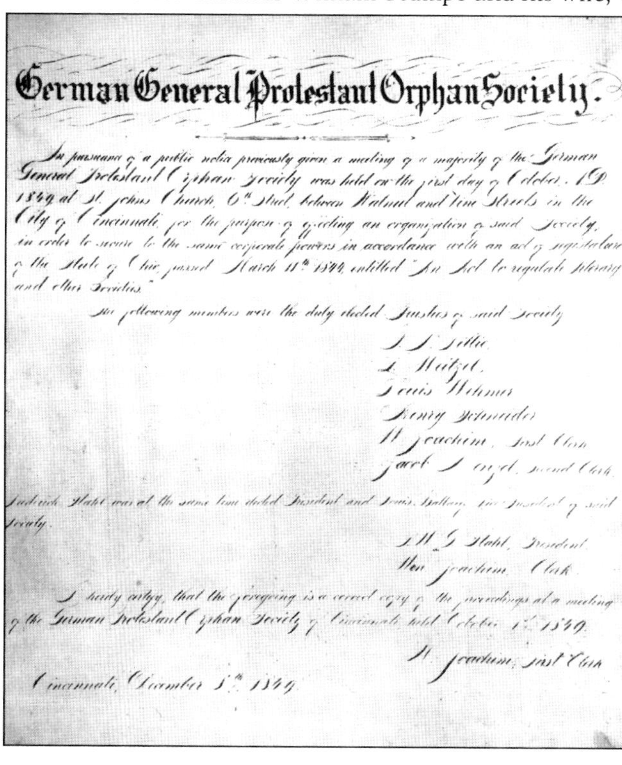

German General Protestant Orphan Society.

In pursuance of a public notice previously given a meeting of a majority of the German General Protestant Orphan Society was held on the first day of October A.D. 1849 at St. Johns Church, 6th Street, between Walnut and Vine Streets in the City of Cincinnati for the purpose of effecting an organization of said Society, in order to secure to the same corporate powers in accordance with an act of legislature of the State of Ohio, passed March 11th 1844, entitled "An Act to regulate literary and other Societies."

The following members were then duly elected Trustees of said Society

J. J. [illegible]
L. Weitzel,
Louis Wehmer
Henry Schneider
W. Joachim, First Clerk
Jacob [illegible] Engel, Second Clerk

Frederick Hahl was at the same time elected President and Louis Ballauf Vice President of said Society.

J. H. G. Hahl, President
Wm Joachim, Clerk

I hereby certify, that the foregoing is a correct copy of the proceedings at a meeting of the German Protestant Orphan Society of Cincinnati held October 1st 1849.

W. Joachim, First Clerk

Cincinnati, December 5th 1849

The vote to erect an orphans' asylum was cast by Cincinnati's German Protestants on Sunday, July 29, 1849, in the North German Church (presently the Third German Protestant congregation). A constitution was adopted and signatures gathered from members supporting the organization. The original articles of incorporation of the German General Protestant Orphan Asylum, dated to October 8, 1849 (shown here), are proudly displayed at Beech Acres Parenting Center today.

Jacob Menzel selected a committee to take on the task of raising funds for the orphan asylum. In 1849, he addressed the German Protestant ministers throughout the city, begging them to speak from the pulpit about the proposed institution and seek donations. Menzel personally delivered letters to various pastors seeking assurance of financial support for the endeavor.

Die folgenden Gründer des Waisen-Vereins
sind ununterbrochen jetzt noch
Active Mitglieder:

Jacob Menzel,
Franz Nolte,
H. G. Rabbe,
H. Schroerlueke,
F. W. Schwenker.

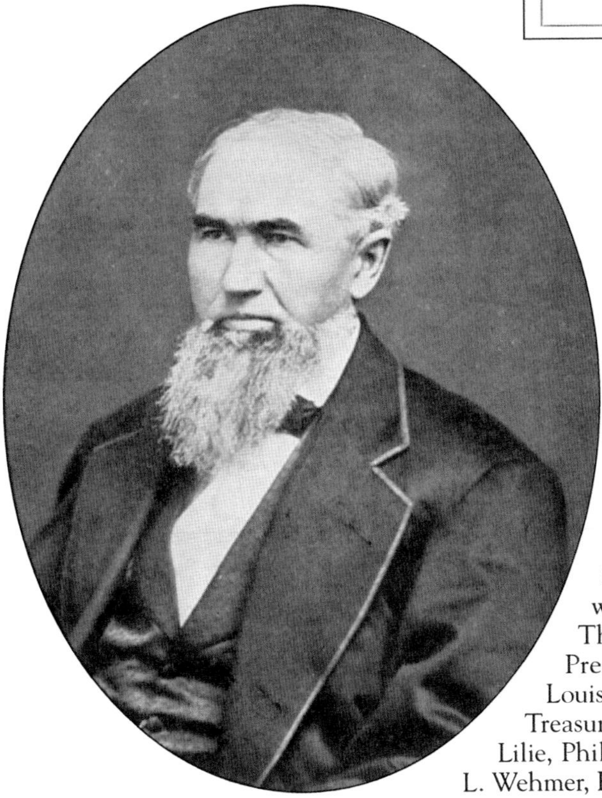

Jacob Menzel, founder of the Orphan Society, was named second secretary when the board of directors was elected. The additional permanent officers included President Frederick Stahl, Vice President Louis Ballauf, First Secretary W. Joachim, and Treasurer John N. Siebern. Trustees were F.H. Lilie, Philip Reiss, Louis Weitzel, St. W. Siebern, L. Wehmer, Frank Nolte, and Henry Snyder.

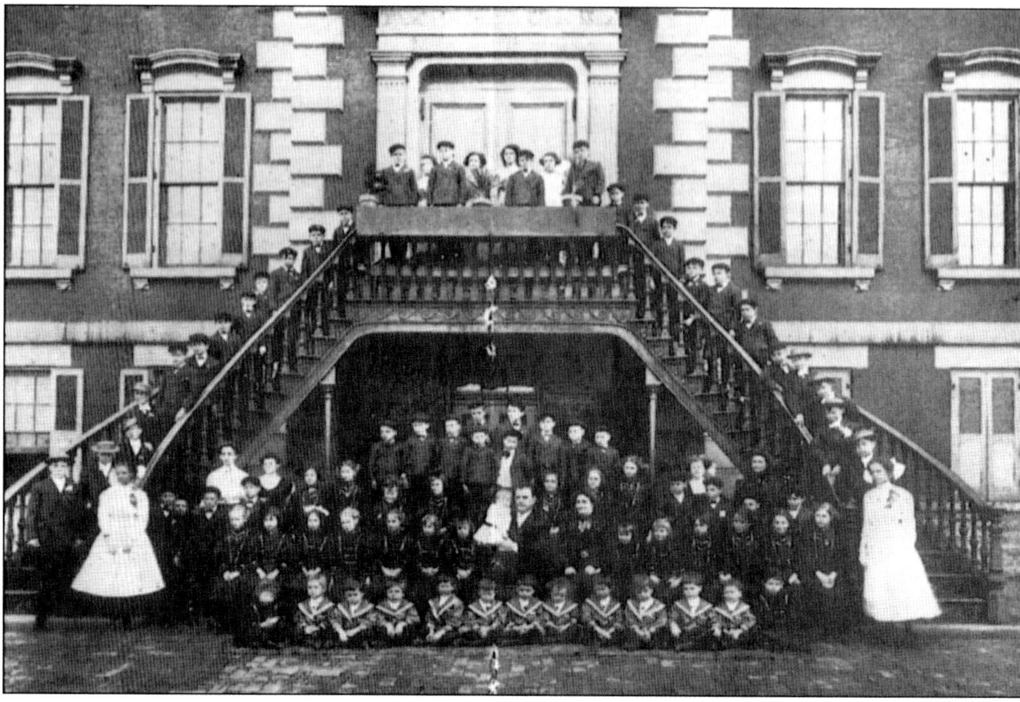

All are baptized
Anytime in the Evening

Recommended by Harry Porfmann

Cincinnati, Ohio. Nov. 17, 1921 No. ____

To The General Protestant Orphans Society
of Cincinnati, Ohio.

Name of child: Earl Henry Brown

Date of birth: March 14, 1916 Place of birth, city: Cinti

County: Hamilton State: Ohio

School record of Child. Has child attended school: Kindergarten Which school did attend: Mt. Auburn

What is conduct report from School: ____

The undersigned ____ hereby makes application for the admission to your Orphanage for the Children hereinafter named and sets forth the following facts in support of this application.

	NAME	AGE	RESIDENCE
Brothers and Sisters	Hazel June Brown	4	529 Channing St.
	Charles J. Brown	3	"
	Mabel Brown	1	"

	FATHER OF CHILD	MOTHER OF CHILD
Full name	Charles H. Brown	Lona (Brandenburg)
Date of birth	May 25, 1890	~~Oct.~~ Nov. 13 1891
Place of birth	Standish, Michigan	Kentucky
Address, if living	529 Channing St.	
Creed	Prot.	Prot.
Occupation	Glazer	
Employer	Neuer Glass Co.	
Income	$25.00 per week	
Intemperate		
Consumptive		
Mentally or physically defective		
Spasms or spells or epilepsy		
Syphilitic		
Sexual pervert		
Sentenced to jail or prision		
Inmate of any other institution—name		
If dead, date		Aug. 11, 1921
Age at death		31 yrs
Cause of death		Appendicitis

All Children accepted are on 60 days probation.

By 1900, most children were registered as "half orphans"—they had one living parent who was unable to provide for them, often due to poverty. Each child was admitted to the orphanage upon acceptance of an application. The application contained information about the child's parents, schooling, and religion. All the children who came to the orphanage were required to get baptized and attend school.

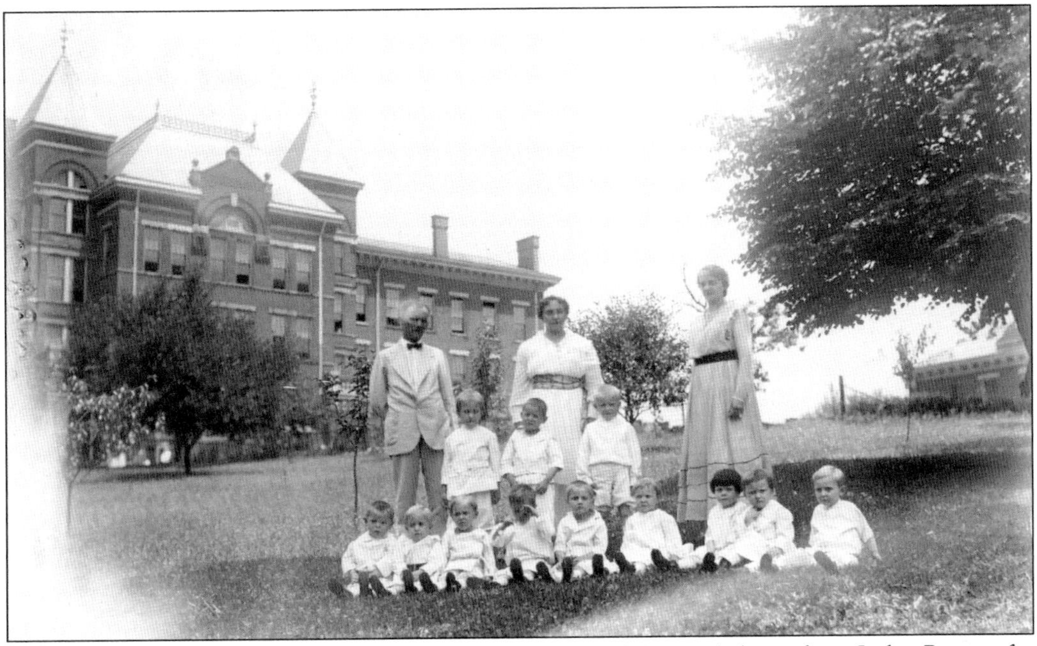

On October 28, 1849, the board purchased four acres in Mount Auburn from Judge Burnet for $4,000, which spanned the modern area between Martin Luther King Drive, Burnet Avenue, East University Avenue, and Highland Avenue. A new brick building was constructed, and the first orphans moved in during 1851. The first floor held sleeping rooms for young children, a schoolroom that also served as an assembly hall, a dining hall, and an apartment for the superintendent. A churning machine was located in the basement so that the orphanage could make its own soap. The second story was divided into separate sleeping rooms for the boys and girls. The third floor housed servants and the 15 housemaids, who were also residents of the institution. The building was sold to Rollman Psychiatric Institute in 1949 and was later demolished in 1977.

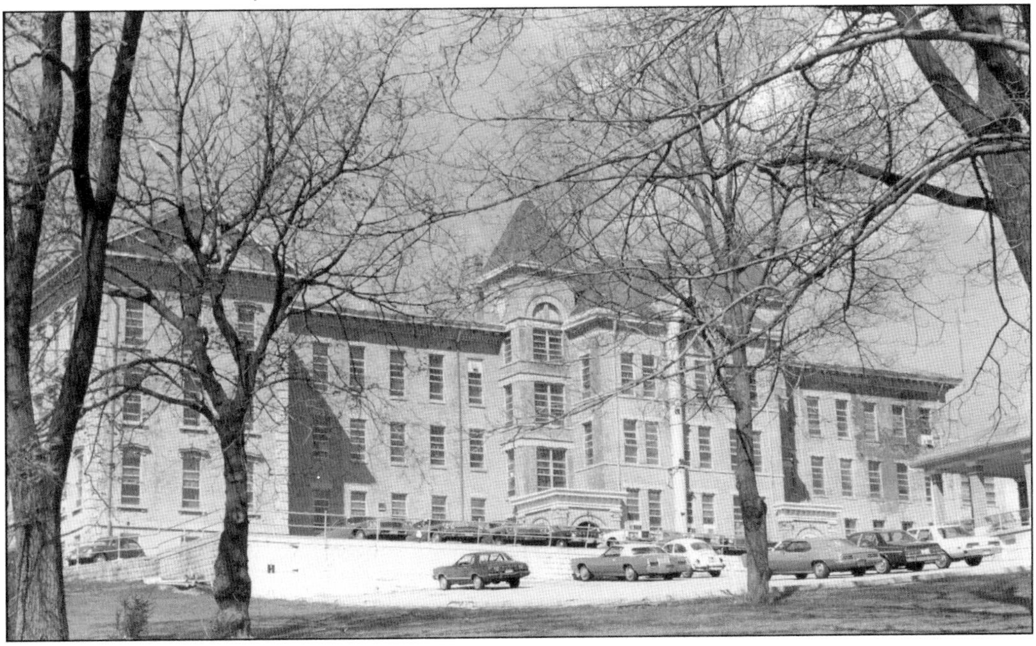

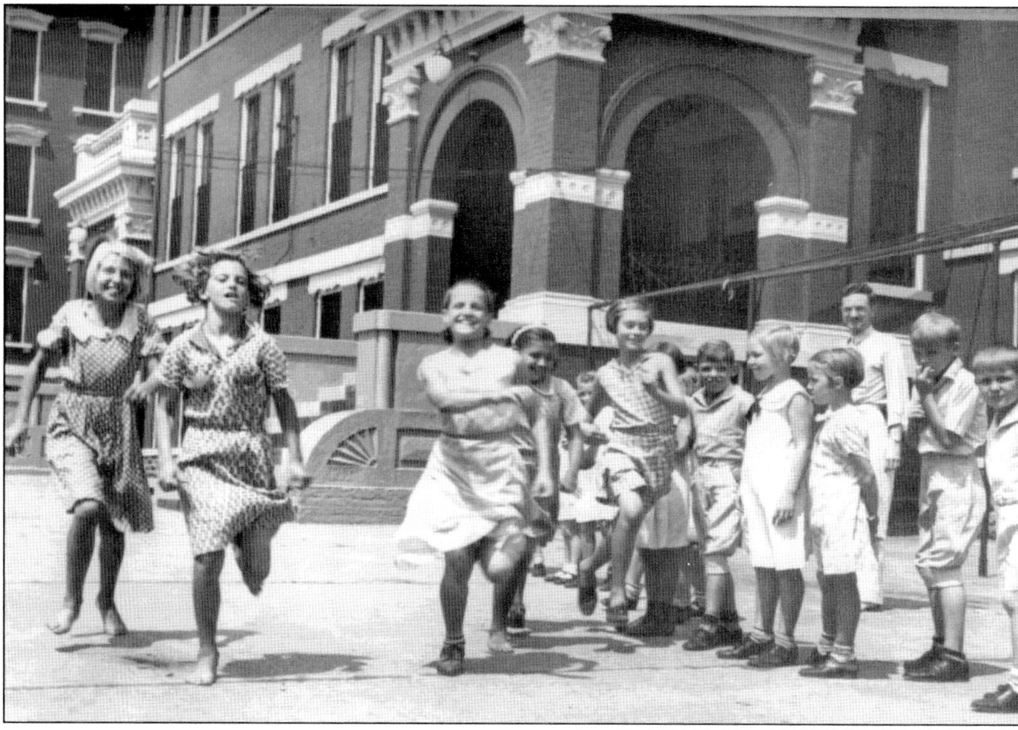

Boys and girls living at the orphanage played outside on separate playgrounds. Boys had a basketball court, baseball field, and an area for running around; girls had the hill in front of the home to play games, including practicing their manners by carrying books on their heads. Former inmates (residents) reported that girls and boys often met secretly along the side of the building for a chat through the bushes. Many sibling groups lived in the home, but they too were segregated by their ages and genders. Siblings were mostly left to connect with each other informally. Periodically, they were permitted more extensive contact.

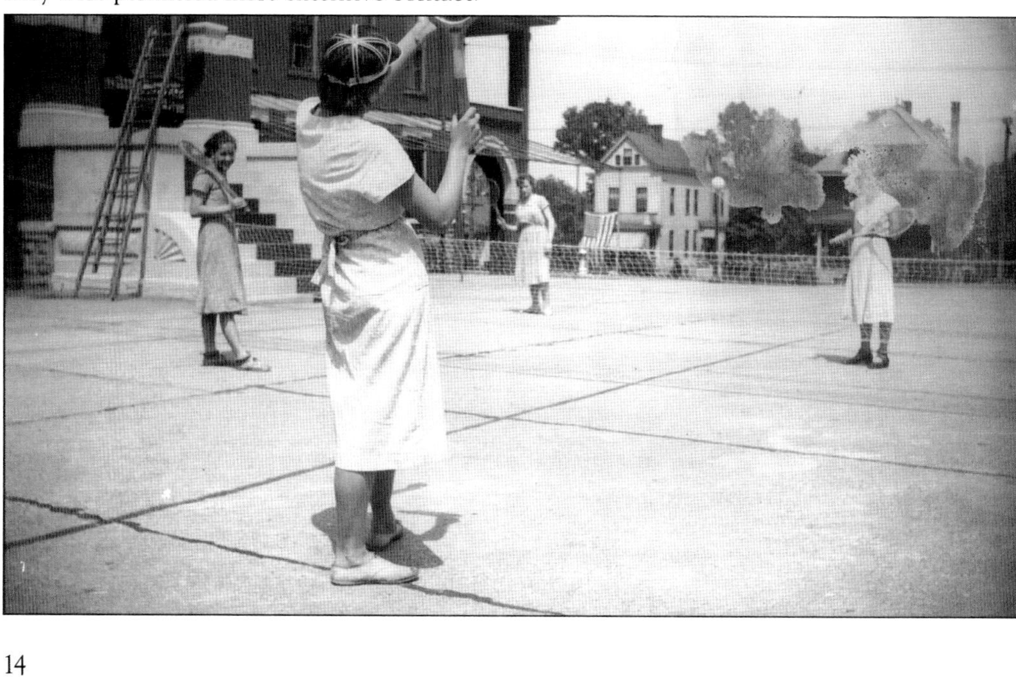

The Home provided order, routine, and consistency for the orphans. Children wore uniforms, lived in quarters based on their ages, and participated in activities with their peers. Routines at the Home ensured a warm place to sleep, eat, get an education, and learn manners. Children rose at 6:00 a.m. to wash and dress for breakfast. All children were required to have a neat appearance and schoolbooks ready before receiving their coffee and roll. (An additional roll served as lunch.) After school, they changed their apparel, brushed their teeth, and prepared for an early supper of soup, meat, and vegetables. Wednesday and Sunday featured a roast or homemade sausage. The children then tended to their schoolwork and cleaned their quarters. A bedtime ritual followed a snack of mostly bread and tea.

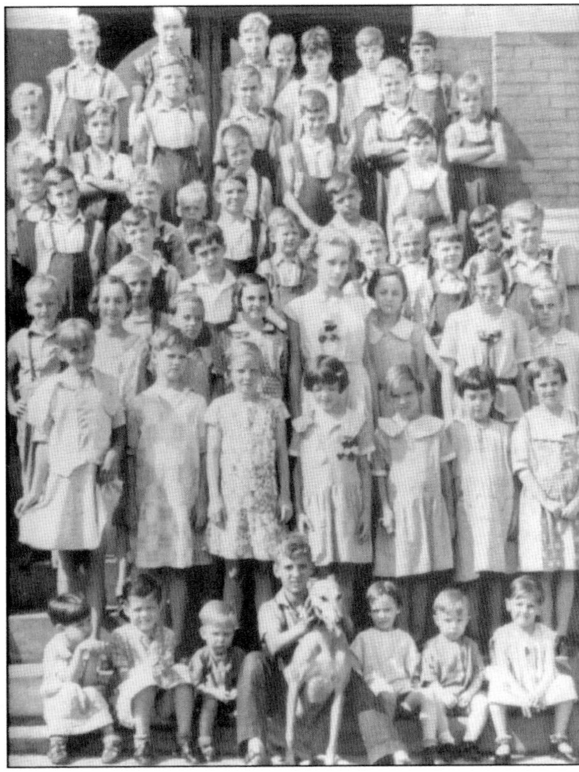

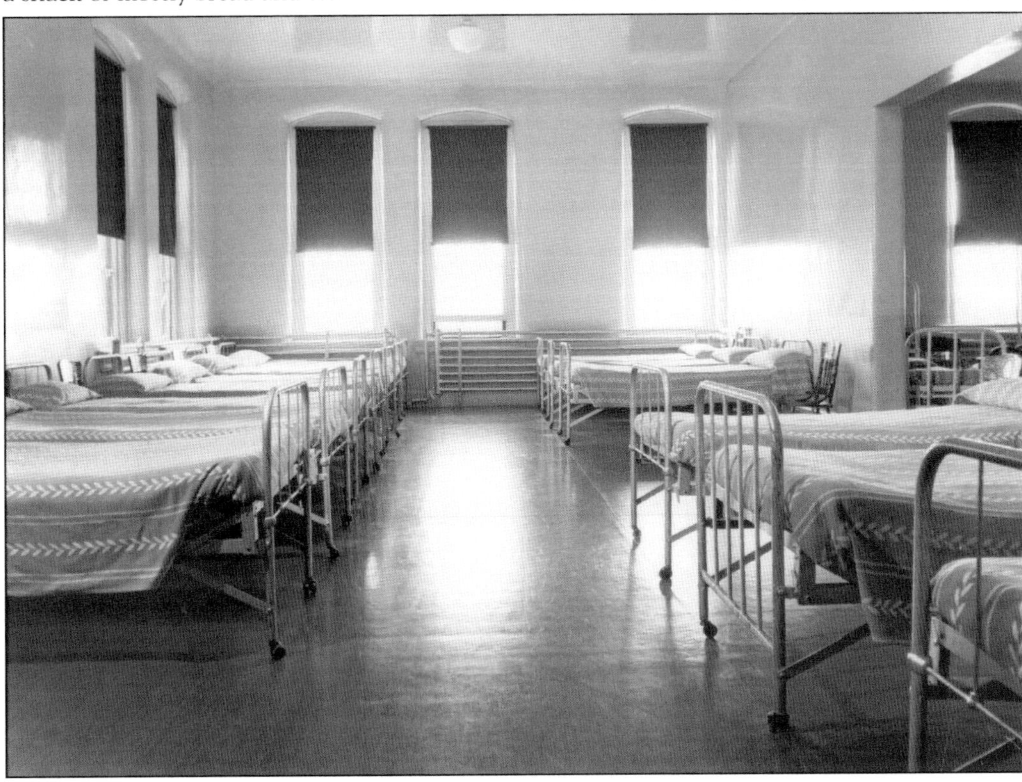

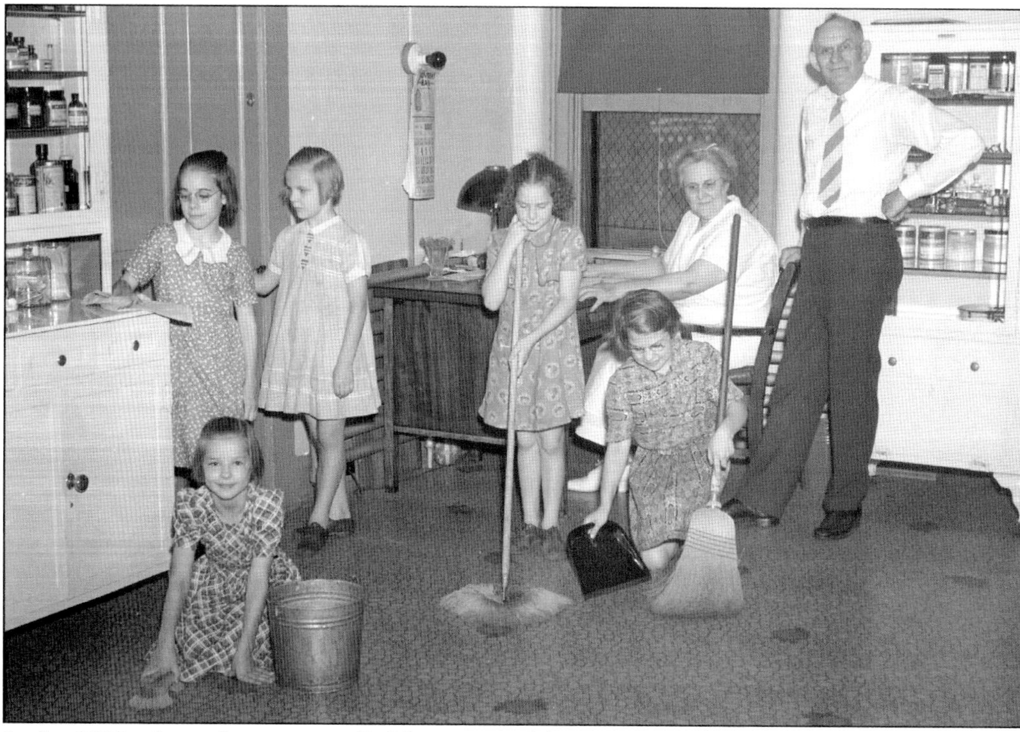

In the 1800s, the orphans were called "inmates" of the Home. Inmates were required to help with chores. The laundry room, located in the basement, is what several young ladies called "home" more than the upstairs residence halls. Inmates served as full-time staff when they reached their teens, assisting with house duties that gave them transferable life skills once they left. At the time, very few women attended school after their teenage years, so teaching residents domestic skills prepared them for life outside the Home.

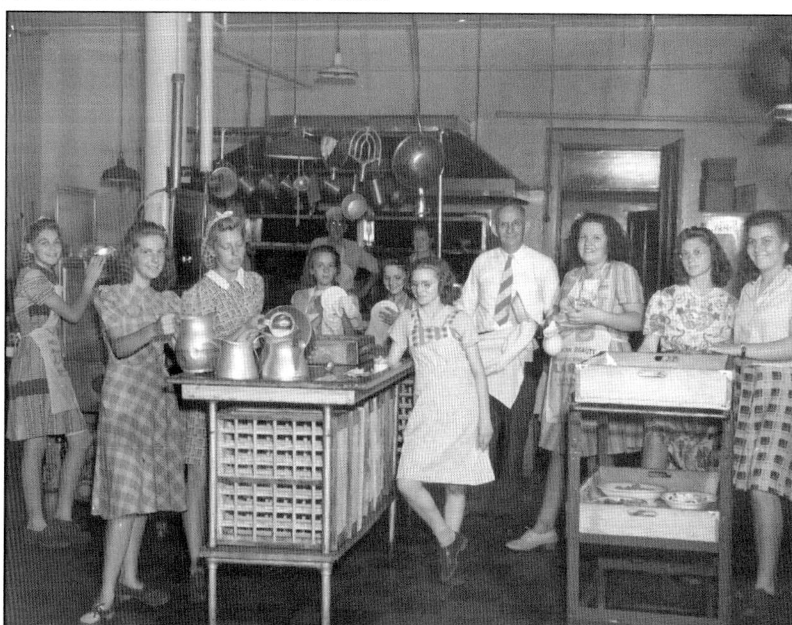

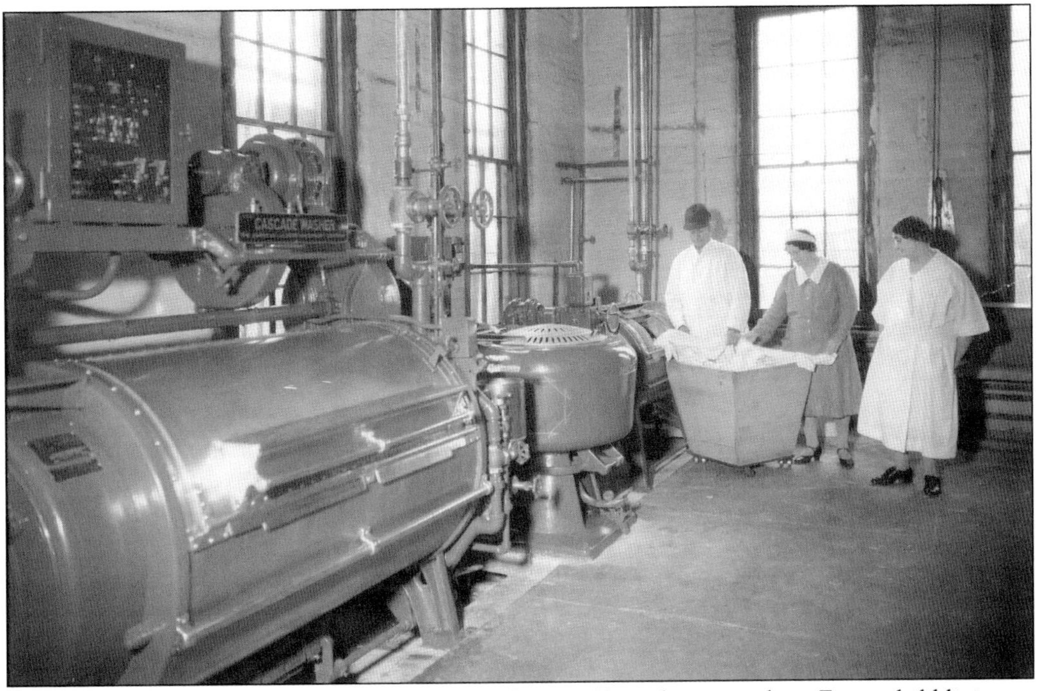

Washing, folding, ironing, and delivery were all part of laundry-room duty. Every child living at the Home received a number to identify his or her laundry. To this day, several former residents remember their assigned numbers. They were admitted by signing the register book, numbered, handed their stack of clothes, and given a cubby and bed to call their own. Accordingly, all of the laundry was sorted by numbers.

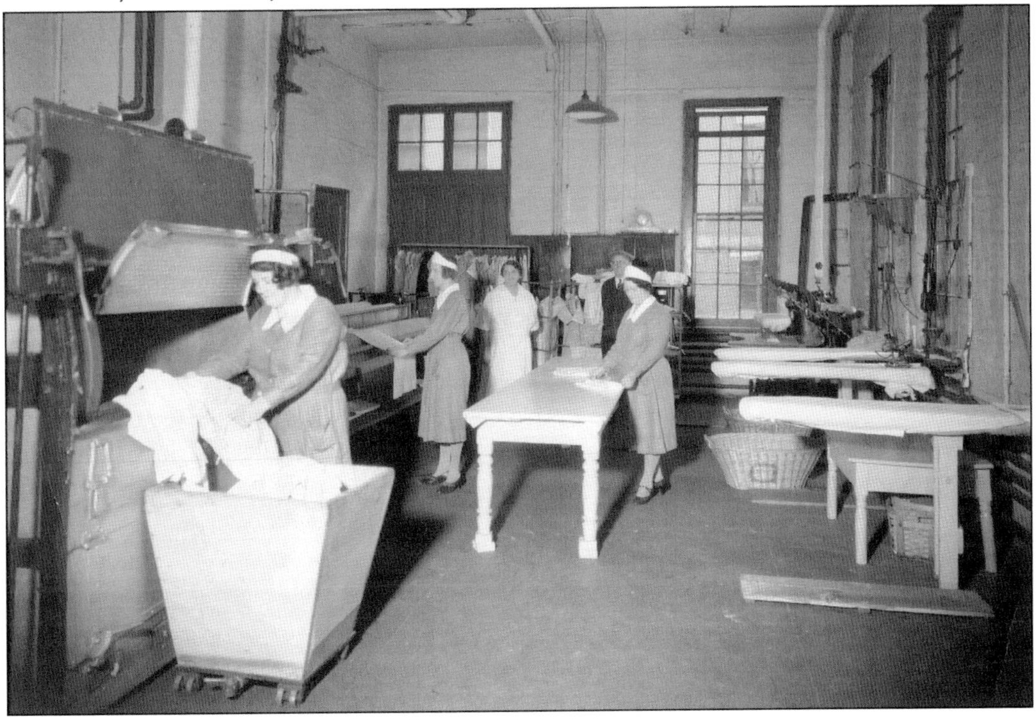

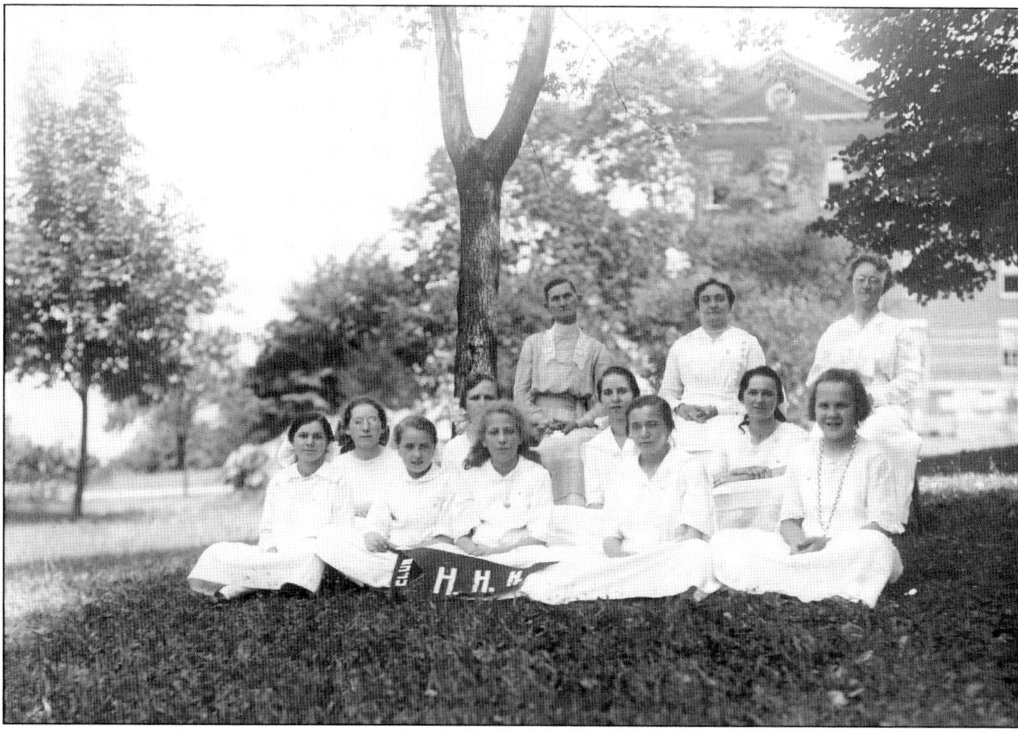

In the 1800s and early 1900s, the children, housemothers, and other staff, such as nurses, were required to be neat and orderly in appearance every day. No one was allowed to enter the dining hall without a tidy appearance. The superintendent would pass by the assembled children to check their appearance and make sure their schoolbooks were in order before departing for school. Dr. Charles Aring, who was a resident in the early 1900s, recalled all the boys wearing matching blue denim overalls in grade school and second-hand mailman pants in high school.

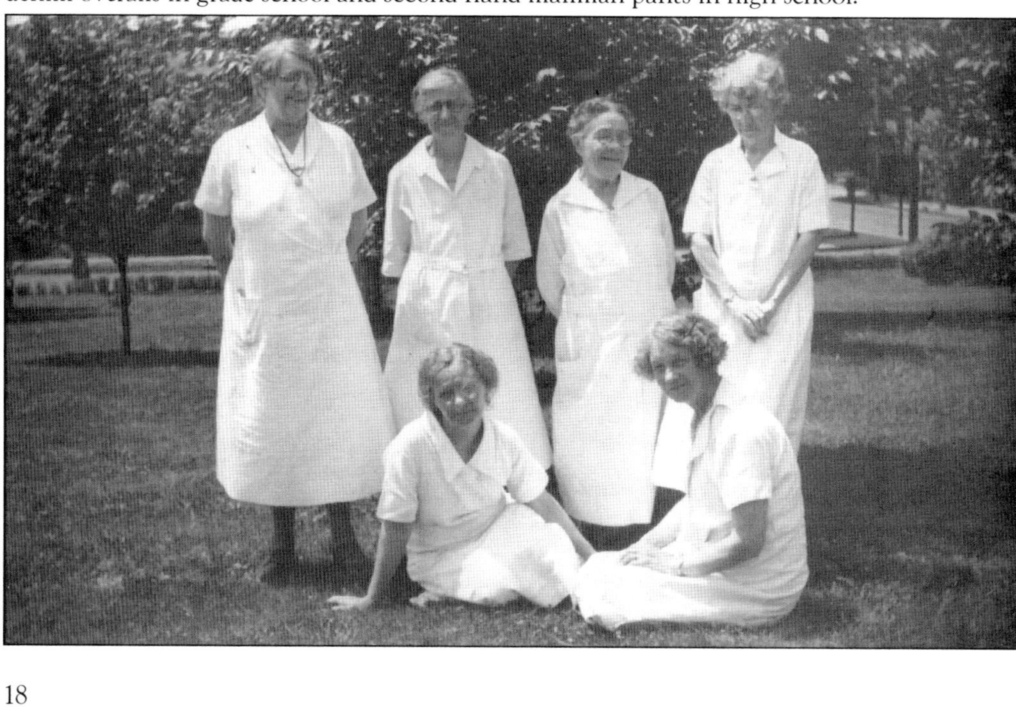

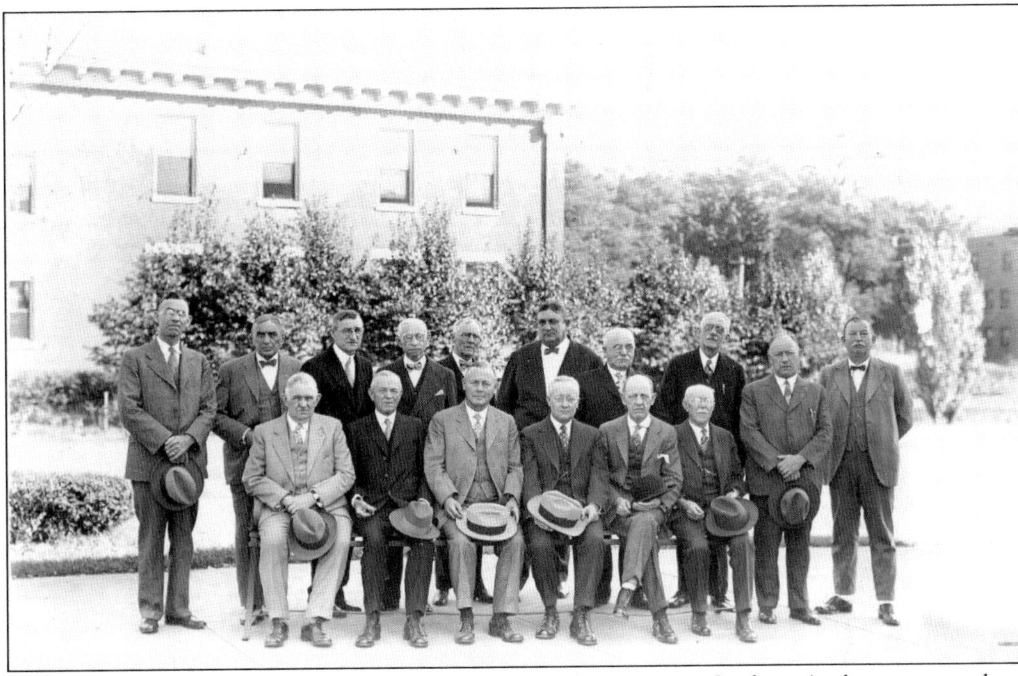

The 1929 Board of Directors of the German General Protestant Orphan Asylum poses to have its portrait taken.

CHARTER.

AN ACT

To Incorporate The German Protestant Orphans' Home.

BE IT ENACTED by the General Assembly of the State of Missouri as follows:

SEC. 1. An Institution to be called the "GERMAN PROTESTANT ORPHANS' HOME" shall be and is hereby established in the city of St. Louis and shall be deemed and held to be a benevolent institution.

SEC. 2. LOUIS E. NOLLAU, FREDERICK MASCHMEIER, T. FRED. MASSMANN, MICHAEL VOEPEL and FRANCIS HACKEMEIER, and such persons as they associate with themselves, not exceeding ten in all, shall be and are hereby made the corporators, or board of Trustees.

SEC. 3. The object of this corporation shall be to establish, sustain and conduct an Asylum for the care, maintenance, support and education of minors, and children under age, who by reason of the loss of one or both of their parents, or from any other cause are not otherwise provided for.

SEC. 4. The corporators or board of Trustees shall have the power to fill vacancies and appoint successors, so as to perpetuate their corporate existence.

SEC. 5. They shall at their first meeting organize and select their officers, and these officers shall perform the duties usually imposed upon officers of a similar character, and as the by-laws may provide.

SEC. 6. The square or block, or part of the square or block or tract not exceeding ten acres, in the county

— 15 —

of St. Louis, on which the corporation hereby chartered shall have, or erect its buildings, shall, so long and so far as used or occupied by this corporation, together with said buildings, yard or yards, walk or walks, garden or gardens, furniture, beds and other necessary apparatus, be exempted from taxation of every kind.

SEC. 7. The corporators or board of Trustees shall frame by-laws and regulations for systematizing the operation of the institution herein named, and they may from time to time amend such by-laws and regulations.

SEC. 8. The corporators or board of Trustees shall have the entire control of all the property of the corporation, of the receipts and disbursements, and of the orphans and destitute children under its care. They shall have power and authority to accept a surrender in writing by the father, and where there is no father or where he has abandoned his family, by the mother of a child or children being minors and unmarried, to the care of said corporation, and bind out to any virtuous and suitable person by written articles of indenture any female child so surrendered until the age of eighteen, and any male child until the age of twenty-one years; provided, that any parent who shall have surrendered such child, shall have liberty to receive said again at any time before such child shall be bound out as aforesaid, upon paying to the Treasurer of this corporation the amount expended by it in the care, maintenance and education thereof.

This Act shall take effect and be in force from and after its passage.

Approved, March 23rd, 1861.

This is the original charter of the German General Protestant Orphan Asylum.

Stehende Committeen.

1887—1888.

Finanzen:
C. Guckenberger, H. Finke, J. F. Moser.
Präsident H. Kreimer, Schatzmeister H. W. Koch.

Ausgebundene Kinder:
H. Steinmeier, J. F. Moser, Michael Gramp.

Schulen:
C. F. Muth, Michael Gramp, L. Langhorn.

Dienstboten:
H. Eschmeyer, P. H. Pentermann, Fr. Lücke.

Spezereien:
L. Langhorn, H. Eschmeyer, W. D. Feuß.

Verbesserungen und Möbel:
Fr. Lücke, Aug. Kreimer, C. Guckenberger.

Feuerungen:
H. Finke, L. Langhorn, Wm. Guckenberger.

Kranke:
Aug. Kreimer, F. Hillebrand, Wm. Guckenberger.

Vieh und Futter:
F. Hillebrand, C. F. Muth, Julius Brinkmann.

Vermächtnisse:
Julius Brinkmann, H. Pentermann, W. D. Feuß.

The Guckenberger family has made innumerable contributions to the success of Beech Acres—The General Protestant Orphan Home. In 1866, Charles Guckenberger became a board member of the German Protestant Orphan Association. He served on the board of directors until 1901 and was board president from 1896 to 1900. His son George also served on the board at the turn of the century. George's sons George Jr. and Herman both were Orphan Feast officers of the day, in 1938 and 1956 respectively. Herman also served on the board from 1940 to 1961.

Beech Acres Honors Families At Open House

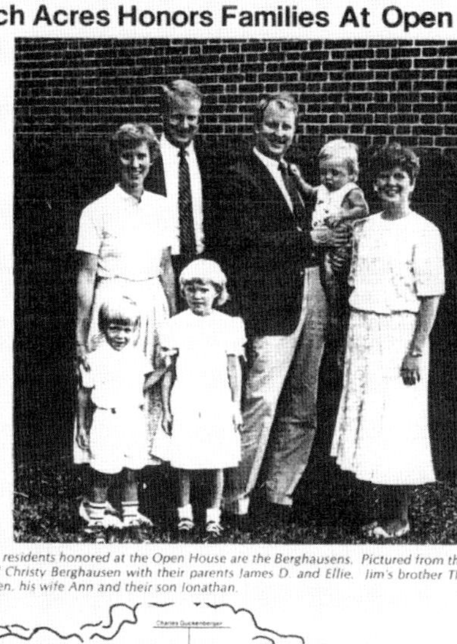

Anderson residents honored at the Open House are the Berghausens. Pictured from the left are Mark and Christy Berghausen with their parents James D. and Ellie. Jim's brother Thomas A. Berghausen, his wife Ann and their son Jonathan.

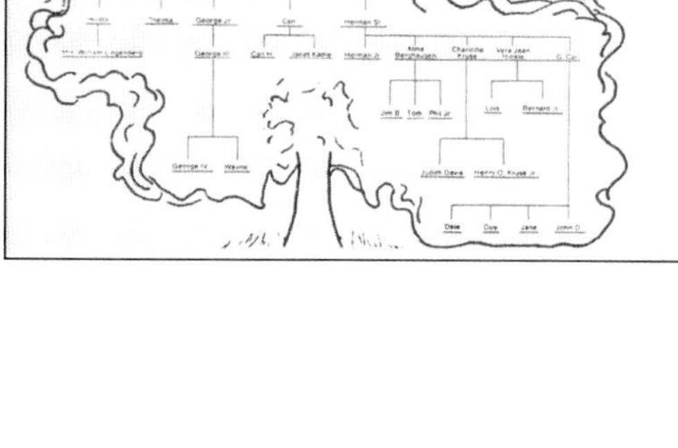

Herman Guckenberger's son Herman J. Guckenberger Jr. served on the board from 1961 to 1985, including as its president from 1976 to 1979. He served as Orphan Feast vice chairman in 1972. In 1985, Herman was honored for a lifetime of commitment to the well-being of children and families. As a prominent attorney, Herman encouraged many to remember the home in their wills.

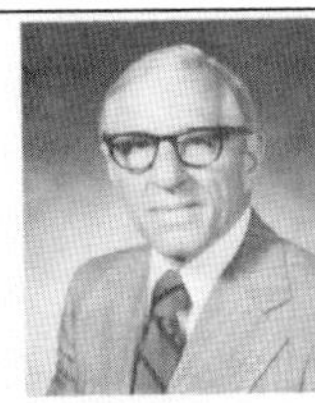

letter from the president

Season's Greetings!

On behalf of the Children, Staff and Board of Directors, I extend our best wishes for the New Year and Holiday Season. This is a special time for thanksgiving and reflection on our many blessings. We deeply appreciate your loyal support of our efforts to provide valuable services for children in our community. As we anticipate the holiday festivities, you will be included in our thoughts.

The children in our residential program and group home program are looking forward to being with their families during Christmas, if possible, or with special friends—Sponsor Families, Big Sisters and Big Brothers. All the children will enjoy the annual Christmas dinner and celebration at Beech Acres along with the many special activities. The generosity of those who share our love and concern for children makes these opportunities possible for each child through our Christmas Fund.

The Annual Meeting of Beech Acres-The General Protestant Orphan Home will be Tuesday, January 22, 1980, at 7 p.m. Members and friends are invited to attend. The progress of our Agency in 1979 will be reported at this time.

Members of five years or more are eligible to vote in the election of the Board of Directors. The names of the nominees are listed on page 10 in this issue. As President of the Beech Acres Board, I am looking forward to seeing you at the Annual Meeting.

Sincerely,

Herman J. Guckenberger Jr.

Our services for children

Beech Acres-The General Protestant Orphan Home aids children and their families (including children with little or no family involvement) in the Greater Cincinnati community. We are a child care/family service agency providing residential care, foster care, group home care, preventive care, aftercare, child and family counseling. All services are available to the public regardless of race, creed, national origin or financial standing.

In 1978 we served 494 children in our programs and related services.

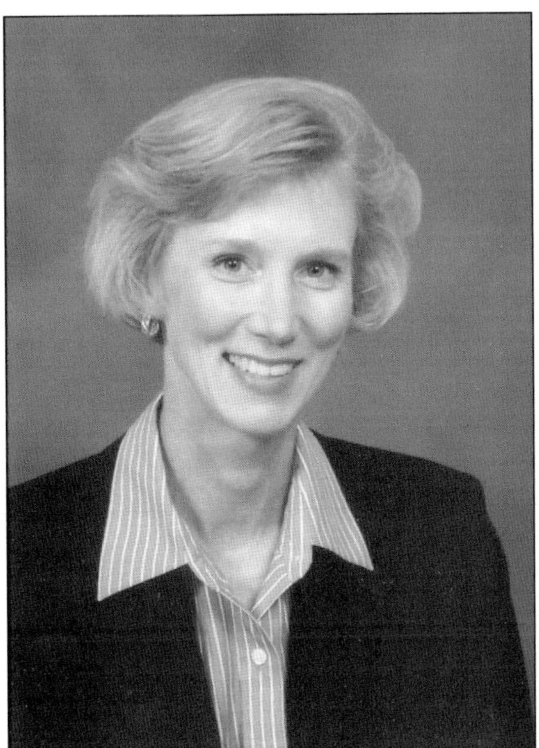

Herman Guckenberger Jr.'s sister Alma married Philip Berghausen, who served on the board from 1970 to 1989. Their sons, Jim, Tom, and Phil Jr., and families remain supportive today. Jim's wife, Ellie Berghausen (pictured), served on the board from 1993 to 2004 and as its chair from 2001 to 2003. Ellie provided leadership during the creation of the parenting center, defining the future focus on strengthening the relationship between parents and their children. Ellie remains involved today.

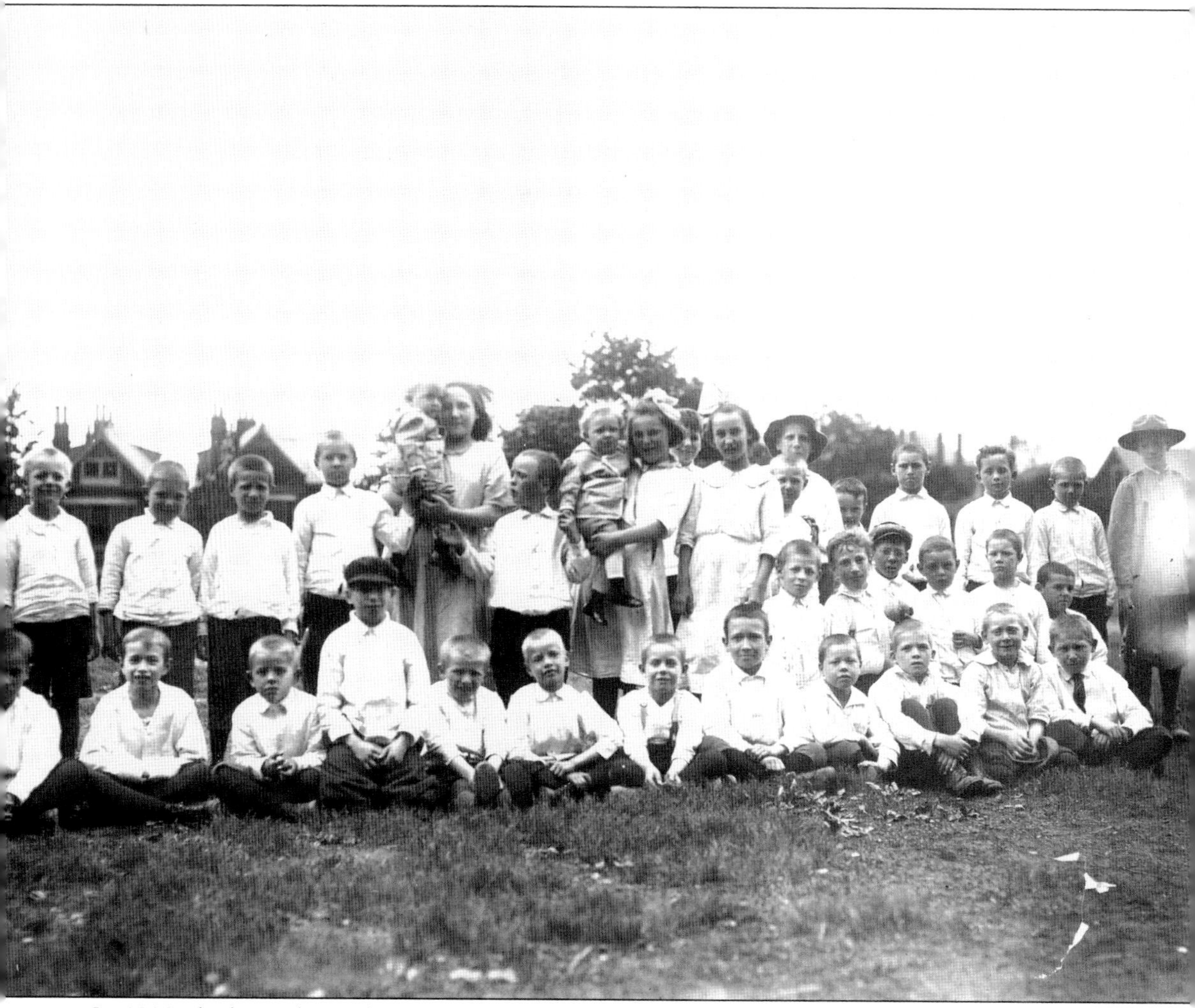

In 1900, the home housed 170 children, six cows, one horse, and 13 small hogs. Board meeting minutes mention the failure of the mulberry tree/silk-worm project, success of the fruit tree orchard, and the construction of a greenhouse. Residents were out-placed at 14 years of age in the early years of the decade and at 16 years by 1911. Girls were generally placed as mother's helpers or worked in the home as maids for $10 per month. Boys were placed with a tradesman and in some cases attended high school. Placements included farms, print shops, shoe stores, and grocers. George Hammerlein was taught to repair shoes and provided that service to the home for many years. After he returned from the Navy, he served as chairman of the Orphan Feast and returned his $300 compensation to the home.

Two

THE SPECIAL ROLE OF WOMEN

Women have always played significant roles in the life of the General Protestant Orphan Home (GPOH) and its children. As early as 1849, women orchestrated a fundraising event to support the construction of the Home. The event became the annual Orphan Feast, which grew to become an important part of the Home's history, so much so that it earned a chapter of its own in this book.

When the first children moved into the orphanage in 1851, the Benevolent Association of German Women elected officers and created the Orphan Society of the German Protestant Women of Cincinnati. Membership was open to "every adult female of unblemished reputation on condition of paying regular dues." The right to vote was acquired by the monthly payment of 10¢.

The first officers were Mrs. Luise Schneider, president; Mrs. Kinsbach, vice president; Mrs. Carolina Hornung, secretary; and Mrs. Anna Maria Phister, treasurer. Committee members included Mesdames Krucher, Klotter, Fieber, Alms, Wolff, Hoffsimmer, Hoffner, Reis, Peters, Graff, Weitzel, Rechel, and Kroll. Meetings were conducted in German until 1918, after which English was used. At the same time, the name was changed to the Ladies Board of the General Protestant Orphan Home.

In 1966, the ladies board transitioned to the Women's Committee. Mrs. Marian Eckert was the first chair of the committee and was given a "virtue of office" seat on the Home's board of directors. The committee ended after women began serving as full members of the board. After joining the board in 1983, Mrs. Linda J. Smith became the first female board president (1989–1990) and led numerous organizational improvements, including the creation of the For the Love of Kids® parenting conference.

Margy Richards (1997–1998) and Ellie Berghausen (2001–2003) followed as female board chairs. Margy instituted policy governance practices, improving the agency's ability to adapt in a rapidly changing environment. Ellie continued her family's legacy of leadership; the involvement of the Guckenberger/Berghausen family dates to 1866. She chaired the board during its second major transformation, becoming a parenting center. That transformation has been significantly guided by women serving on the organization's staff during the 2000s, notably Diane Jordan-Grizzard, Pam McKie, Ruthann Zins, Chandra Mathews-Smith, Christine Hall, and Roseann Hassey.

Today, many staff, board, and leadership positions are held by women. While too many to mention, their daily contributions allow the parenting center to provide services to over 11,000 children, parents, and families each year.

Officers of the Ladies Board of the GPOH

Founders: Misses Kecher, Siebern, Schepp, Naut, Wehmer, Rapp, Horwing, Mrs. Woodrough, Mrs. Pfisterer, Mrs. Ficke, Philomena Diemann, Louis Peters, Caroline Harter, Mrs. Hurst, Mrs. Peters, Dorothea Stegner, Mrs. Johns, Mrs. Monkhoff and Miss Urbach

Presidents:

1851-1876	Louise Ballauf Schneider
1877-1880	Dorothy Hohnstedt
1881-1882	Maria Fels
1883-1884	Maria Lackmann
1885-1888	Barbara Herancourt
1889-1890	Dora Kruse
1891-1898	Katharine Widmann
1899-1917	Elise Deppe
1918-1953	Miss Susanna Dater
1954-1955	Mrs. Edna Schille
1956-1967	Mrs. Lillian Kratt
1968-1971	Mrs. George Pellens
1972-1975	Mrs. Donald Eckert
1976-1979	Mrs. Thomas Scott
1980-1985	Mrs. Donna Hull
1986-1997	Mrs. Roberta Arnold
1998	Vera Juergens

In 1849, the German General Protestant Orphan Society planned a fair to raise funds to build the orphan home. A group of women prepared the fair, taking charge of the tables, assigning the lots, and organizing the event. Original members included Louisa Haller, Mrs. Johns, Mrs. Weitzel, Mrs. Urbach, Amelia Pfau, Mrs. Hust, Mrs. Ficke, Dorothea Stegner, Mrs. Woodrough, Mrs. Krucker, Philomena Diemann, Mrs. Monkhof, Mrs. Pfisterer, Christina Techner, Caroline Harter, Miss Horwing, Louisa Peters, Katharine Siebern, and Mary Schepp.

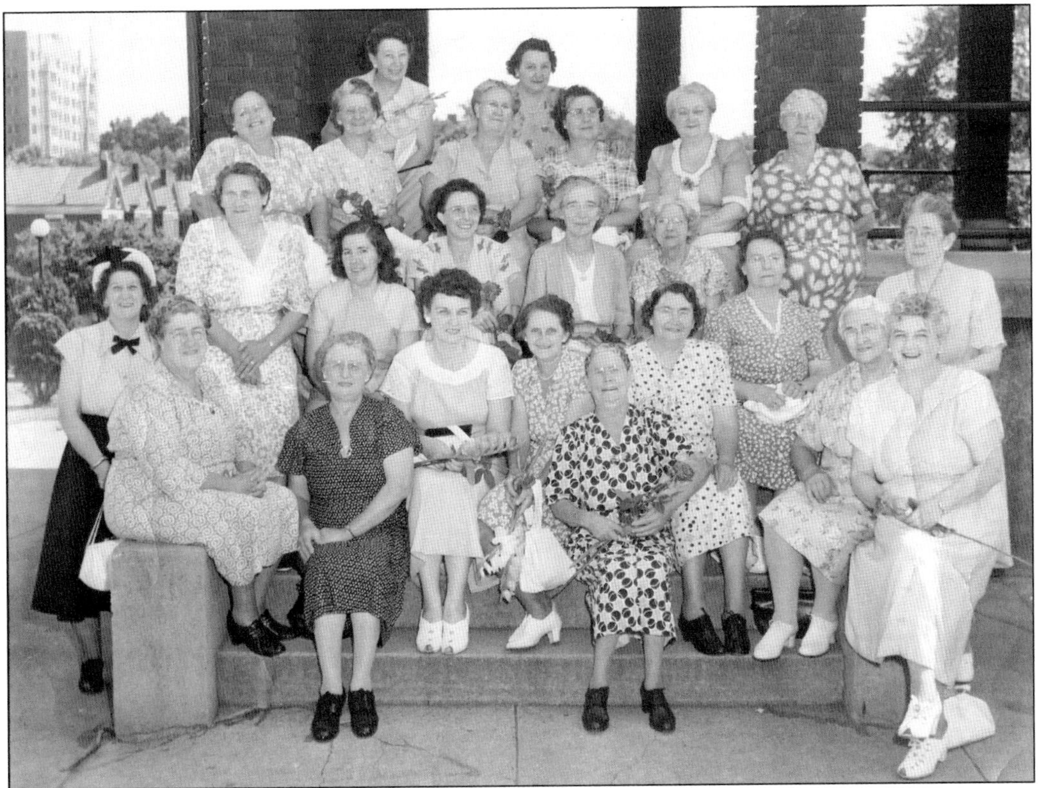

The Orphan Society of the German Protestant Women of Cincinnati was organized in 1851 "to assist in the supervision and care of the orphans in the German General Protestant Orphan Asylum and to furnish, as far as possible, their wearing apparel." Membership was open to adult females of "unblemished reputation" who were willing to pay the annual dues of $1.20. They became the Women's Committee and were active in furnishing dormitory rooms, covering the floors with linoleum, and putting new curtains on all windows and renovating the dining room in the Old Orphanage in Mount Auburn. Every child received a birthday card with a dollar in it, and parties for the children provided by the committee were the highlights of the holiday season and summertime. Seen here are members of the Women's Committee from 1940 and 1959.

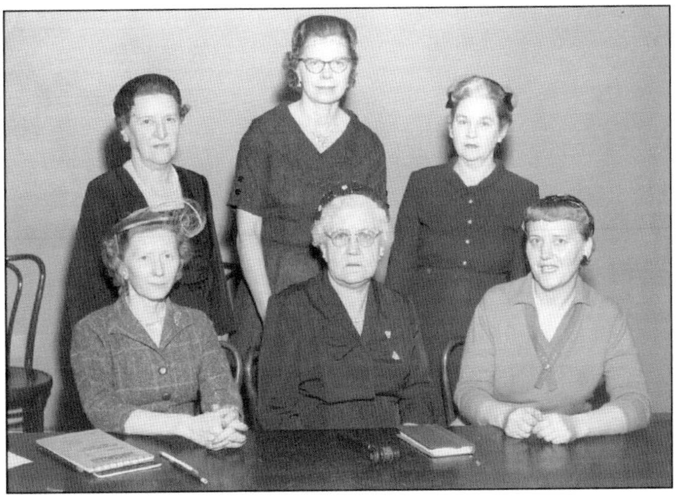

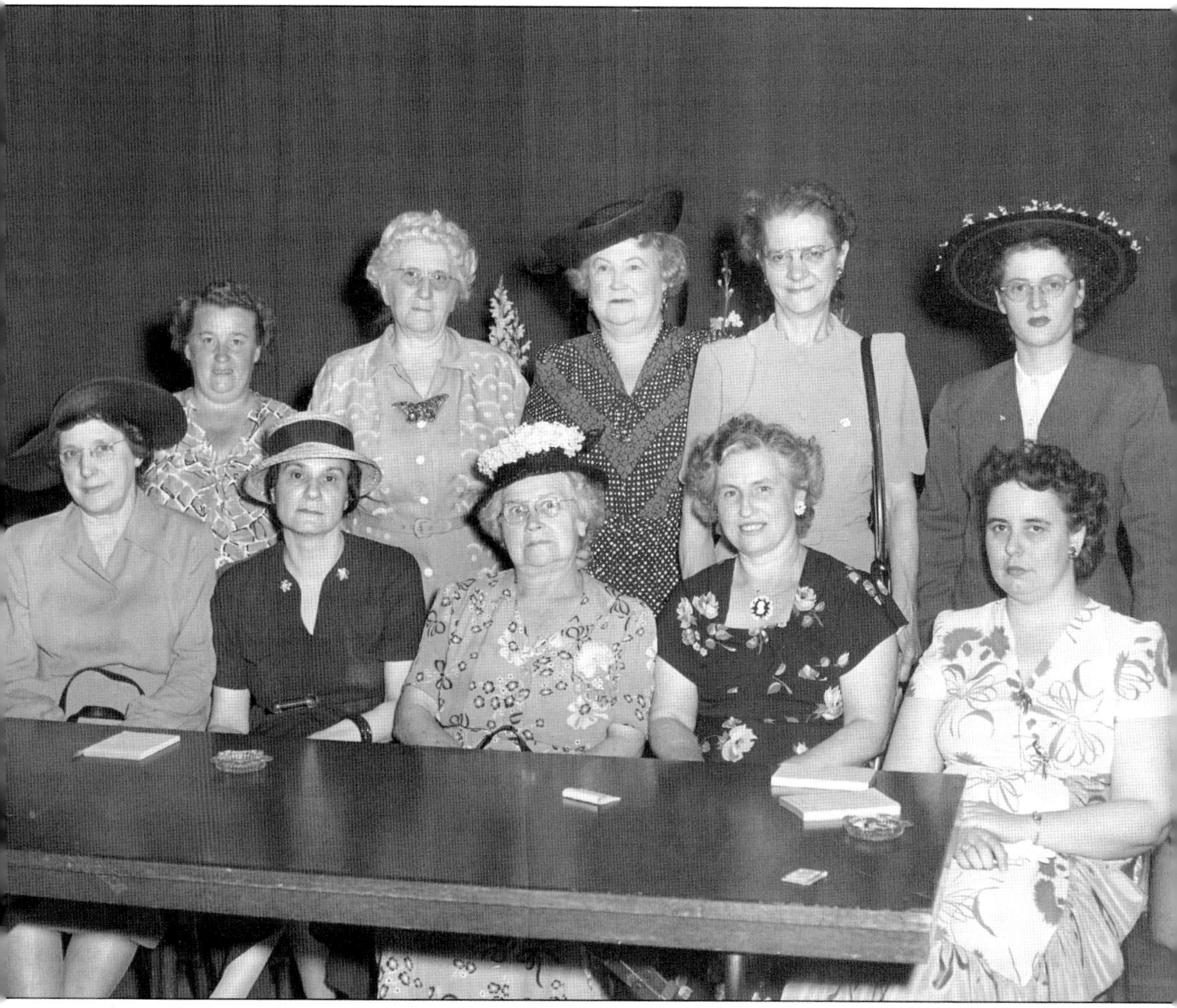

The Ladies Board consisted of women from area churches and was headed by Susanna Dater. Members chaired booths at the annual Orphan Feast, campaigned for funds, and organized workers to solicit funds for the children's stay. The Ladies Board also managed the volunteers for the Orphan Feast, which tallied up to over 1,000 people annually. This is a photograph of the women's booth chairwomen from the centennial Orphan Feast in 1949.

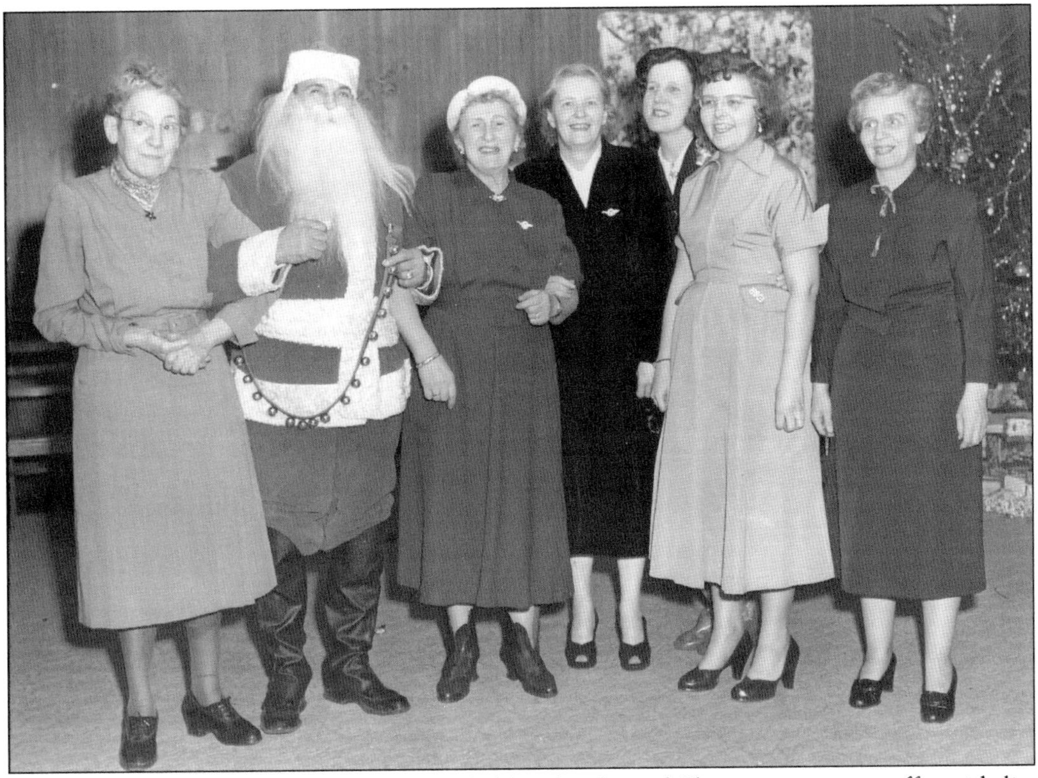

The Women's Committee provided each child with a box of Christmas presents off a wish list that the children had made. Several former residents recall receiving "everything that we wrote on the list!" Since many families had several siblings living at the orphanage, each family received a large box full of new clothing. Above, the Women's Committee of 1951 shares a moment with Santa. At Christmas time, the committee hosted a large dinner for the children.

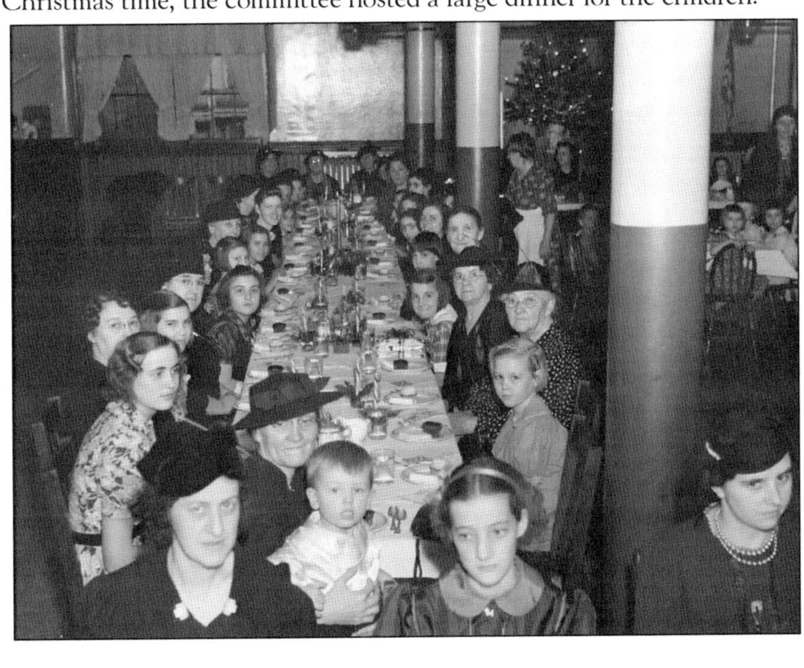

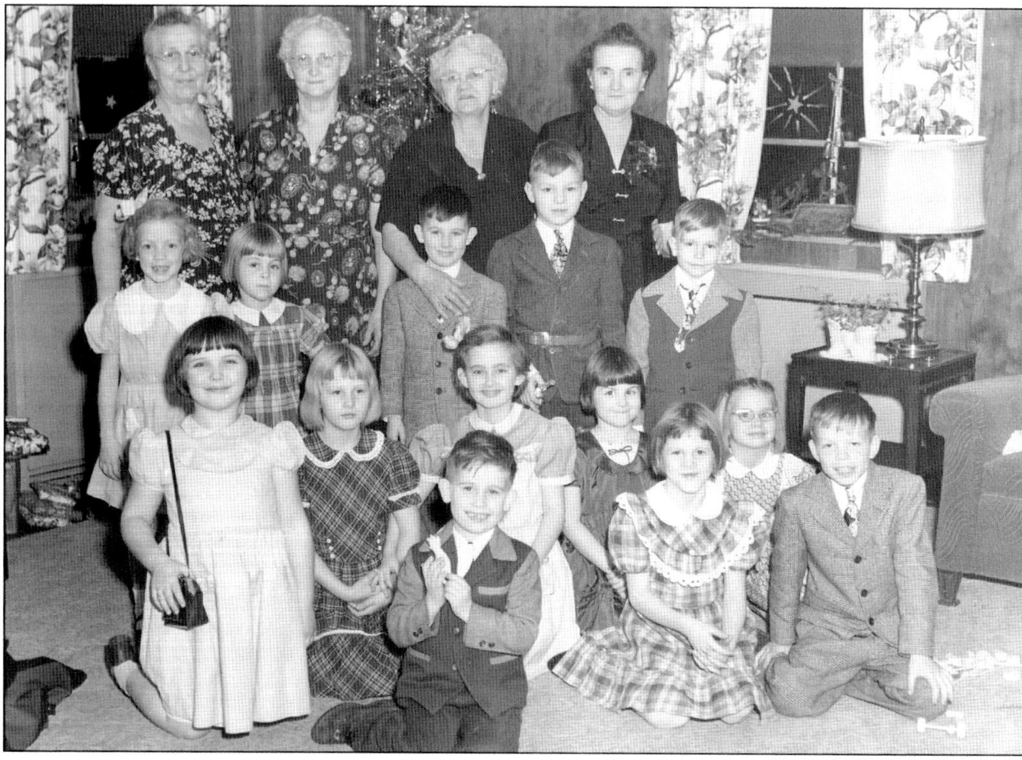

After the move to Anderson Township, housemothers cared for the children in each cottage. They taught children domestic skills such as ironing, cooking, and sewing. Three different mothers staffed each cottage; one mother had the day shift, one the evening, and the third worked the weekend shift. Each mother ensured the children did their daily chores and homework, as well as managed their behavior. Housemothers lived on the property and were compensated with room, board, and wages. In 1957, it is recorded that there were 70 children in the Home, representing 28 families with nine housemothers caring for them.

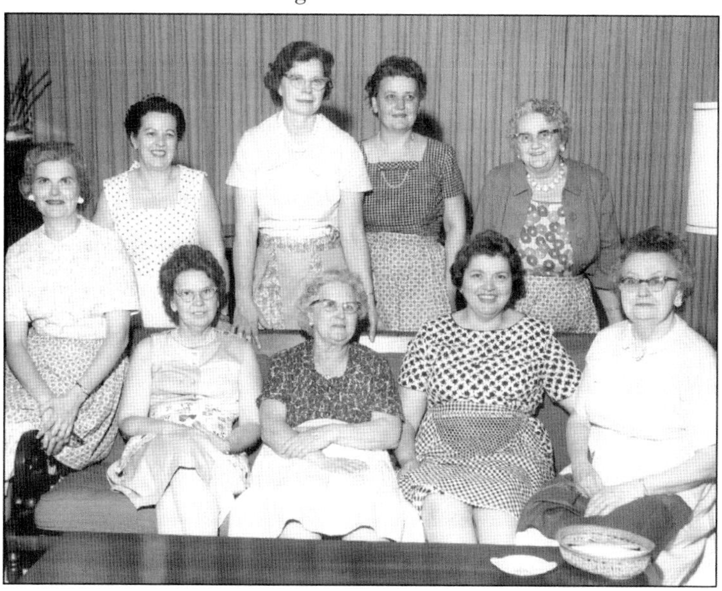

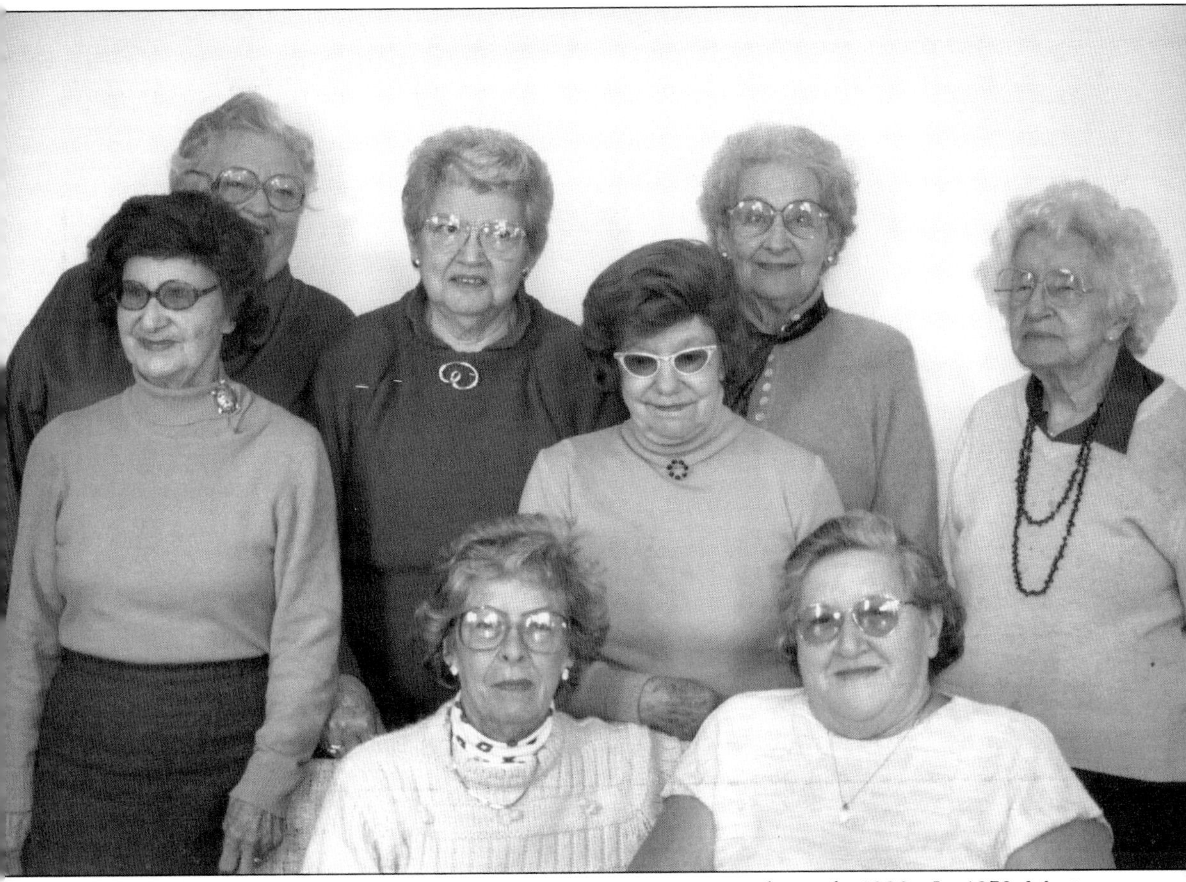

The Women's Committee continued its generous support into the early 1990s. In 1970, Marian Eckert (third row, second from left) became the first woman to join the board of directors. Marian was the chairwoman of the Women's Committee and was placed on the board of directors, ex officio, to represent the committee. She was the first female to have voting rights on the board of directors.

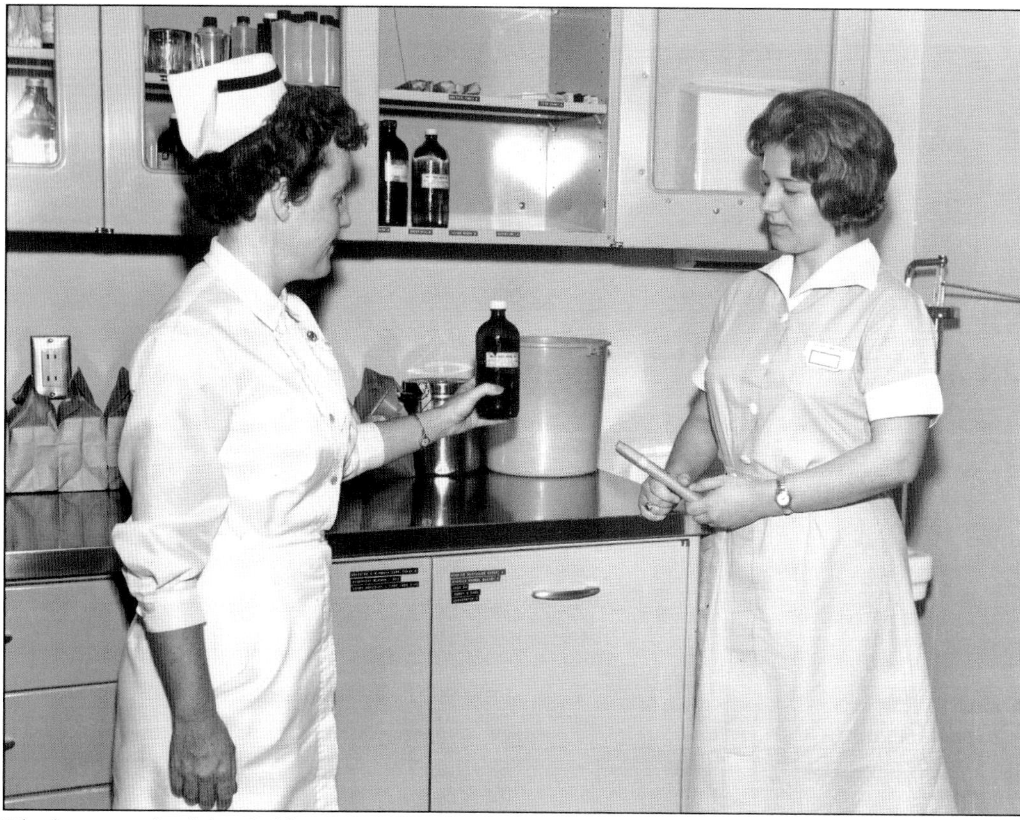

The basic needs of the children were met, including health care, from nurses and staff. As children aged, each had duties around the Home. One former resident recalled that when she entered the Home at age 12, she immediately began to work in the infirmary. There were 6 to 10 beds available, as well as a quarantine area for any children with communicable diseases. She did not associate with many of the children, as her responsibility was to work in the unit and assist the nurses. First a resident, she later became an employee with room and board as pay. She later went on to marry another resident from the home. They are still living in Cincinnati after 60 years of marriage.

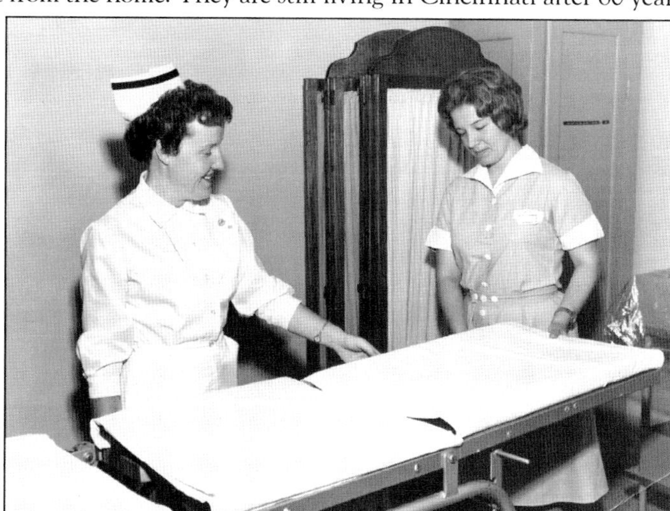

Three

The Orphan Feast

The Home's founders and the Ladies Board were very pleased with the success of the mid-December 1849 festival, which raised over $4,000 to support land purchase and construction of the orphanage. The highly successful event was repeated annually for 137 years and became known to many as the Orphan Feast.

The earliest mention in print, cited in a local German newspaper, of an event called the Orphan Feast was in 1852, when an unidentified man noted that "turning out on silk hat and Prince Alberts to march in the parade was an event to be participated in." By the spring of 1886, the Orphan Feast netted $1,957.21. This was a great success, as the cost of caring for a child per year was merely $79.50.

The Orphan Feast became Cincinnati's big fall event each year. An Officer of the Day was elected to be in charge of raising money. The city's residents could plan their attendance a year in advance, as it was always held the Sunday immediately following Labor Day. The event was popular, and leadership roles were coveted. In 1930, Congressman William E. Hess was chosen as Officer of the Day. George W. Huston, chairman of the soft-drink booths, cut short his trip to Europe to ensure his presence at the event.

By the 1940s, the feast had become so popular it netted over $50,000. It was a community-wide event, involving large numbers of vendors, business owners, politicians, and well-known citizens. A record number attended in 1950, the year the orphanage was moved to the new campus on the border of Mount Washington and Anderson Township. Oral history has it that over 80,000 people participated in the one-day festivities. Supported by hundreds of volunteers and vendors, the Orphan Feast became known as the largest one-day fundraiser of any not-for-profit organization in the Midwest at the time.

As with many traditions, modern times took its toll. Alternate sources of entertainment and a growing number of not-for-profit fundraising events led to dwindling attendance and support from volunteers. Planning the event was beginning to require significant staff time throughout the year. And, as the problems presented by the children in residence became increasingly severe, it became clear that the nature of the event and the month-long disruption it created in their routines was too much for the children. Booths were put away and betting wheels taken down for the last time after the 1986 Orphan Feast. It made for a sad ending to a very special 137-year tradition.

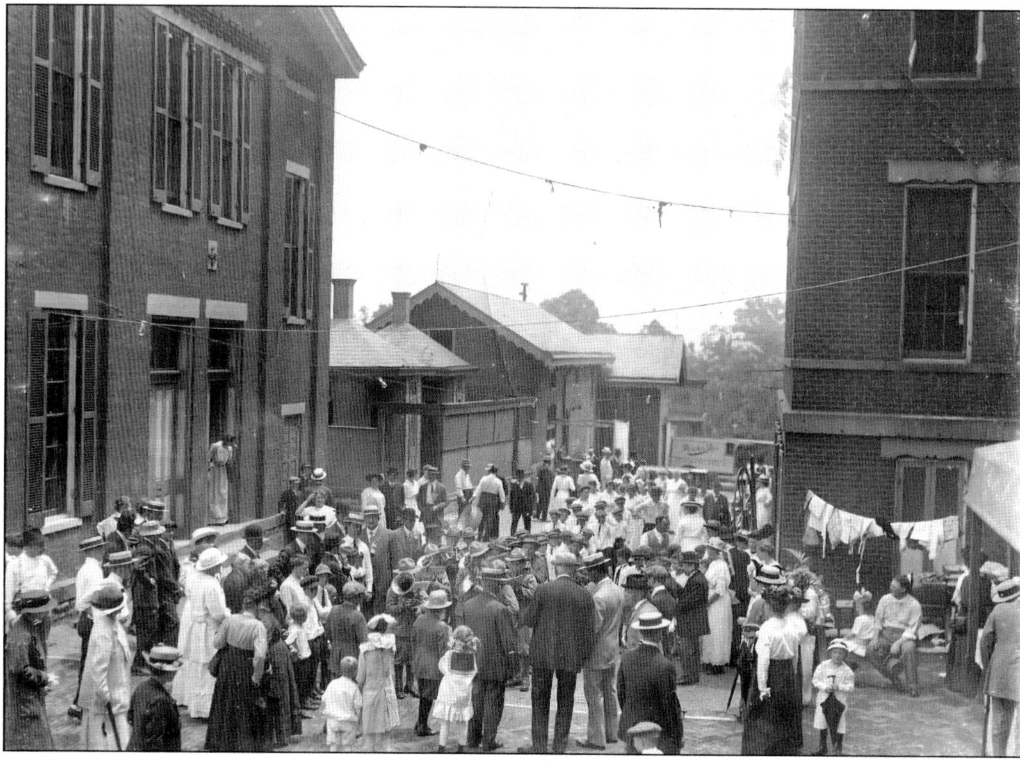

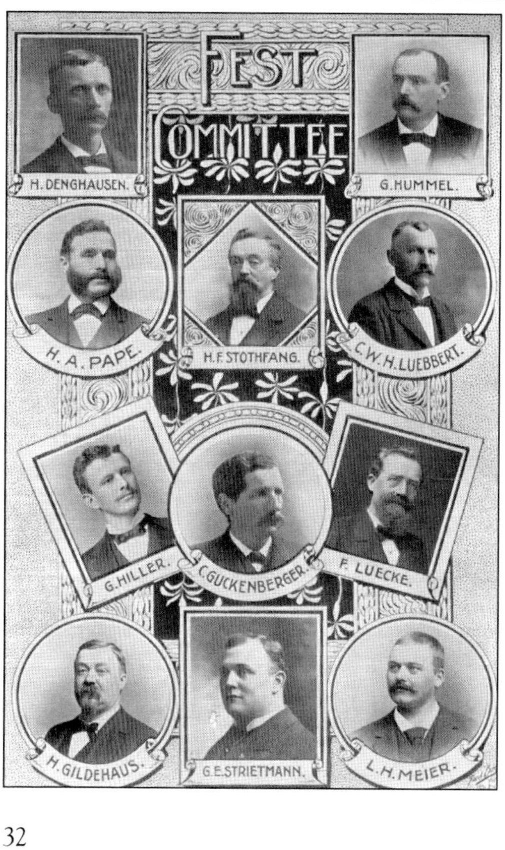

The entrance price to the Orphan Feast in 1849 was only 10¢, yet a total of $1,043.56 was made from admissions. The receipts and donations from the fair were $3,264.37, making a grand total of contributions of $4,651.03. The expenses for the hall ($95) and music, which had been furnished by John Geyer's band ($110), left a surplus from the fair of $4,181.88. Land owned by Judge Burnet had already been chosen as the site of the new orphanage. With the cost of the land at $4,000, the fair yielded enough money to pay Judge Burnet in cash. The annual Orphan Feast had claimed its honored place in the history of the Home.

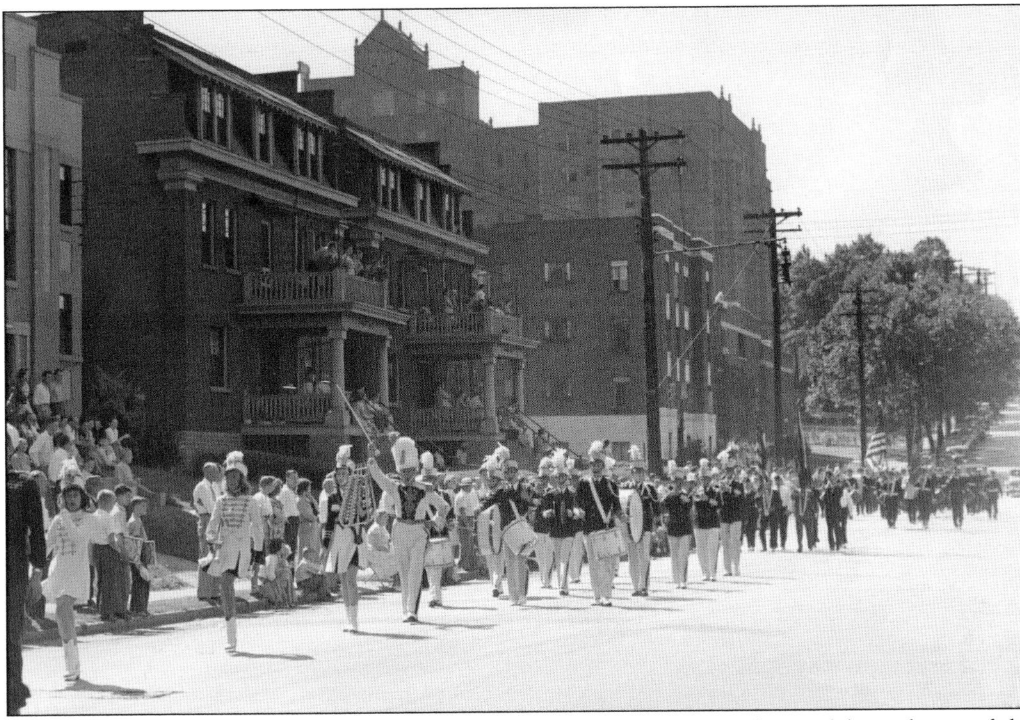

The annual parade kicked off the Orphan Feast each year. The parade, a celebrated part of the feast due to its size and scope of participants, began on what is now East McMillan Street and went through the entire neighborhood of Mount Auburn until it reached the Home. The parade drew large crowds and expanded every year. When the Orphan Home moved to the border of Mount Washington and Anderson Township, oral history has it that the parade was known nationally as the largest, one-day parade organized by a nonprofit.

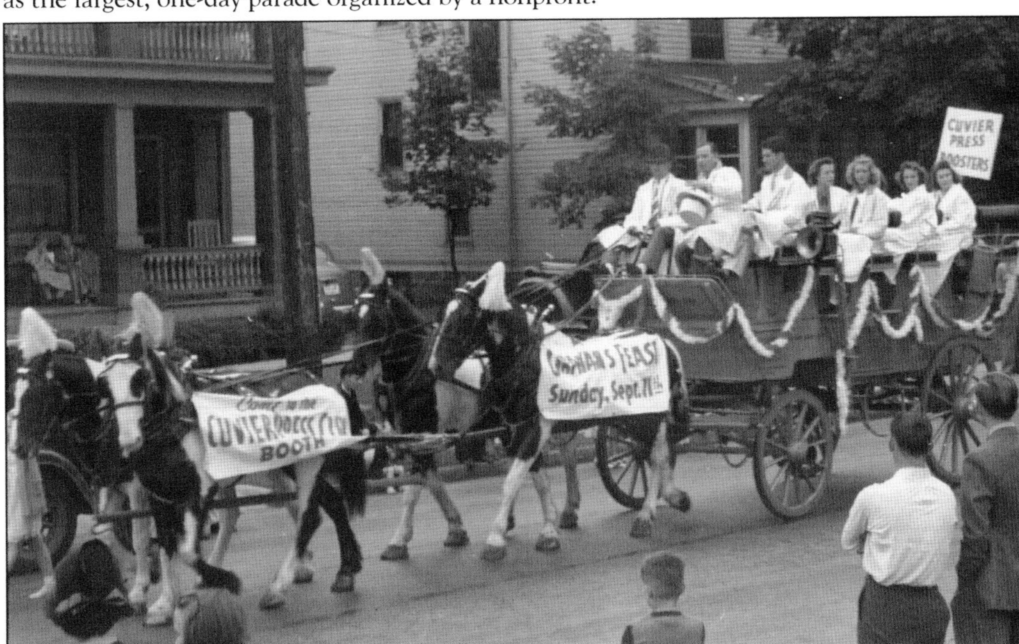

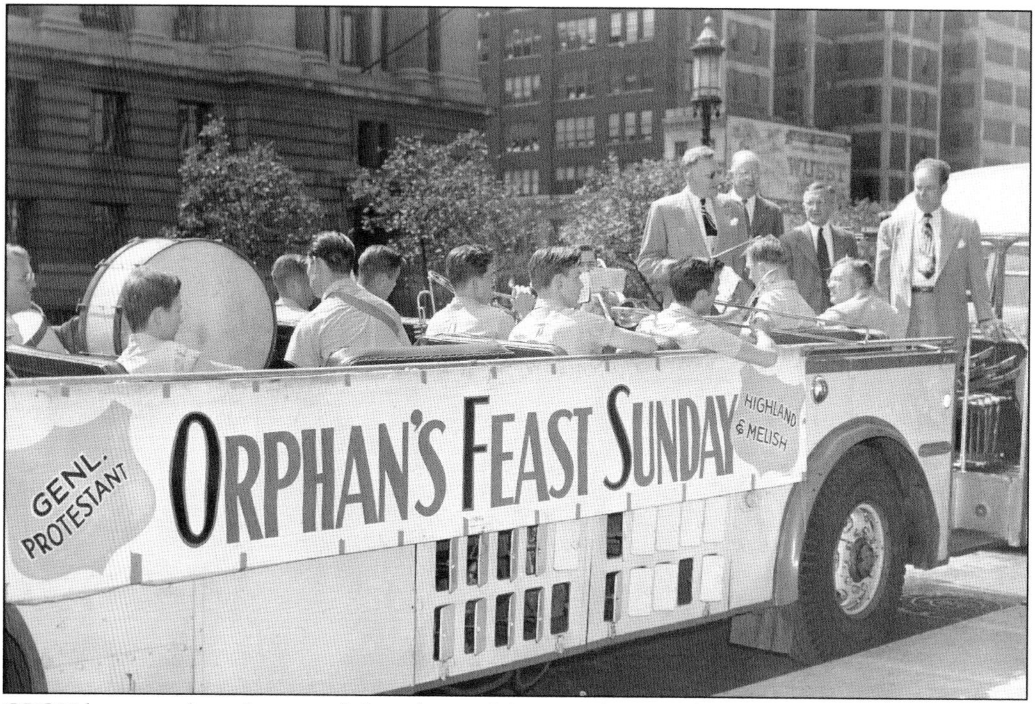

GPOH housemothers showcased the talents of their residents in the Orphan Feast band car. The parade, which opened the festival, originated the year the Home was built in 1851. This annual gathering was the place to be for businesses, individuals, and community partners.

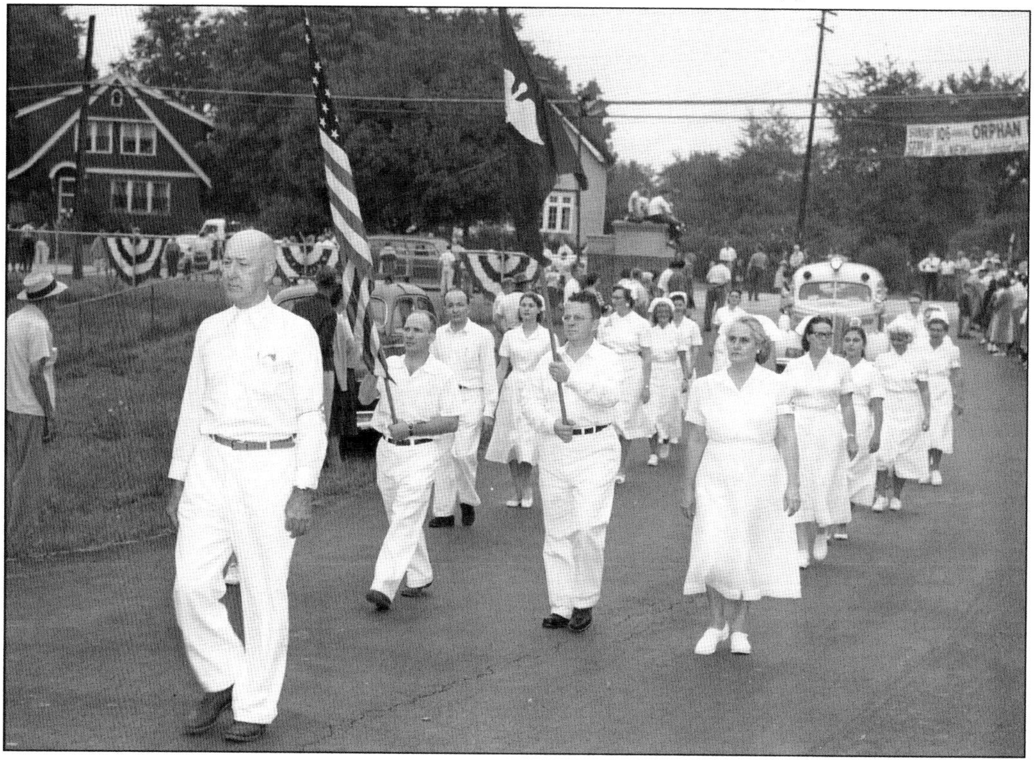

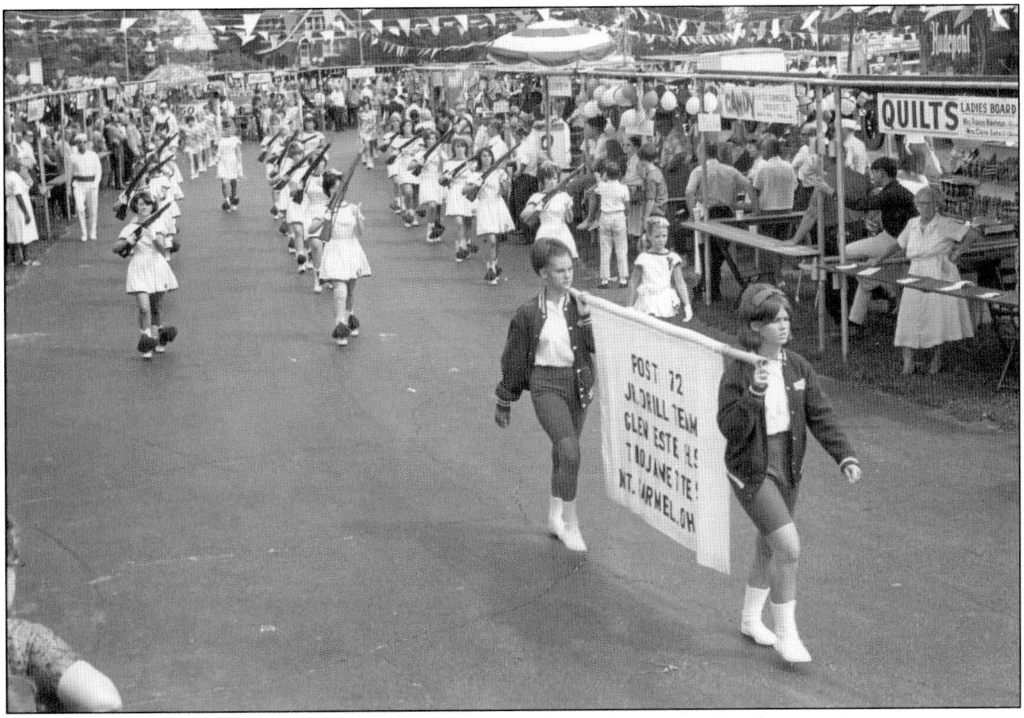

Parade participants included the orphanage band, military, and other performing troupes, community partners, and local politicians. After 1950, the parade began at the Beechmont Levee near Lunken Airport and ended at the Beech Acres campus. The orphanage band led all the way up the Beechmont Avenue hill. For weeks before the Orphan Feast, posters advertising the parade, 35 acres of parking, food, and patriotic ceremonies were hung throughout the city.

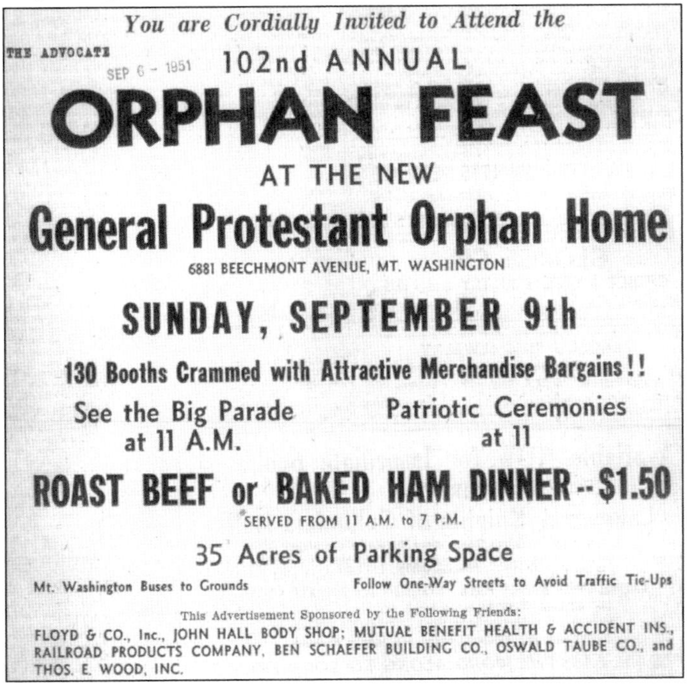

You are Cordially Invited to Attend the

THE ADVOCATE SEP 6 - 1951

102nd ANNUAL

ORPHAN FEAST

AT THE NEW

General Protestant Orphan Home

6881 BEECHMONT AVENUE, MT. WASHINGTON

SUNDAY, SEPTEMBER 9th

130 Booths Crammed with Attractive Merchandise Bargains!!

See the Big Parade at 11 A.M.

Patriotic Ceremonies at 11

ROAST BEEF or BAKED HAM DINNER--$1.50

SERVED FROM 11 A.M. to 7 P.M.

35 Acres of Parking Space

Mt. Washington Buses to Grounds

Follow One-Way Streets to Avoid Traffic Tie-Ups

This Advertisement Sponsored by the Following Friends:

FLOYD & CO., Inc., JOHN HALL BODY SHOP; MUTUAL BENEFIT HEALTH & ACCIDENT INS., RAILROAD PRODUCTS COMPANY, BEN SCHAEFER BUILDING CO., OSWALD TAUBE CO., and THOS. E. WOOD, INC.

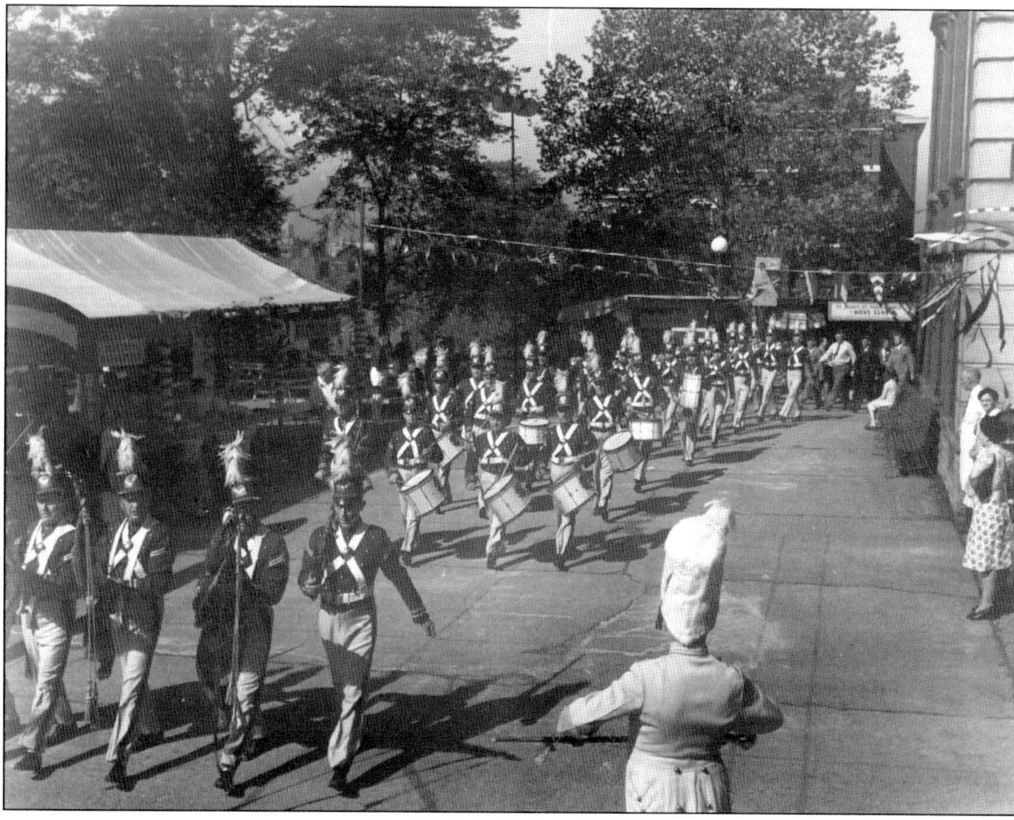

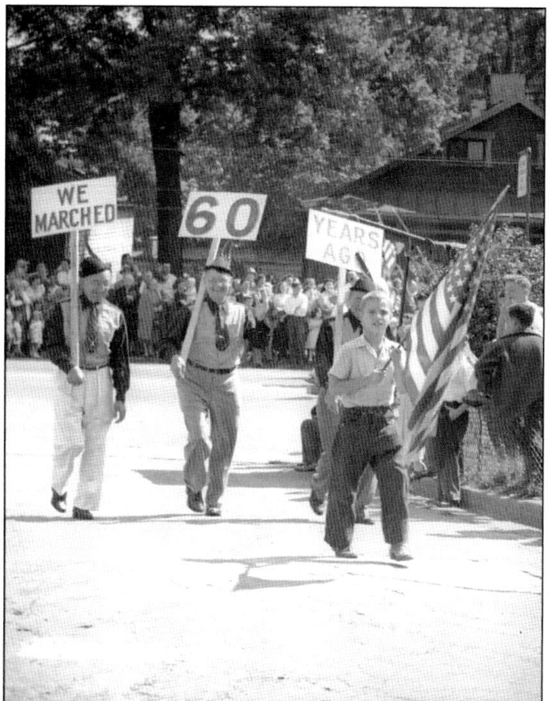

The 1951 parade was led by the American Legion posts, drum corps and rifle squads, the Cumminsville Veterans of World Wars, the Milford school band, the Anderson school band, and the Veterans of Foreign Wars.

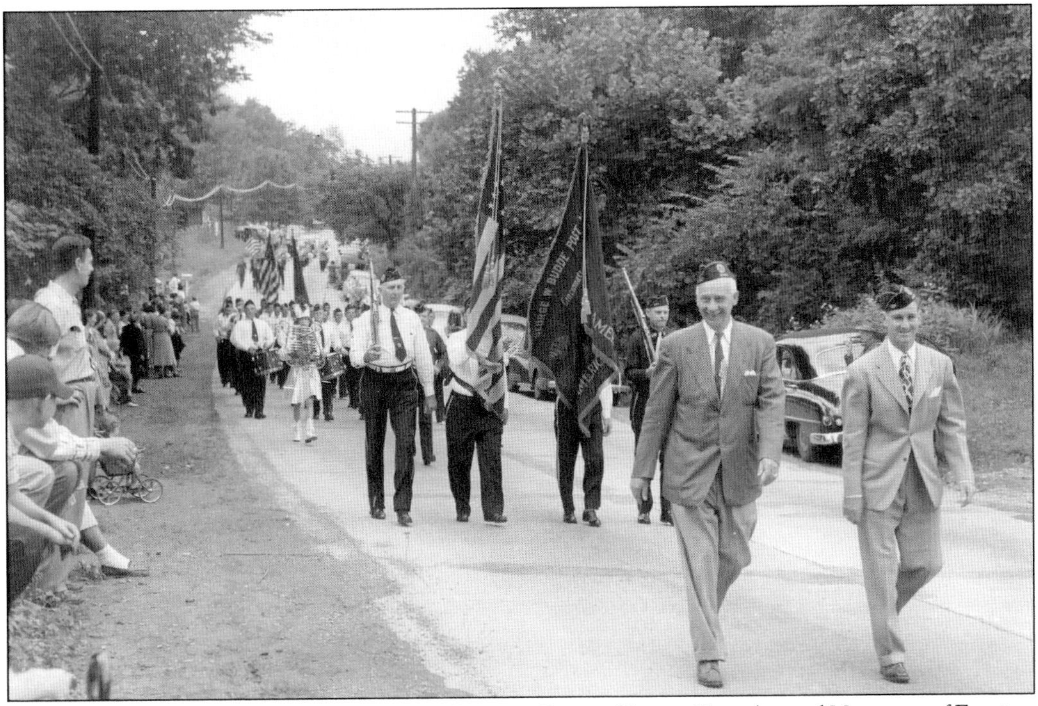

For many years, the men of the American Legion, Syrian Shrine Temple, and Veterans of Foreign Wars joined the ranks of the Orphan Feast, making the parade the largest in the state of Ohio. These units comprised 90 percent of participants in the parade. In addition to their parade duties, many of the units operated booths on the feast grounds.

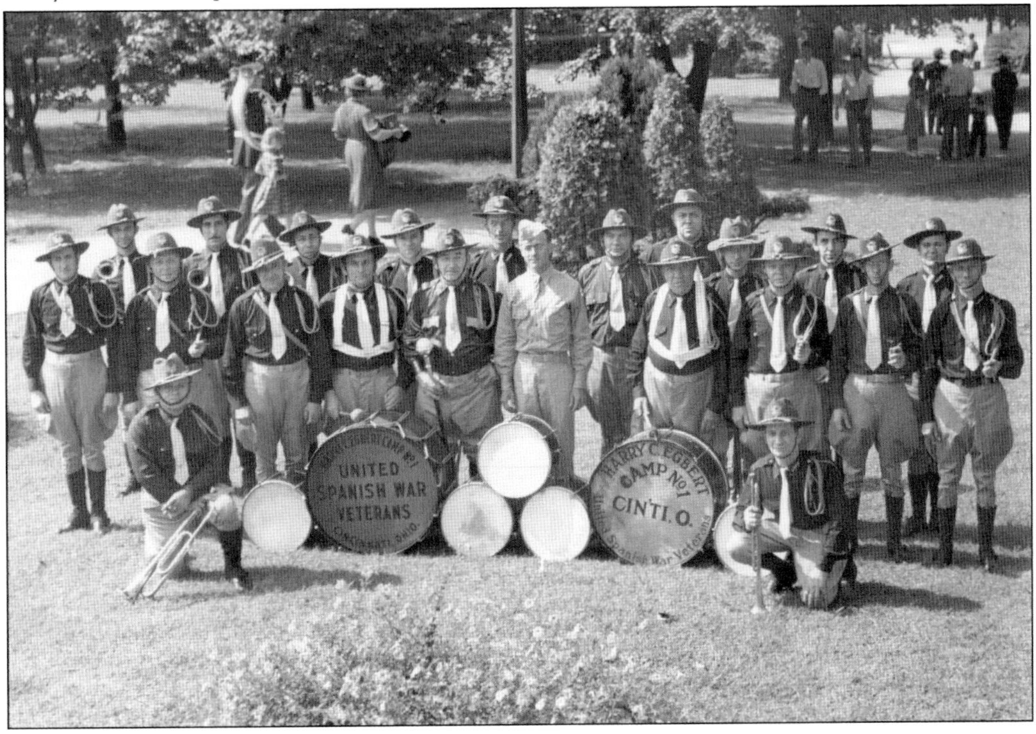

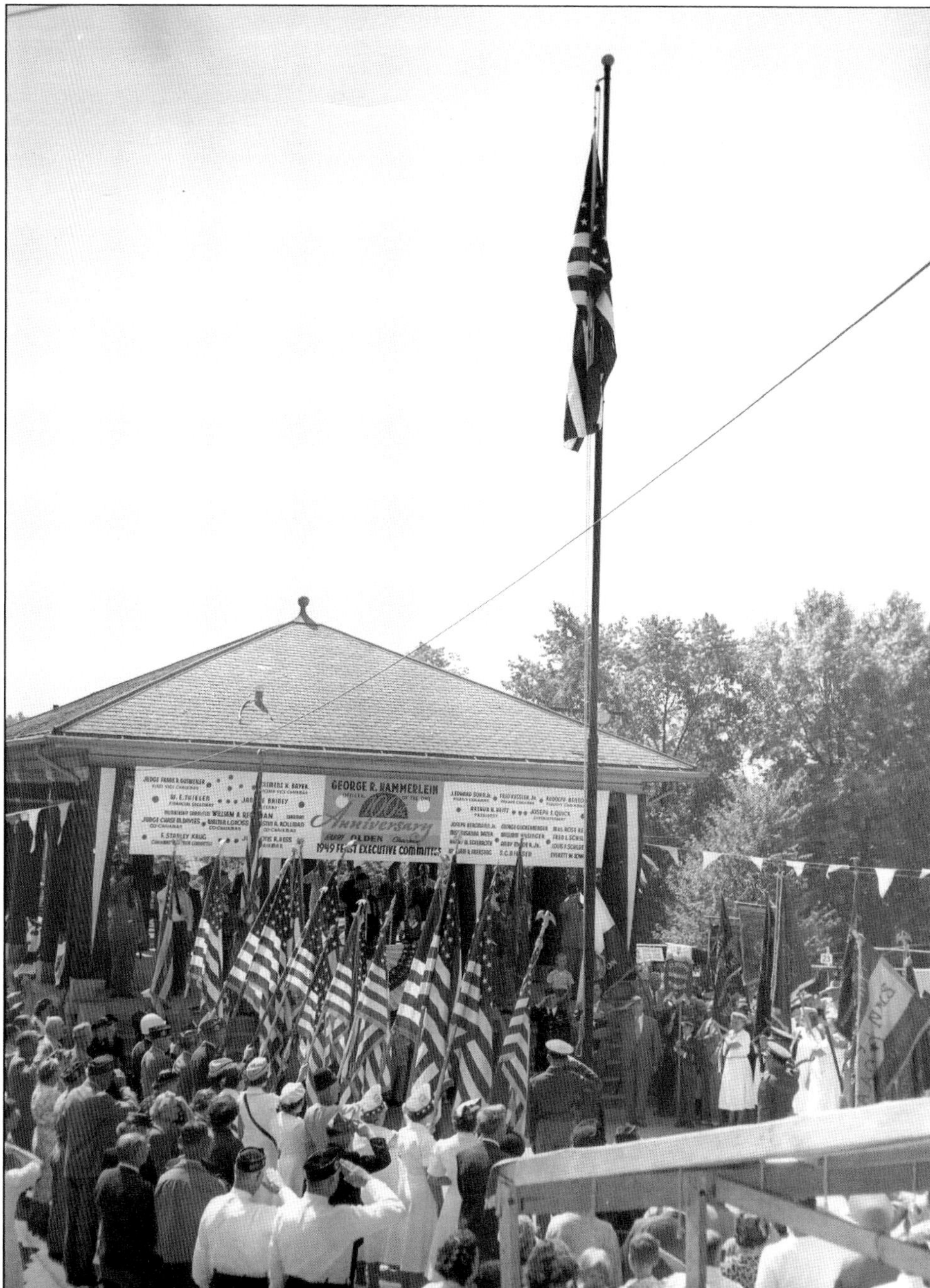

The 100th annual Orphan Feast opened at the new location on Beechmont Avenue, and a new era began for Beech Acres—The General Protestant Home. According to the police, the turnout by patrons caused "the largest traffic congestion in 20 years, and it was a jam that lasted for 11 hours." Cars lined up, double-parked, from Columbia Parkway at the Beechmont Levee to the Orphanage grounds five miles away. An oral history estimates a crowd of 80,000. This photograph shows the official welcome and invocation of the feast in 1949—the last to be held in Mount Auburn.

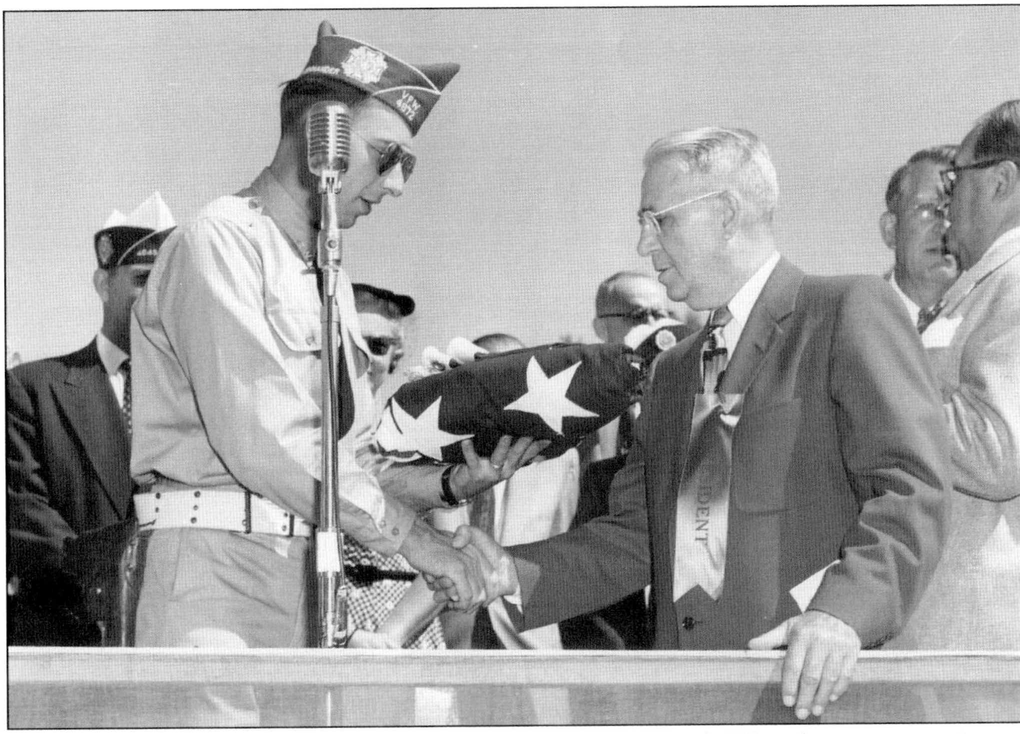

Every Orphan Feast commenced with a patriotic ceremony. A US military veteran is seen presenting a US flag to the feast's Officer of the Day. The Officer of the Day was recognized for his community engagement and the funds he could raise for the Home. In addition to being presented a US flag, his contribution was acknowledged with a life-sized poster of himself near the entrance of the administration building.

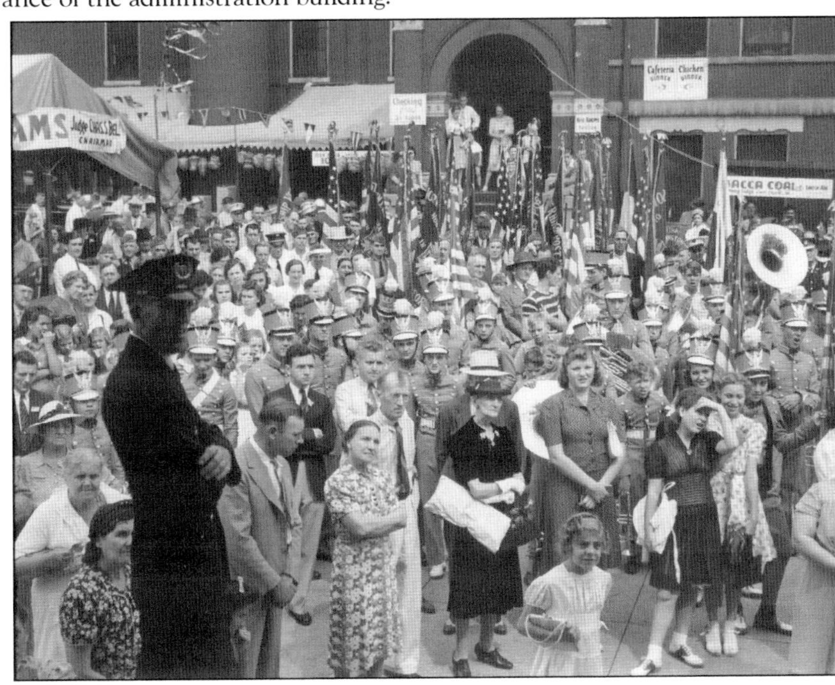

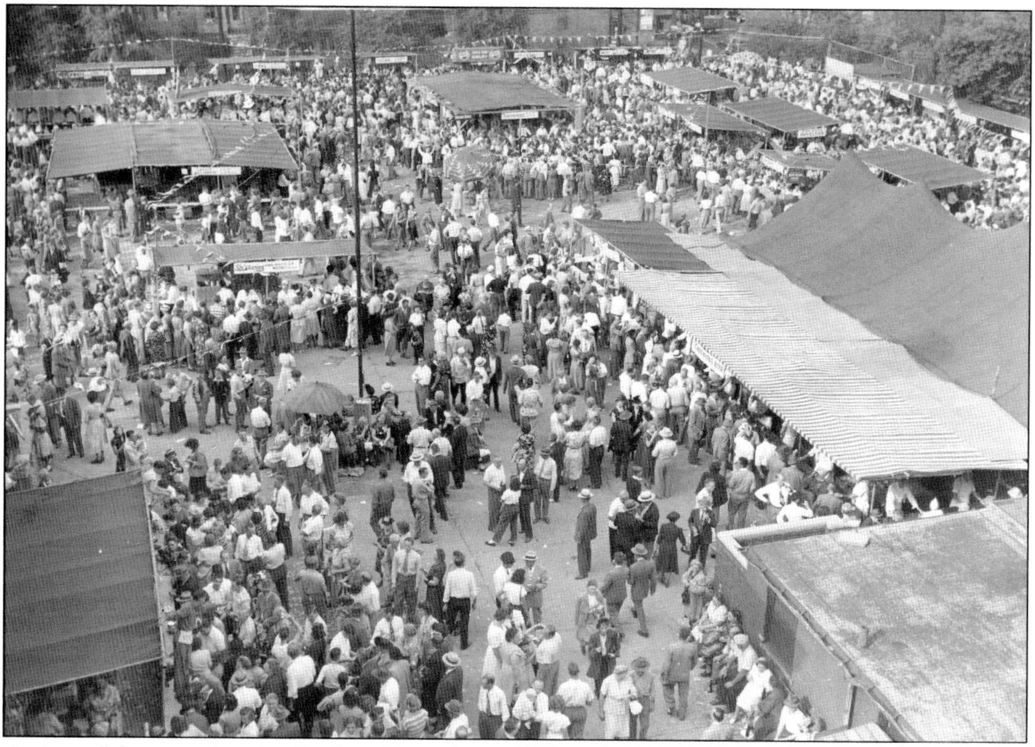

A view of the crowd at the Orphan Feast shows the energy and excitement that surrounded this one-day event. People traveled from all over the city to enjoy entertainment and socialization. From the earliest days of the feast, when people walked to the fair, to the latter days of automobiles, no distance was too far for an Orphan Feast attendee to travel to enjoy the event.

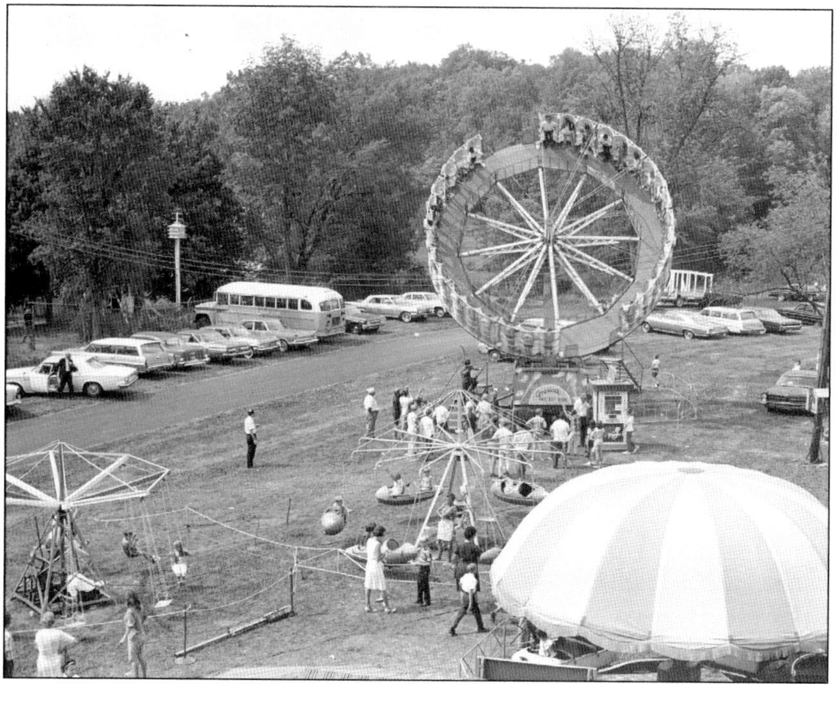

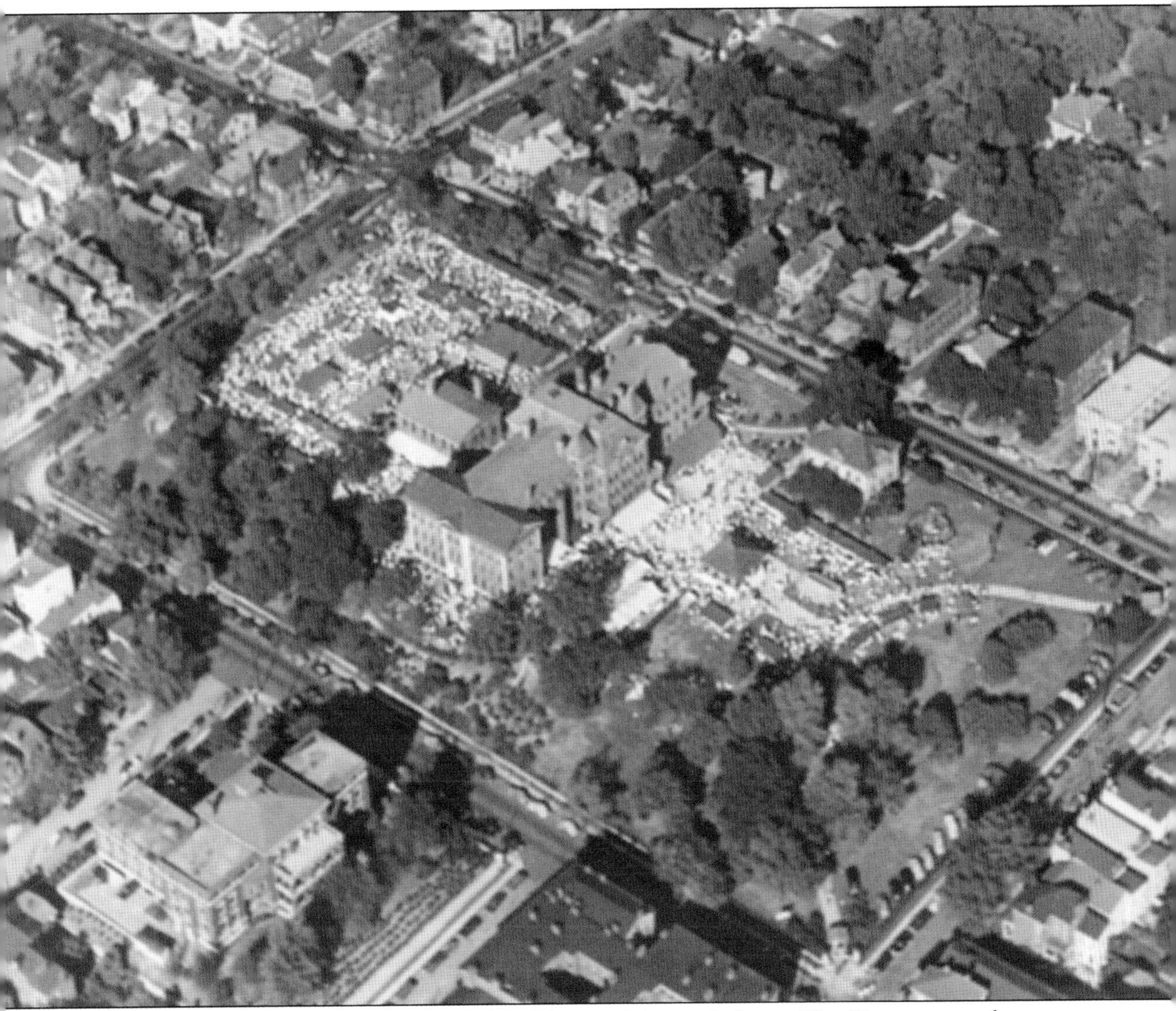

This is a c. 1940 aerial view of the Orphan Feast in Mount Auburn. The Home sat on four acres purchased from Judge Burnet for $4,000 in 1849. Completed in 1851, it spanned the modern area between Martin Luther King Drive at Burnet Avenue and East University at Highland Avenue.

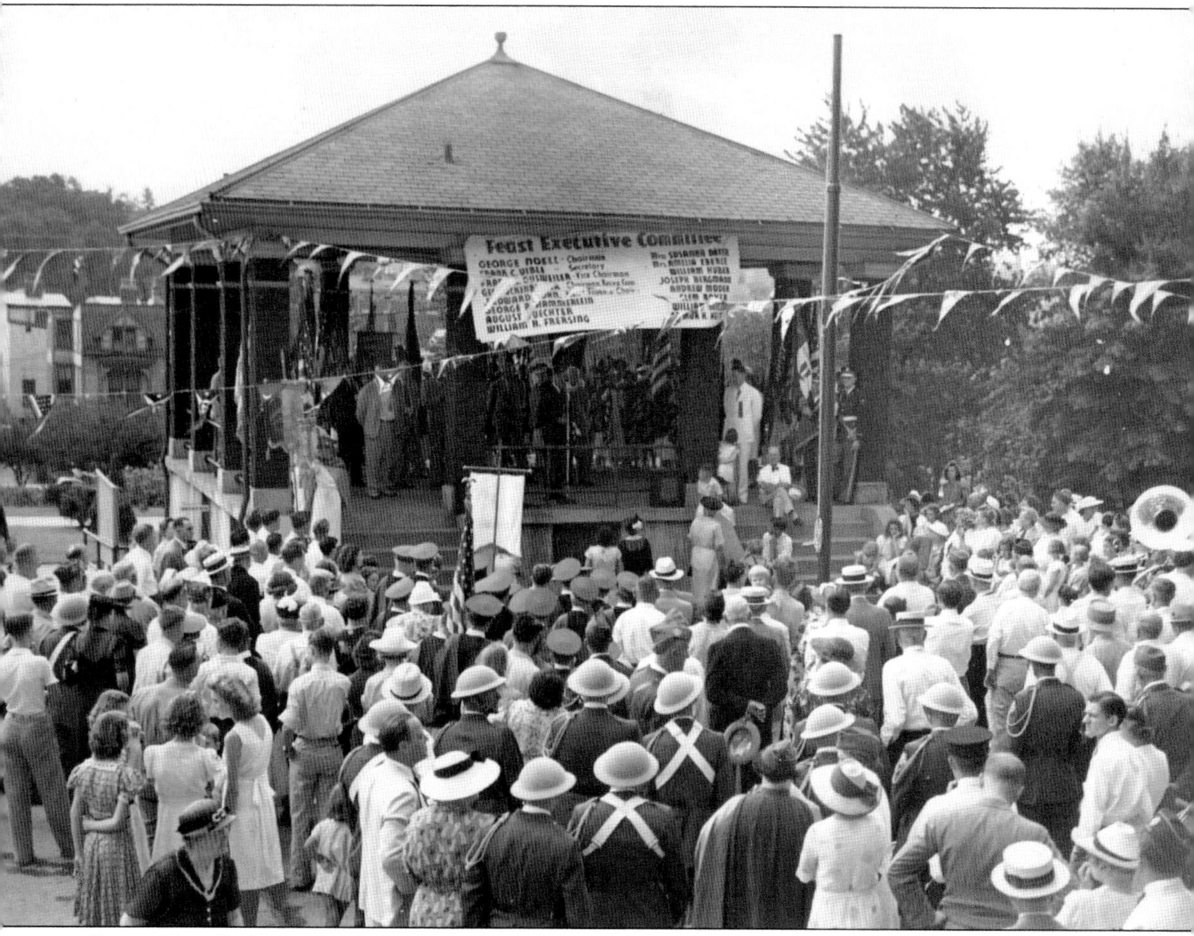

Pictured is the Patriotic Ceremony opening the 1939 Orphan Feast in Mount Auburn.

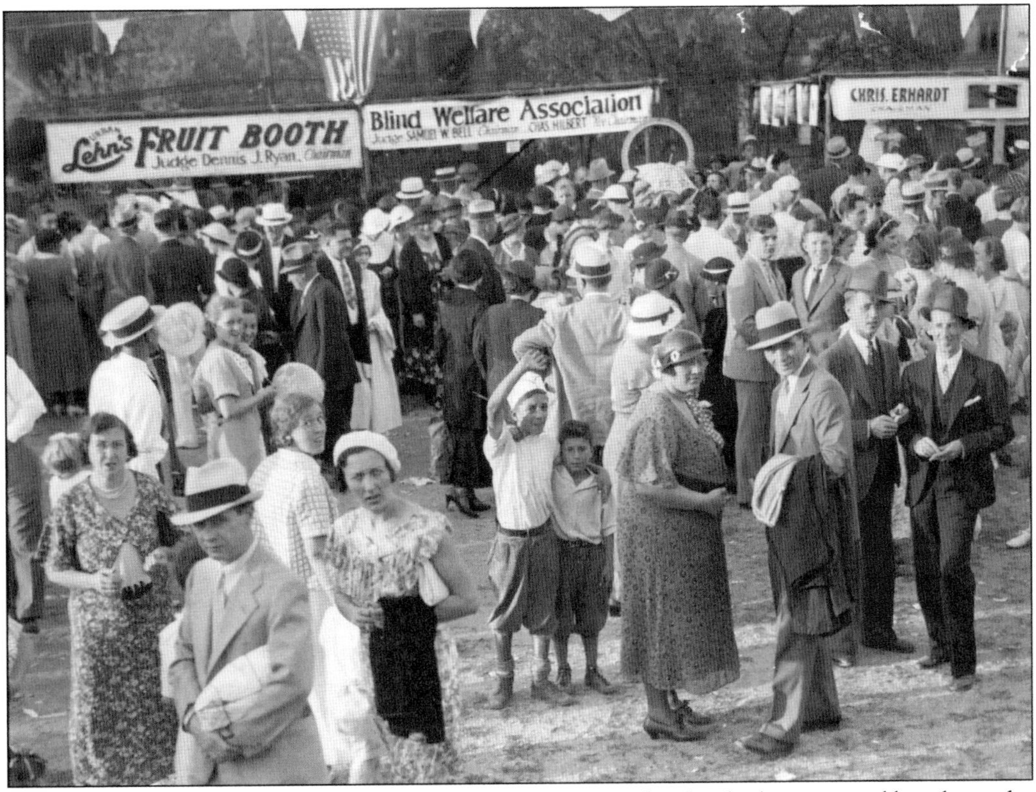

Every year, for 137 consecutive years, businesses, groups, and individuals sponsored booths at the feast. The booths were rented out and proceeds donated to the Home. Booths varied from games, food, prizes, and sales of goods. There was always something for everyone at the feast, especially when it came to winning, taking a chance on a bet, and purchasing items.

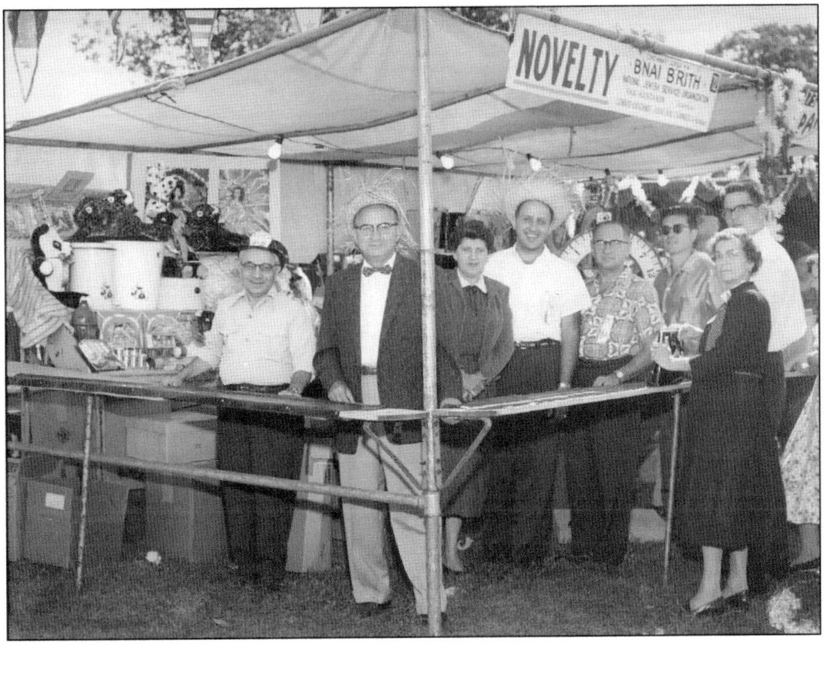

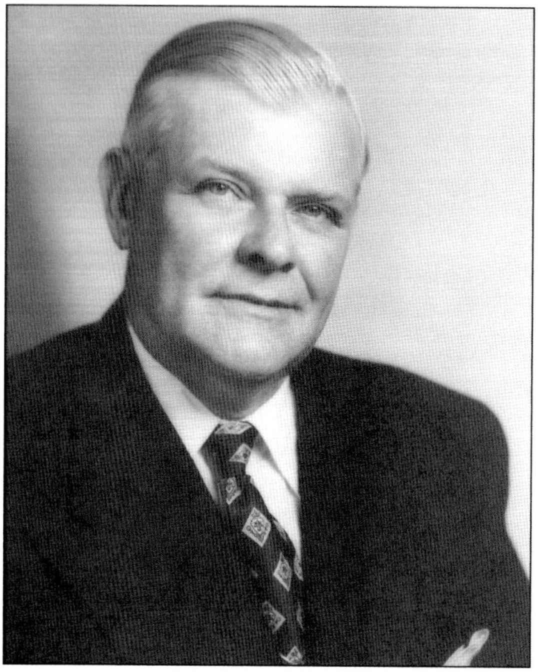

Leadership has been a legacy in the Nielsen family across three generations. Patriarch Simon C. Nielsen (left) served on the board of directors and as Orphan Feast Officer of the Day in 1943. His most important contribution was as chairman of the campaign that raised $350,000 to build a new campus in Mount Washington. Simon's commitment to children was passed on to future generations. Son Eric "Rick" Nielsen (below) also served on the board of directors (1969–1978) and donated printing services to the Home. Grandson Simon C. "Chip" Nielsen III served on the board of directors from 1993 to 2000, including as its treasurer, during a period of significant growth in providing more preventive services. The Nielsen family remains supportive today, exemplifying the power of a consistent commitment to children and the ability to adapt to changing times.

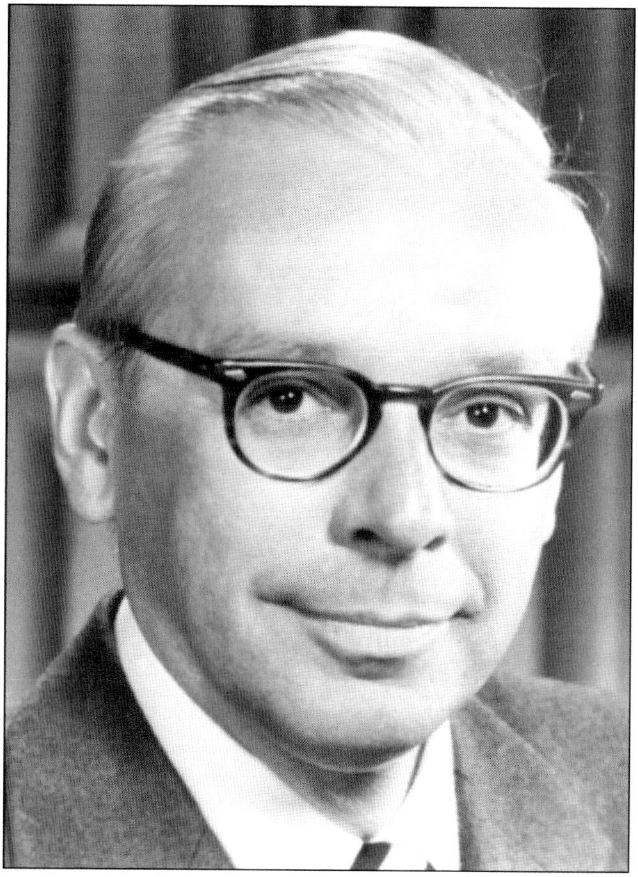

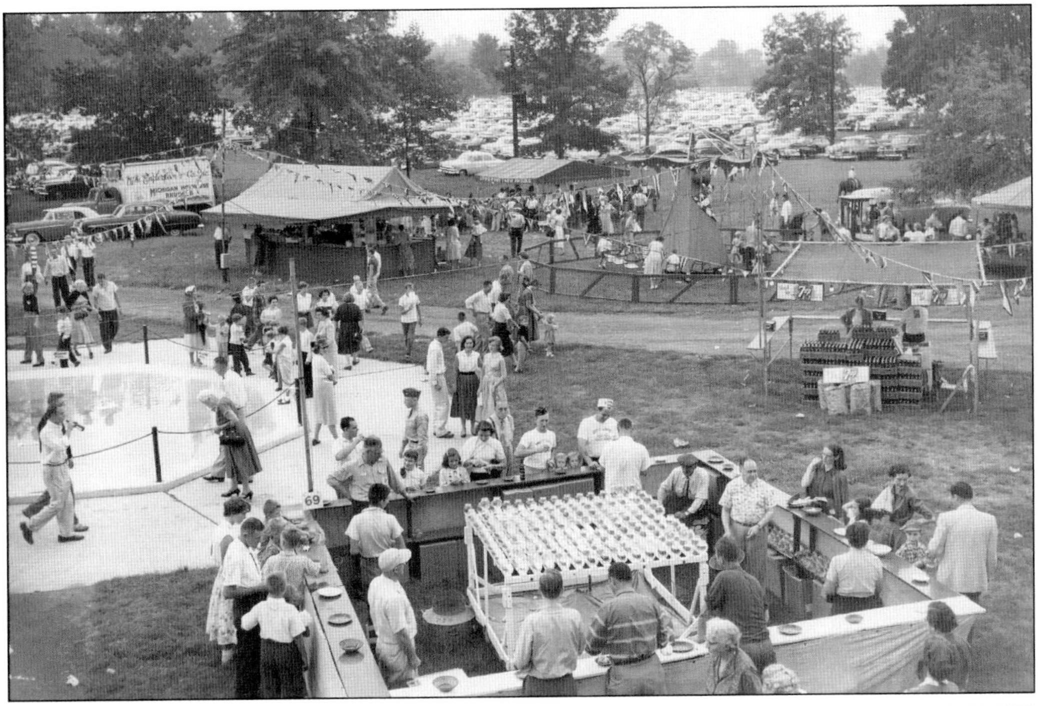

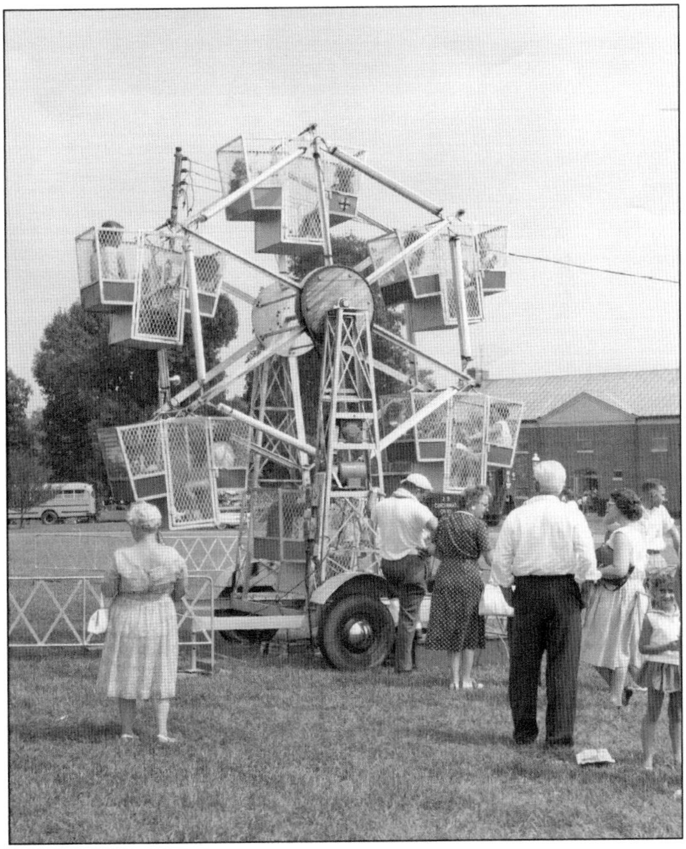

Popular rides were featured at the Orphan Feast for adults and children alike. The famous swing set was an annual requirement, as it passed the test of time for festival enjoyment. The ever-popular Ferris wheel was brought to the Orphan Feast by way of a trailer. Rides gave children the opportunity to release some energy while their parents were participating in gambling games and other festival-related activities. The children of the Home had the opportunity to ride the rides, but they had to do so before the feast began.

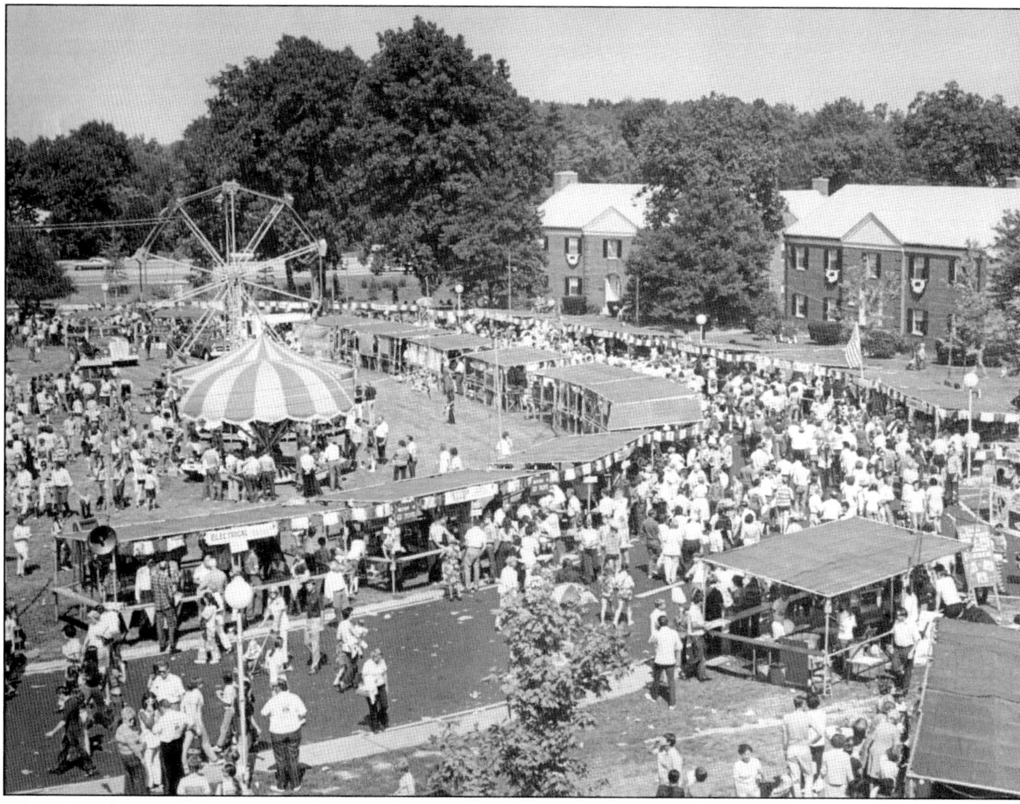

The aerial view below of the Orphan Feast shows current-day Beech Acres Park as the parking lot for the festival. People came from a 50-mile radius, backing up Beechmont Avenue with hours of traffic. Thousands of people attended this popular social outing to support the orphanage.

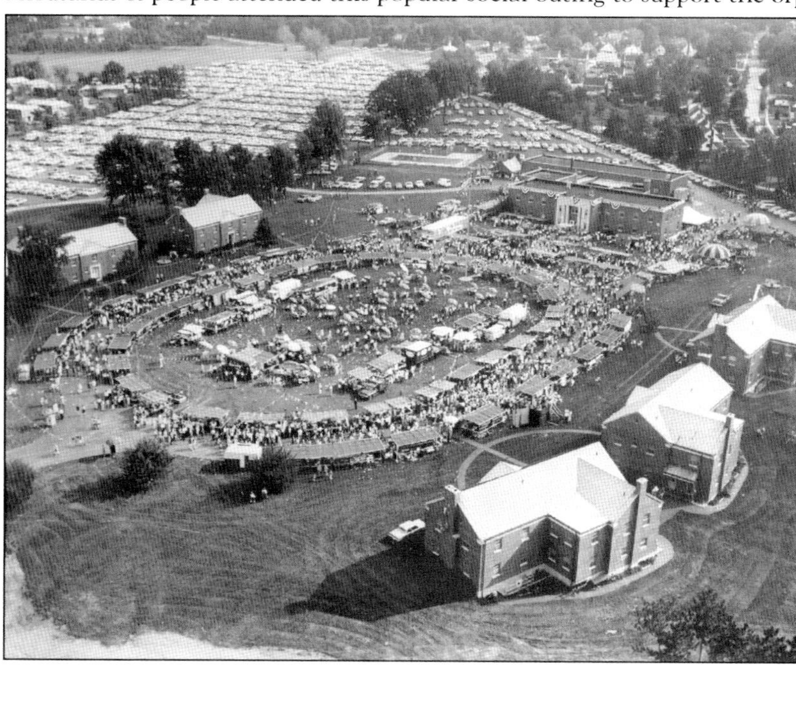

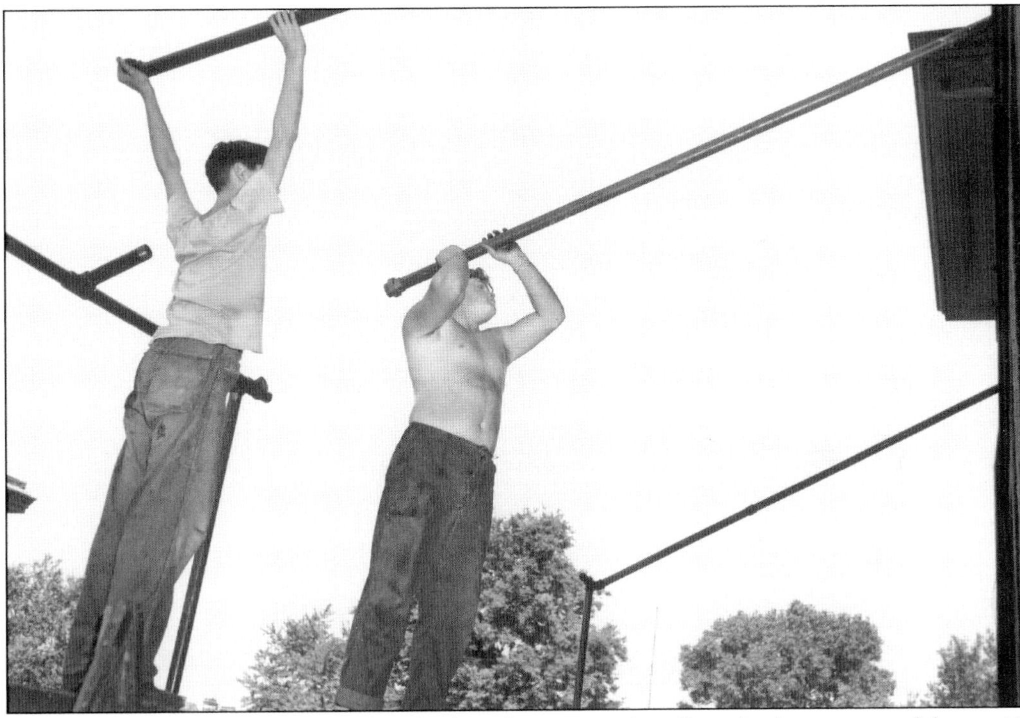

More than 1,000 volunteers were involved in planning and staffing the feast, many of them with the setup and breakdown of the booths. Cincinnati firefighters volunteered eight hours of their time the day before the event. In 1972, under the direction of Capt. Sam Rue, over 100 booths were erected, with all repairs and breakdowns handled by the Cincinnati firemen. Their unselfish efforts included dismantling and storing of the booth equipment as well.

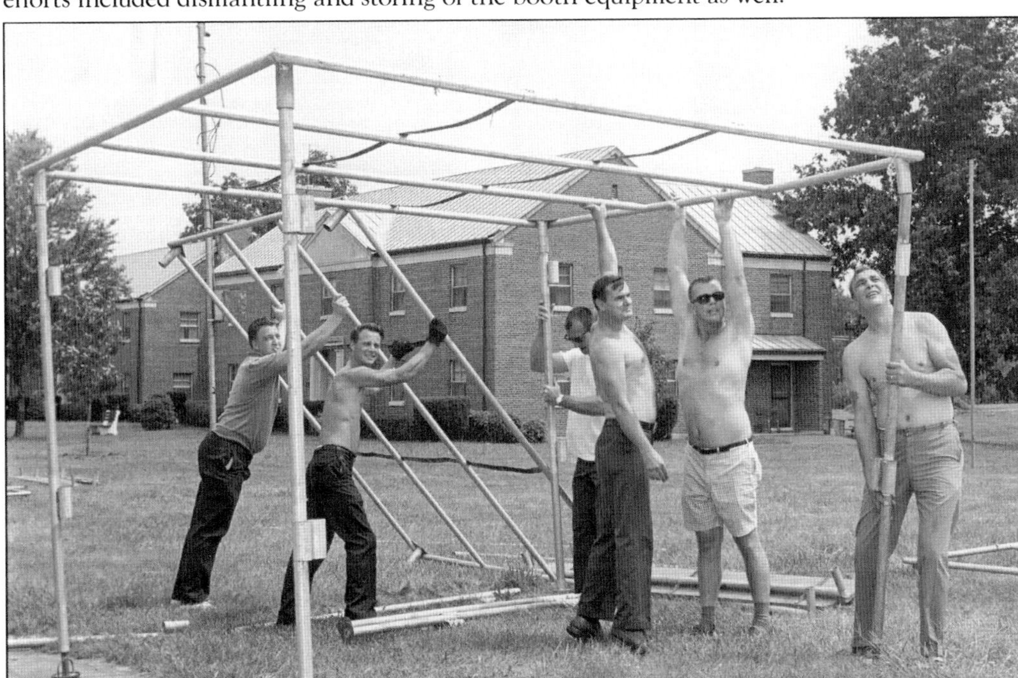

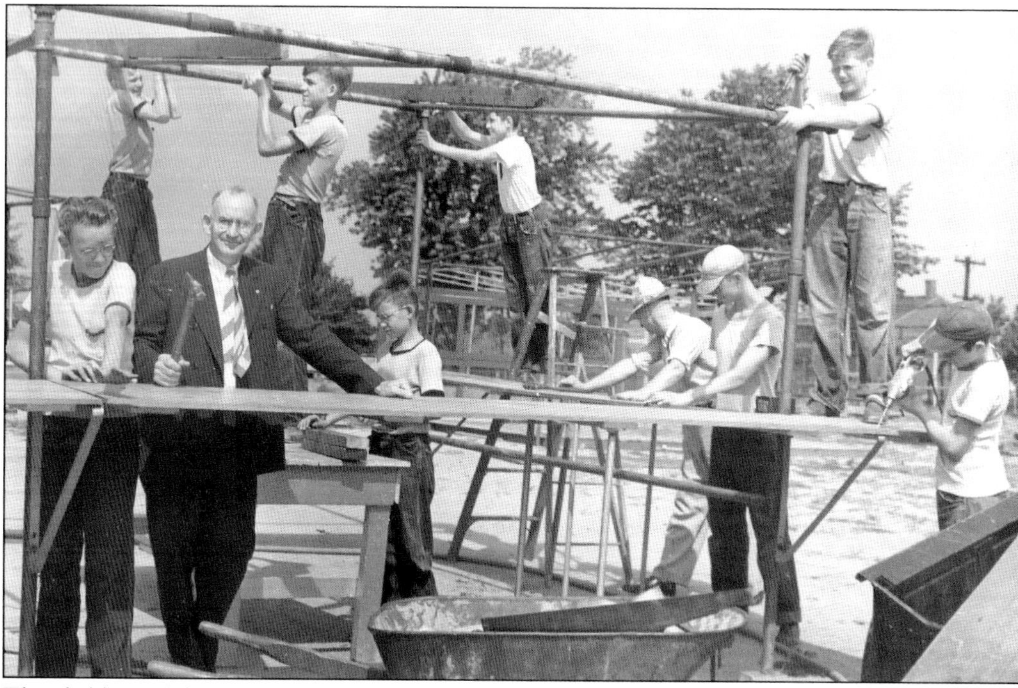

The children of the Home eagerly awaited the annual Orphan Feast. The day not only provided rides, entertainment, guests, and large quantities of food, it also provided an opportunity for the residents to make some money. A former resident recalls that the foreman leading the group of children workers would make 50¢ per hour, while the children in the group made 25¢ per hour. Senior boys assisted in building the booths. Senior girls created crafts to be sold at their booth.

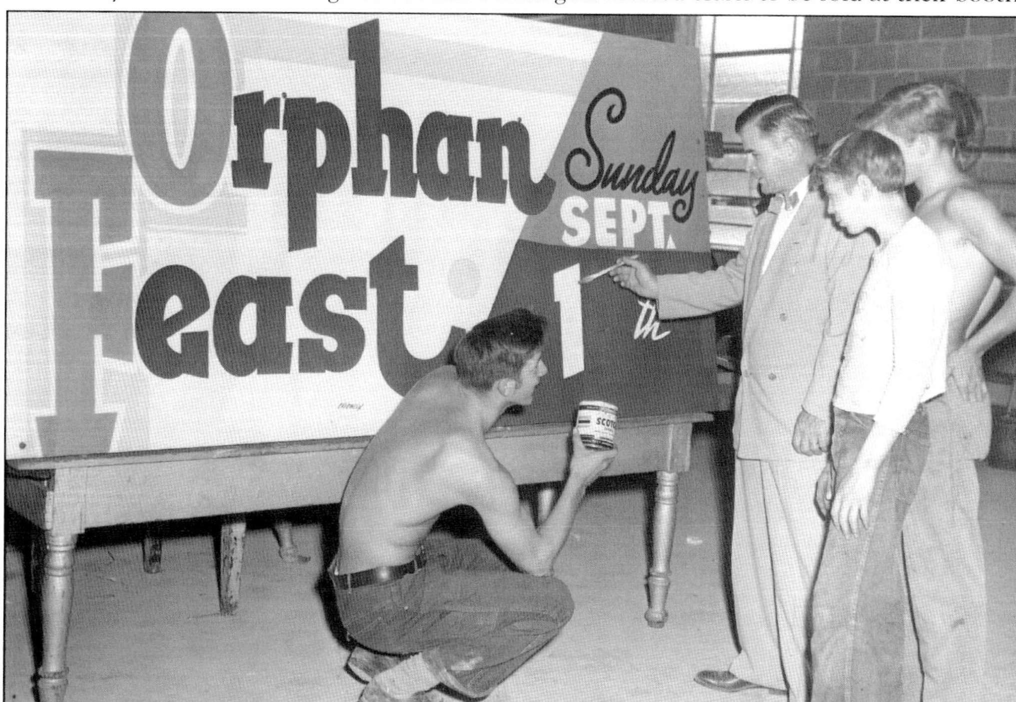

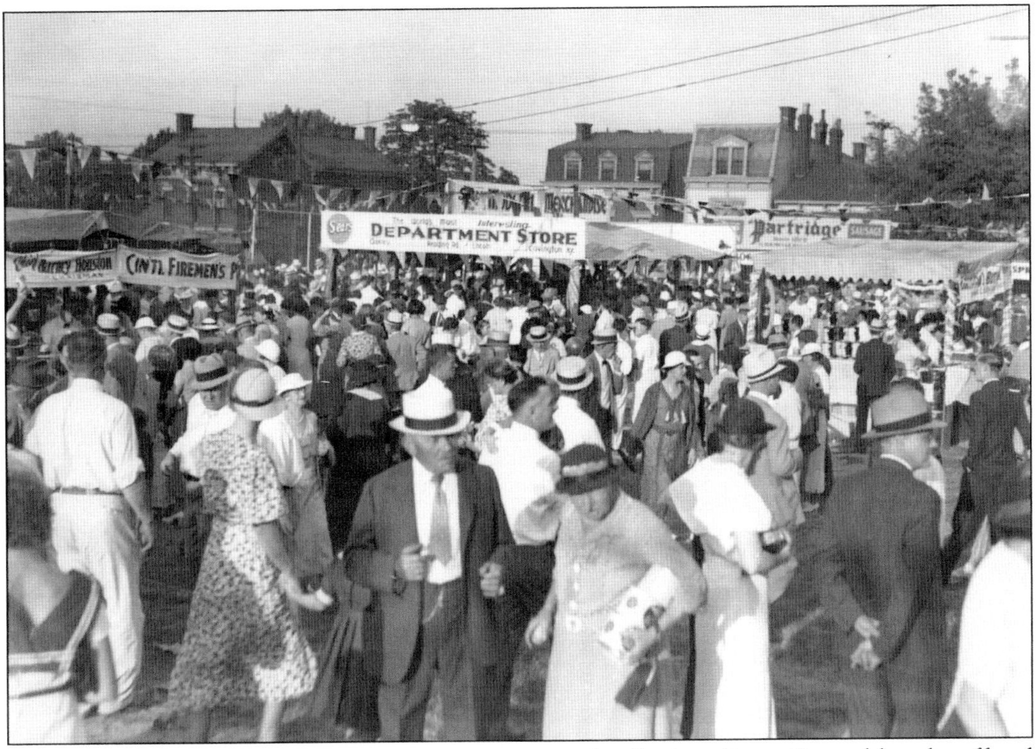

Buying or winning a pig was an exciting prospect at the Orphan Feast. Several booths offered ham as a reward for winning a game or holding the correct raffle ticket.

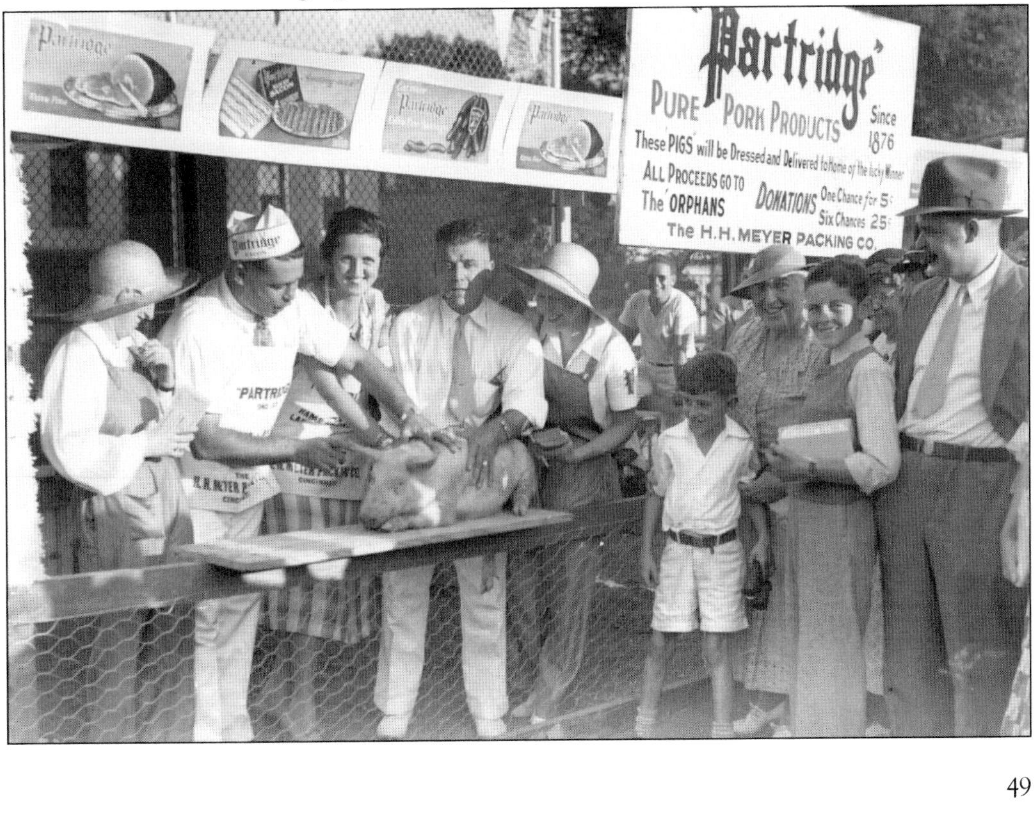

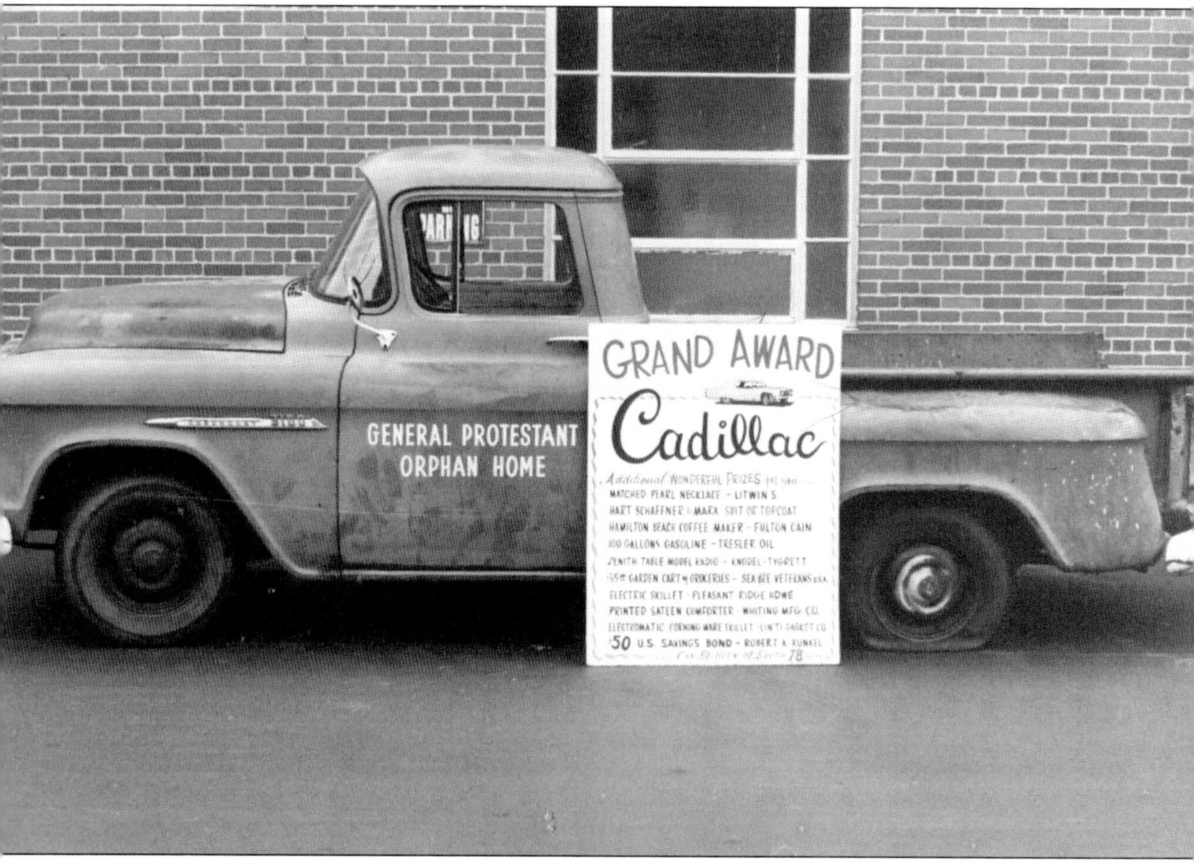

The Orphan Feast Executive Committee offered exciting raffle prizes each year. In 1974, prizes included a new Cadillac, a $50 US Savings Bond, 100 gallons of gasoline, a Zenith table model radio, a Hamilton Beach coffee maker, a printed sateen comforter, a pearl necklace, a Hart, Schaffner and Marx topcoat, and an Electromatic skillet.

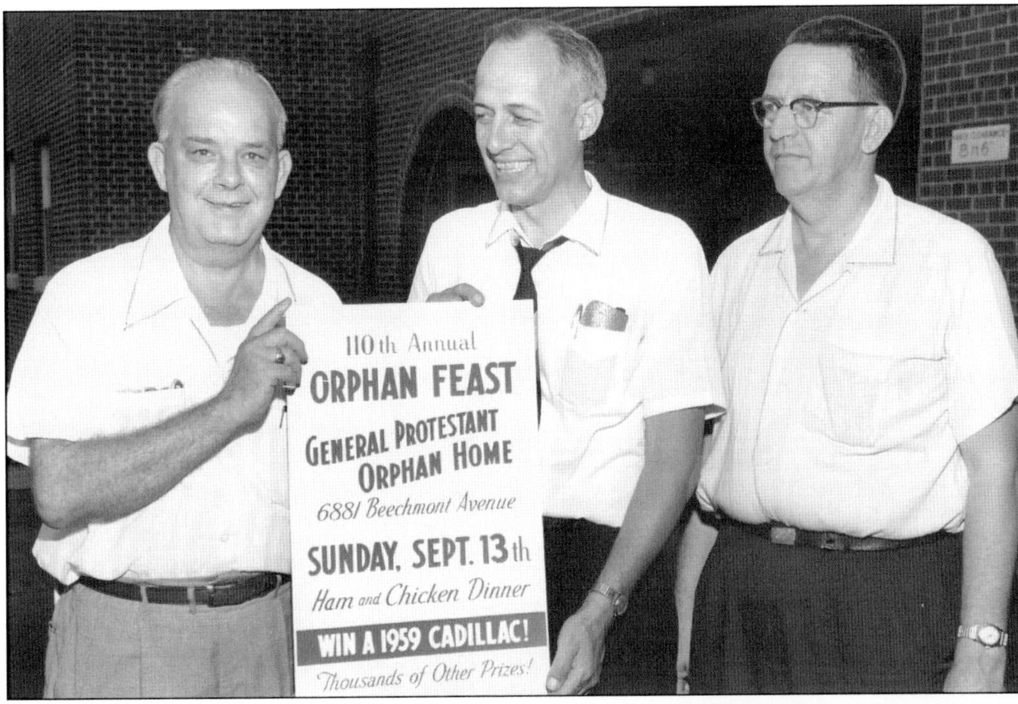

It was well known that the Orphan Feast offered several large raffle prizes. A new Cadillac, available for one fortunate ticket holder, was the highly valued grand prize. The winner of the grand prize in 1972 was Edward Holmes. He is seen above (left) receiving his award from GPOH Board president Carson Whiting (center). The 1972 Orphan Feast theme, "Welcome to Beech Acres—the Gateway to Love and Happiness," helped the annual event break all records with over 100,000 people in attendance. Tickets were sold in advance throughout the community. The image to the right was taken in front of Riverfront Stadium where the Cincinnati Reds and Cincinnati Bengals played.

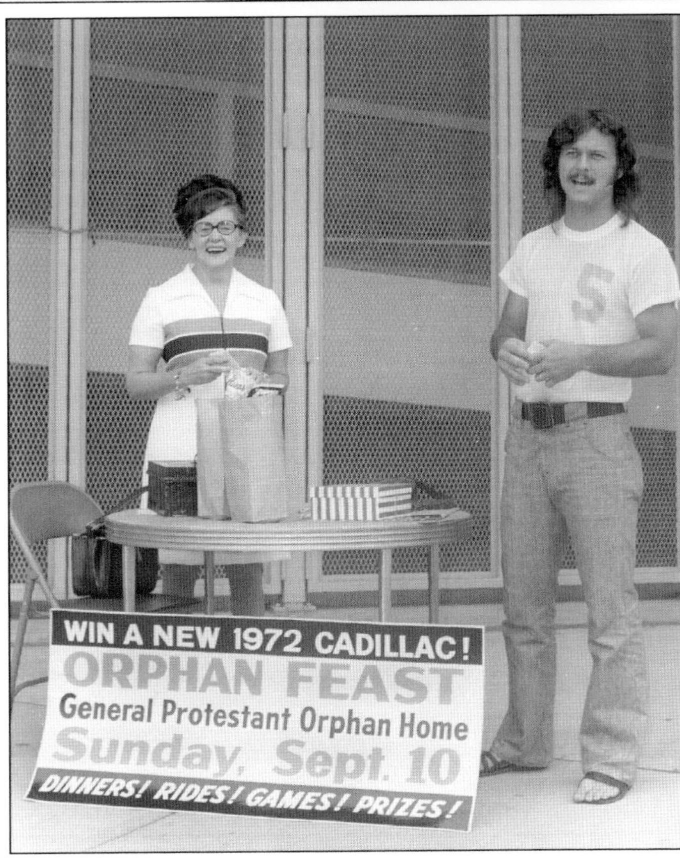

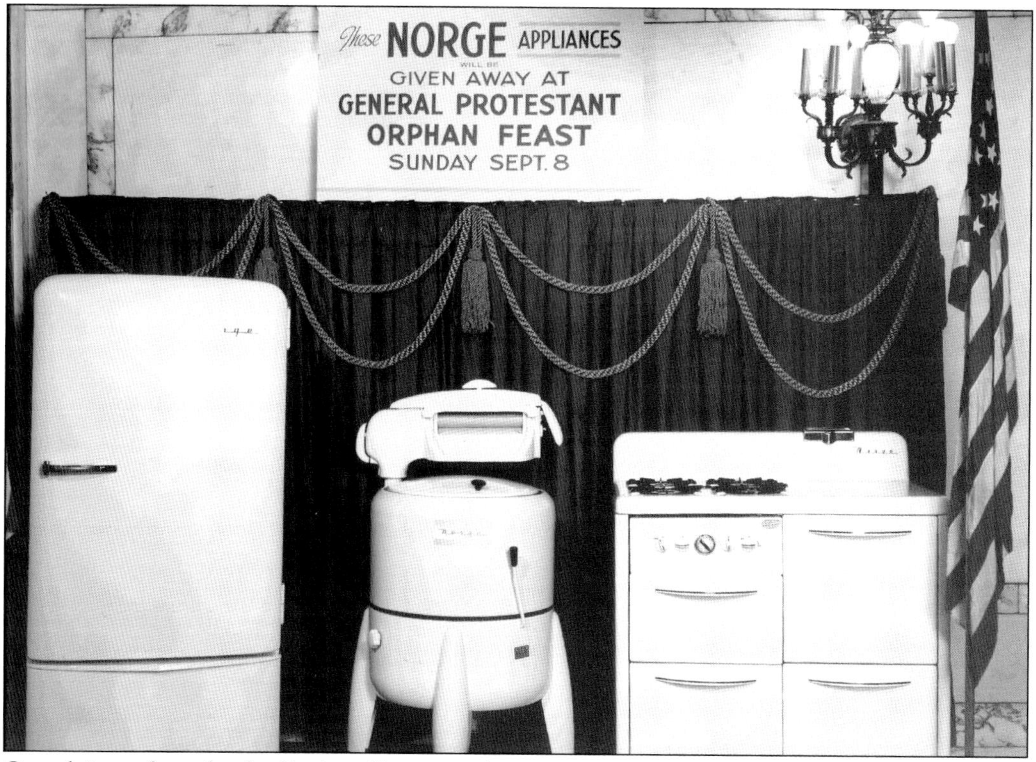

One claim to fame for the Orphan Feast was the many opportunities to win valuable prizes; some included taking home brand-new home appliances, while others included winning a brand-new car. The last chance to win a new 1950 Nash Rambler was available to any of the Orphan Feast attendees for the low price of $1. Each attendee could purchase up to 21 chances to win the new vehicle. Guaranteed to be the car of the future, this car got 50 miles to the gallon. The Nash Dealership of Cincinnati remained in business until the late 1980s, supporting the Orphan Feast every year.

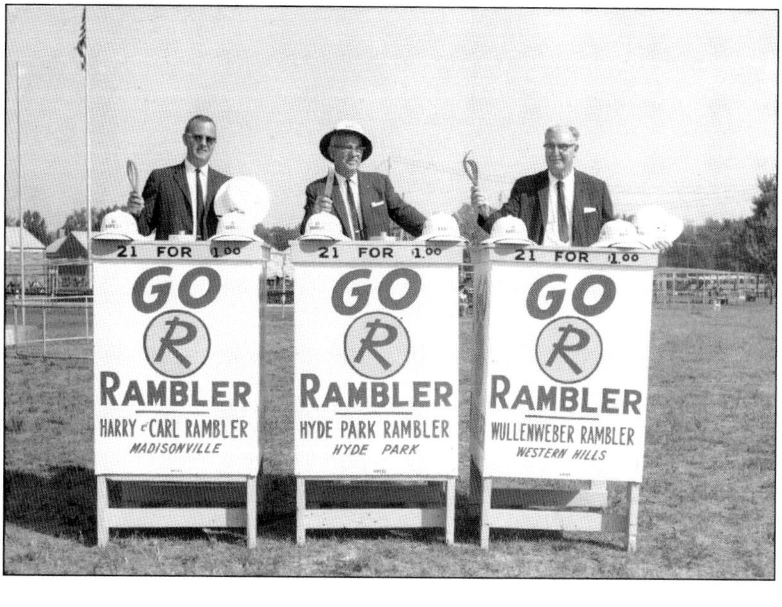

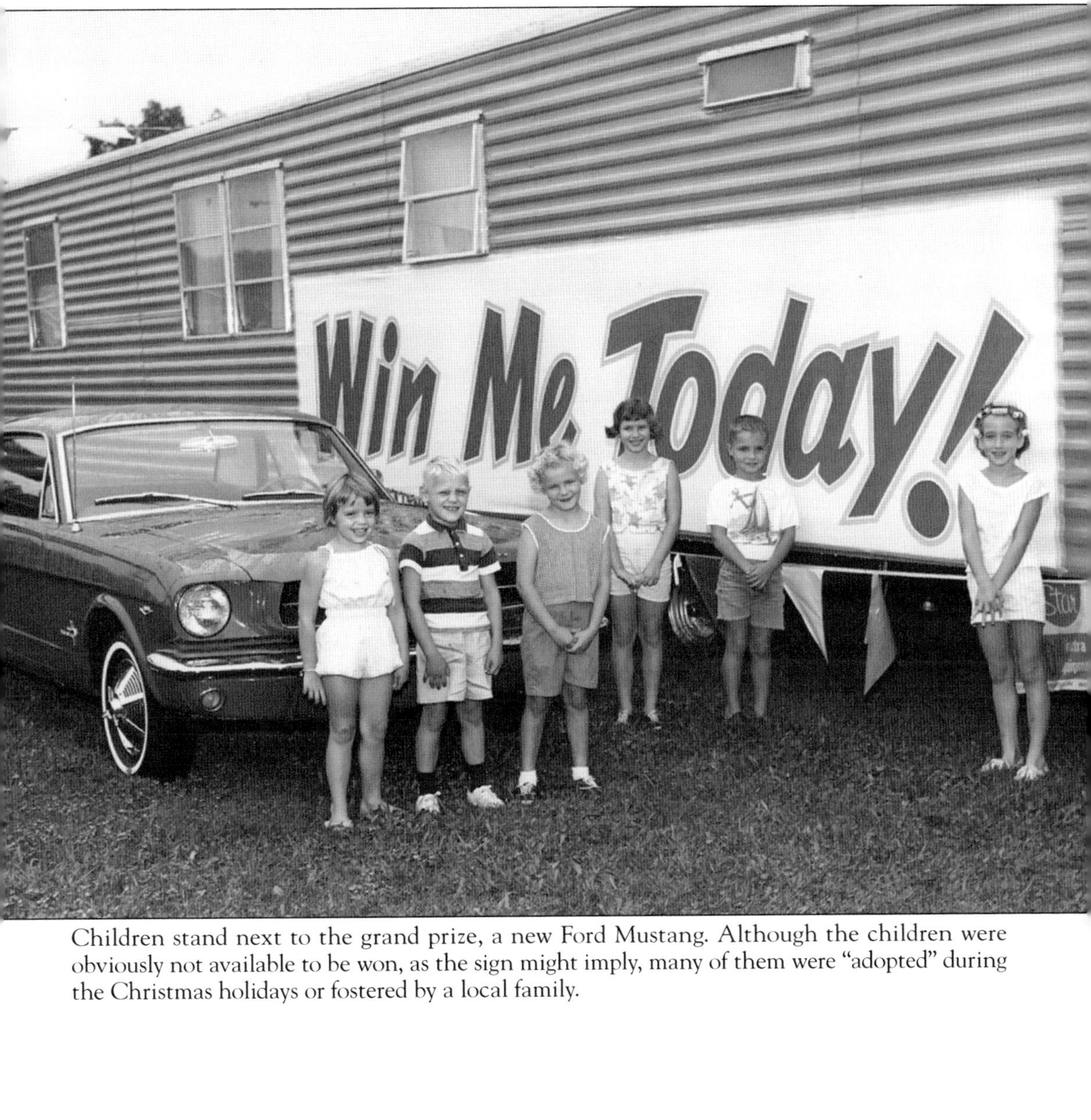

Children stand next to the grand prize, a new Ford Mustang. Although the children were obviously not available to be won, as the sign might imply, many of them were "adopted" during the Christmas holidays or fostered by a local family.

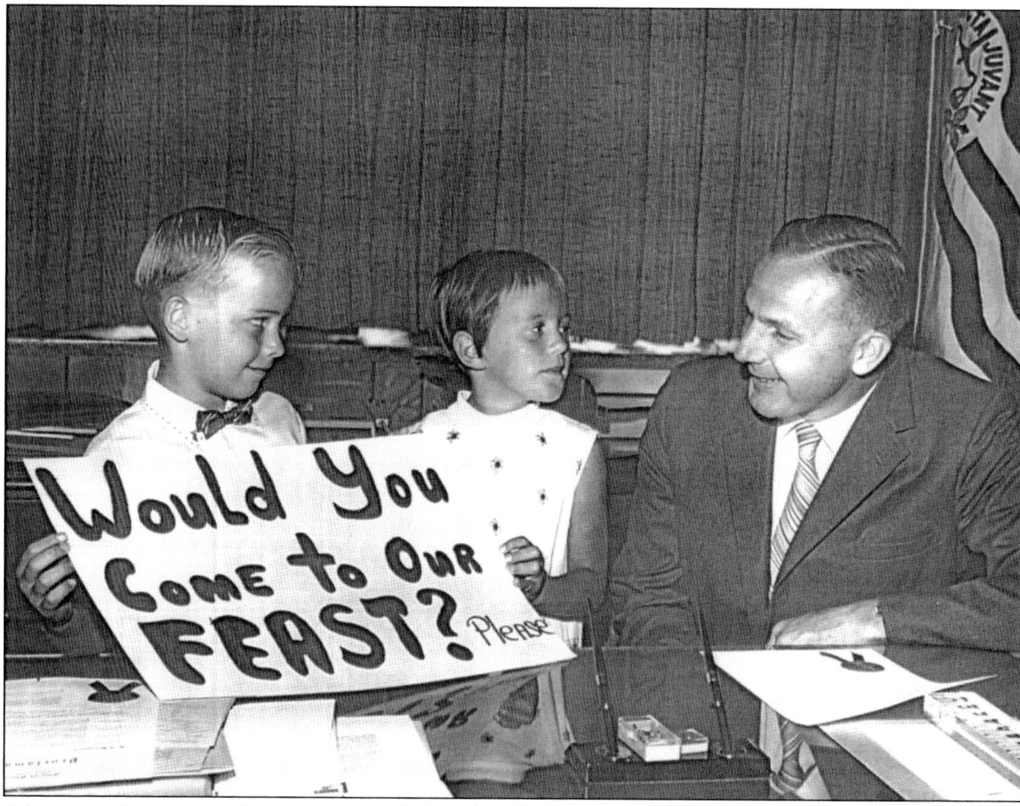

Above, orphans pose for pictures with handcrafted posters. The photographs and posters were shown throughout Cincinnati to build awareness for the annual Orphan Feast. Below, Tom Luken, mayor of Cincinnati, signs a proclamation for the General Protestant Orphan Home's Orphan Feast. Every year, the feast received a proclamation from the City of Cincinnati, naming that day the Day of the Orphan Feast.

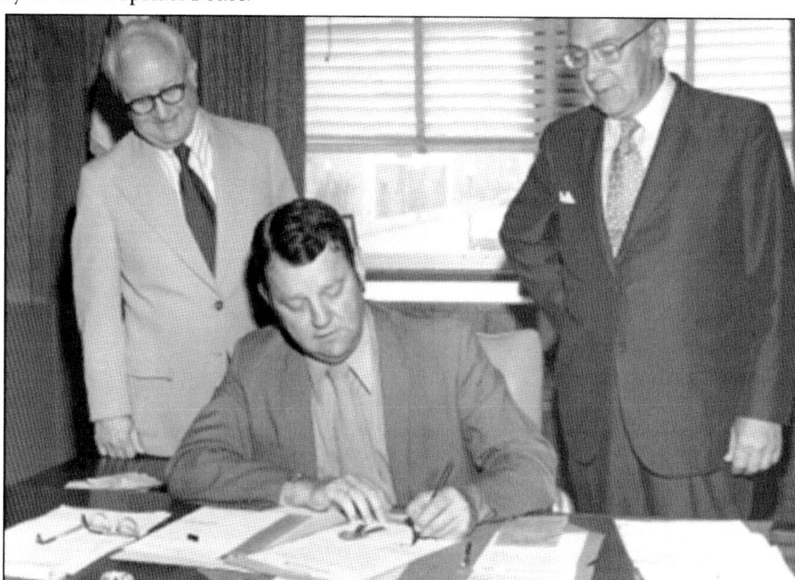

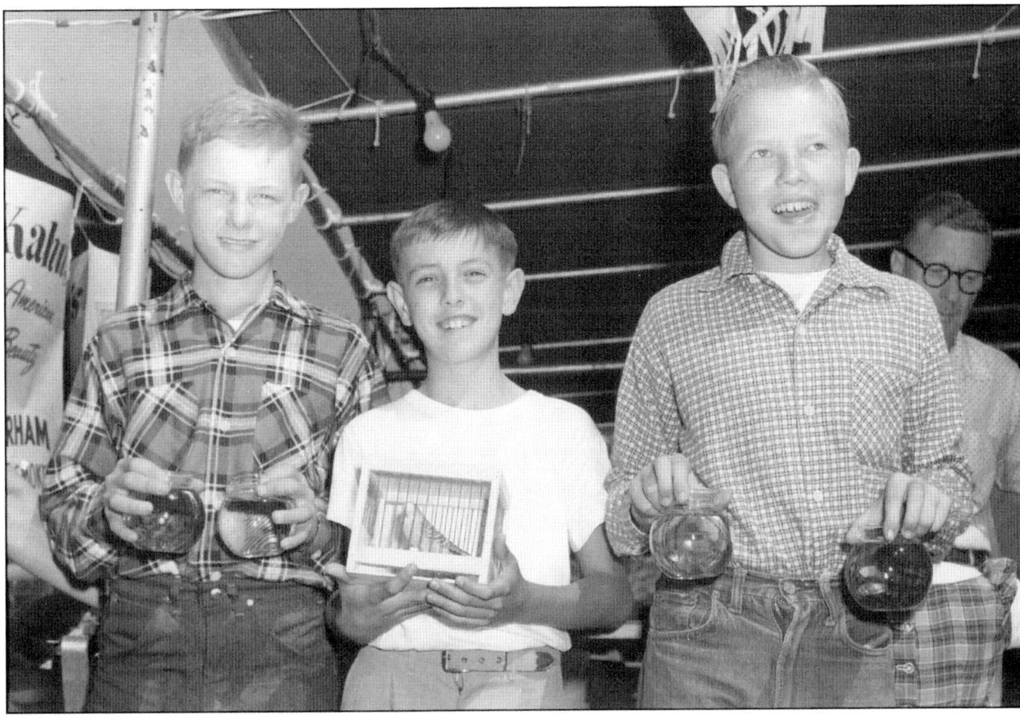

Resident children were often permitted to participate in feast activities after the majority of the attendees had left. With great excitement, the children had the opportunity to win prizes, ride the rides, and enjoy themselves in a carefree manner.

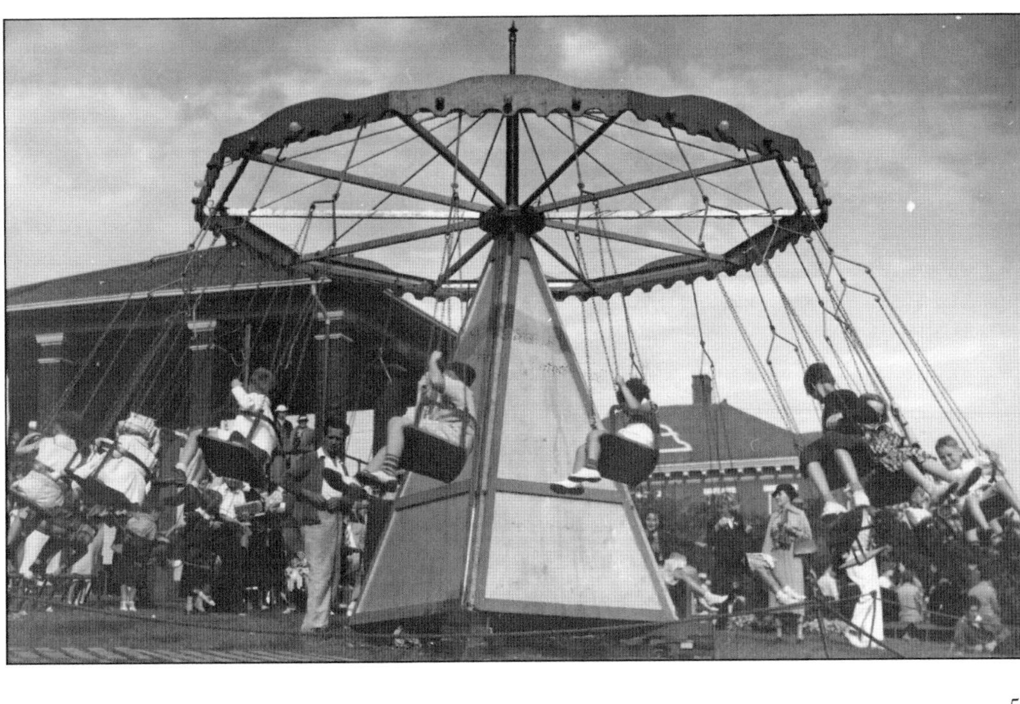

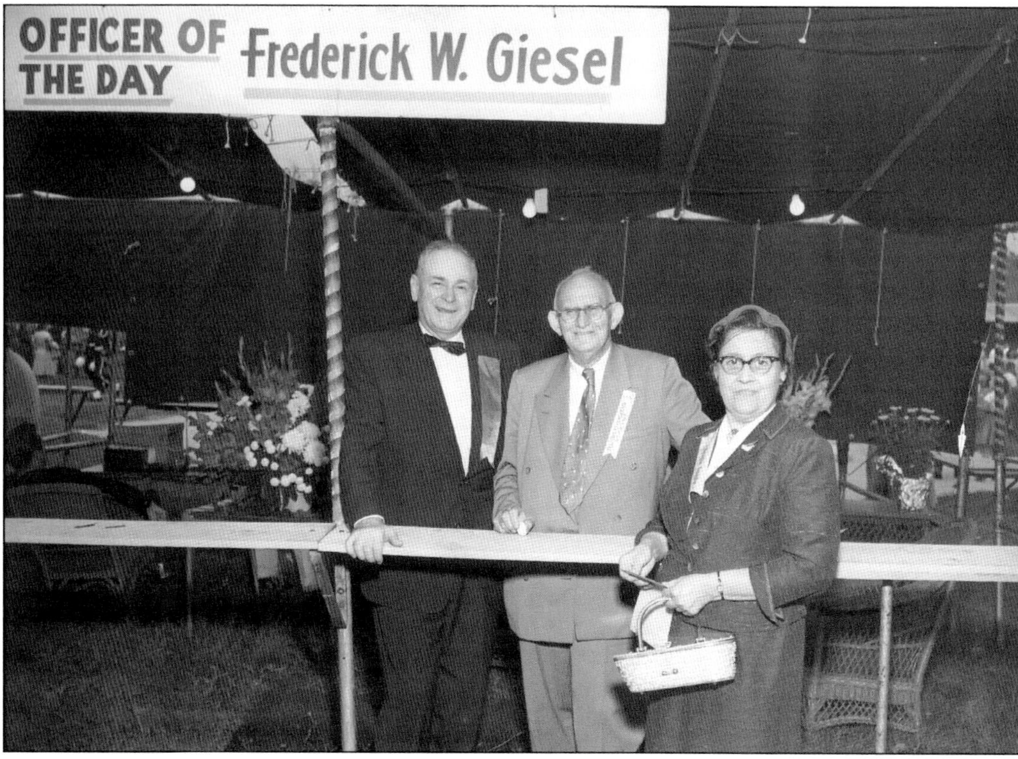

The Officer of the Day of the Orphan Feast was an elite title given to a prominent community member. This person had the responsibility of raising funds for the Orphan Feast through business and individual donations. He or she was also in charge of gaining new lifelong supporters and financial contributors. The Officer of the Day had his or her own special booth at the event and was honored during the opening ceremony.

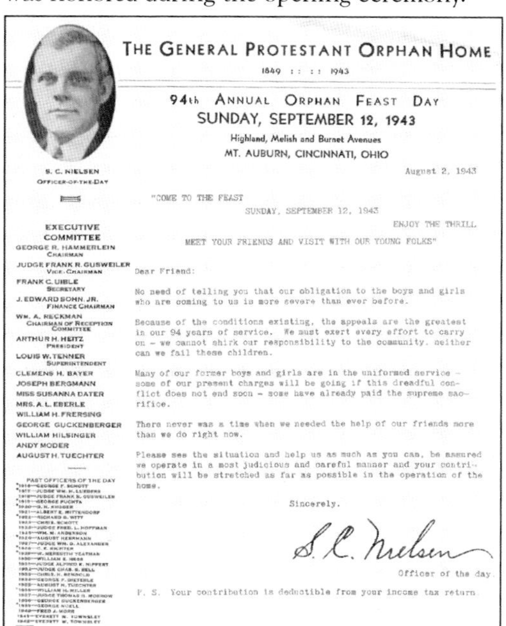

THE GENERAL PROTESTANT ORPHAN HOME

1849 :: :: 1943

94th ANNUAL ORPHAN FEAST DAY

SUNDAY, SEPTEMBER 12, 1943

Highland, Melish and Burnet Avenues

MT. AUBURN, CINCINNATI, OHIO

S. C. NIELSEN
OFFICER-OF-THE-DAY

EXECUTIVE COMMITTEE
GEORGE R. HAMMERLEIN, CHAIRMAN
JUDGE FRANK R. GUSWEILER, VICE-CHAIRMAN
FRANK C. UIBLE, SECRETARY
J. EDWARD BOHN, JR., FINANCE CHAIRMAN
WM. A. RECKMAN, CHAIRMAN OF RECEPTION COMMITTEE
ARTHUR H. HEITZ, PRESIDENT
LOUIS W. TENNER, SUPERINTENDENT
CLEMENS H. BAYER
JOSEPH BERGMANN
MISS SUSANNA DATER
MRS. A. L. EBERLE
WILLIAM H. FRERSING
GEORGE GUCKENBERGER
WILLIAM HILSINGER
ANDY MODER
AUGUST H. TUECHTER

PAST OFFICERS OF THE DAY

August 2, 1943

"COME TO THE FEAST

SUNDAY, SEPTEMBER 12, 1943

ENJOY THE THRILL

MEET YOUR FRIENDS AND VISIT WITH OUR YOUNG FOLKS"

Dear Friend:

No need of telling you that our obligation to the boys and girls who are coming to us is more severe than ever before.

Because of the conditions existing, the appeals are the greatest in our 94 years of service. We must exert every effort to carry on – we cannot shirk our responsibility to the community, neither can we fail these children.

Many of our former boys and girls are in the uniformed service – some of our present charges will be going if this dreadful conflict does not end soon – some have already paid the supreme sacrifice.

There never was a time when we needed the help of our friends more than we do right now.

Please see the situation and help us as much as you can, be assured we operate in a most judicious and careful manner and your contribution will be stretched as far as possible in the operation of the home.

Sincerely,

S. C. Nielsen

Officer of the day.

P. S. Your contribution is deductible from your income tax return

Each year, the Officer of the Day established fundraising goals for the annual Orphan Feast, including support to be generated before the feast and the day of the event. S.C. Nielsen, Officer of the Day in 1943, sent this letter of solicitation to local business owners.

Join us at the Feast on September 6th & 7th!

JAMES P. ORR II
Officer of the Day

CHARLES G. PUCHTA
Membership Chairman

WEST SHELL JR.
Immediate Past Officer of the Day

PAST OFFICERS OF THE DAY

*1917—Judge William H. Leuders
*1918—Judge Frank R. Gusweiler
*1919—George Puchta
*1920—B. H. Kroger
*1921—Albert E. Mittendorf
*1922—Richard B. Witt
*1923—Chris Schott
*1924—Judge Fred L. Hoffman
*1925—William H. Anderson
*1926—August Herrmann
*1927—Judge Wm. D. Alexander
*1928—C. E. Richter
*1929—W. Meredith Yeatman
*1930—William E. Hess
*1931—Judge Alfred K. Nippert
*1932—Judge Charles S. Bell
*1933—Chris H. Rembold
*1934—George F. Dieterle
*1935—August H. Tuechter
*1936—William H. Miller
*1937—Judge Thomas R. Murrow
*1938—George Guckenberger
*1939—George Noell
*1940—Fred J. Morr
*1941—Everett W. Townsley
*1942—Everett W. Townsley
*1943—S. C. Nielsen
*1944—William A. Reckman
*1945—J. Edward Sohn Jr.
*1946—Walter L. Gross
*1947—Harry L. Olden
*1948—Louis F. Schlueter
*1949—George R. Hammerlein
1950—Louis Nippert
*1951—Barney J. Houston
*1952—Wayne P. Westfall
*1953—William L. McGrath
1954—Reuben B. Hays
*1955—Frederick W. Geisel
*1956—Herman Guckenberger Sr.
*1957—Walter C. Beckjord
*1958—Paul M. Arnall
1959—Stanley R. Schrotel
*1960—George H. Streitmann
1960—John A. Lloyd
*1962—Dr. Walter C. Langsam
*1963—John W. Pease
*1964—G. Carlton Hill
*1965—William H. Zimmer
1966—Fletcher E. Nyce
1967—Francis L. Dale
*1968—Warren Giles
*1969—William O. Mashburn Jr.
1970—Charles K. Murdock
1971—Judge Chase M. Davies
1972—B. John Yeager
1973—Dean P. Fite
1974—Bert A. Lugannani
1975—Jane DeSerisy Earley
*1976—Peter J. Palazzolo
1977—James A. D. Geier
1978—Carson R. Whiting
1979—John W. Gantt
1980—W. H. Dickhoner
1981—Frederick A. Hauck
1982—Paul Martin
1983—Dr. Charles M. Barrett
1984—John J. Schiff

*Deceased

We mourn William E. Hess

We are saddened to relate the recent death of William E. Hess. He was Officer of the Day of the Annual Feast in 1930, and was a life member of our agency.

Hess, a Delhi Township resident, was a former U.S. Congressman who served Ohio's 2nd District for more than 28 years.

As a Congressman, he was a member of the Judiciary, Naval Affairs, and Armed Services committees. Upon his retirement from Congress in 1961, Hess returned to private law practice.

We extend our sincerest sympathies to the family of William E. Hess.

Gift Shoppe booth at Annual Feast

The Gift Shoppe Booth, sponsored by The Women's Committee of Beech Acres, features handmade items for Feast patrons! The booth, offering a variety of beautiful items for sale, will be open Saturday and Sunday.

If you have new handmade items that you would like to donate for the Gift Shoppe booth, contact Linda Roberts at 231-6630.

In addition, the committee will raffle a handmade quilt and afghan. The quilt and afghan will be awarded on Sunday, but raffle chances will be sold at the booth on both days. For more information call 661-7661.

All proceeds from the Feast benefit the children and families served by Beech Acres.

This list shows officers of the day since 1917. These men, and one woman—Jane DeSerisy Earley (1975)—were critical to the success of the Orphan Feast. Each one contributed significant time and money, as well as gathered funds and volunteers to support the Home. Each officer is still remembered and appreciated for his or her significant generosity.

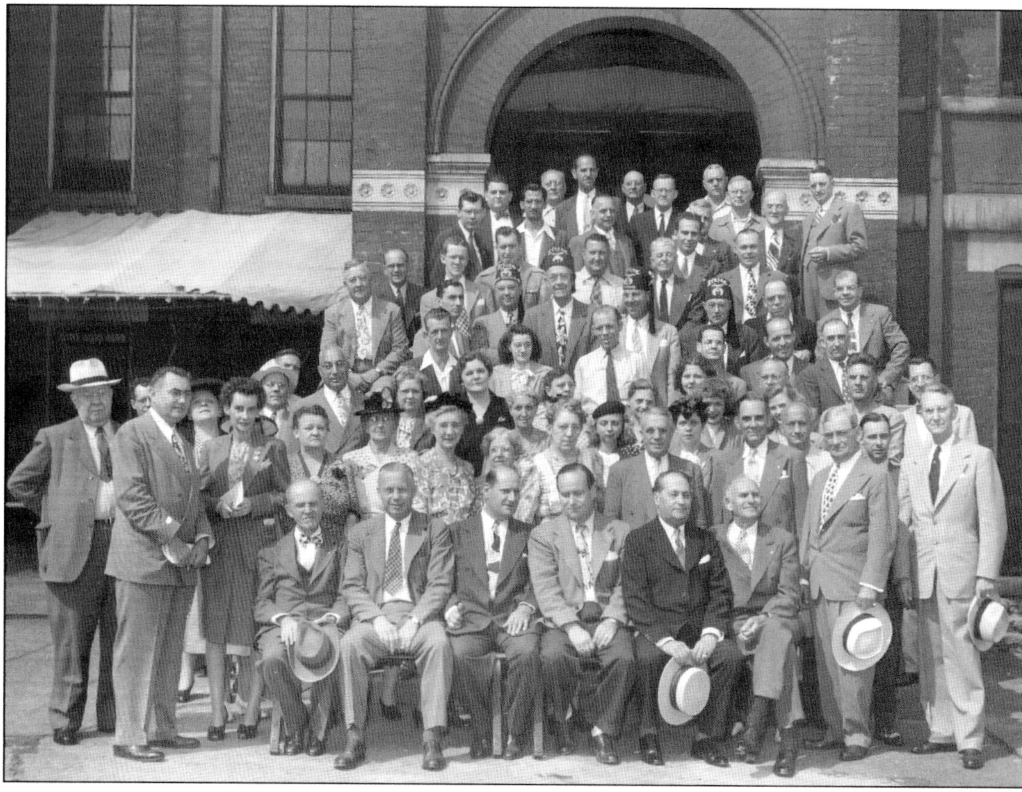

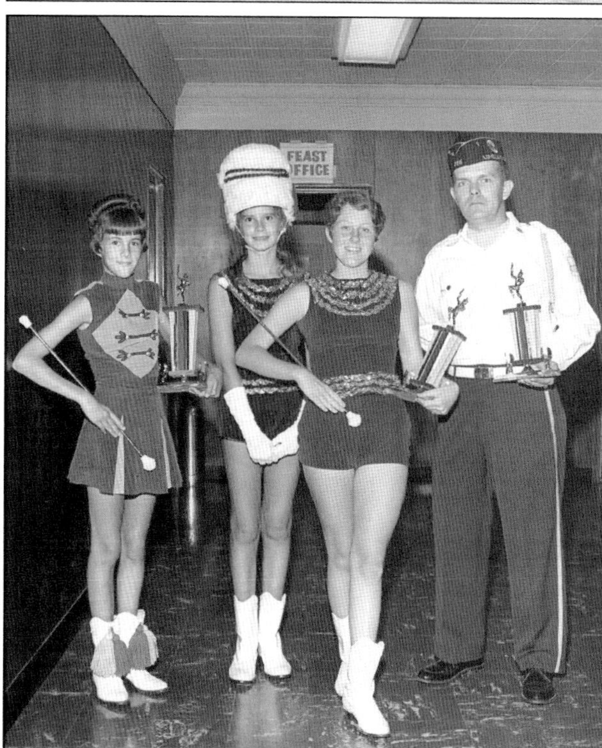

This photograph features the Orphan Feast Committee in Mount Auburn.

Every year, winners were chosen for their performance in the parade. Trophies were given to the director of the band, the director of the patriotic group, and the director of the squad that performed best. These three winners happily displayed their awards.

The Women's Committee contributed significantly to the feast. They prepared chicken dinners to be sold at the event. They also staffed a booth of crafts that committee members made, including embroidered pillowcases and handmade quilts (that won awards). Seen here are Women's Booth chairwomen for the September 8, 1946, feast.

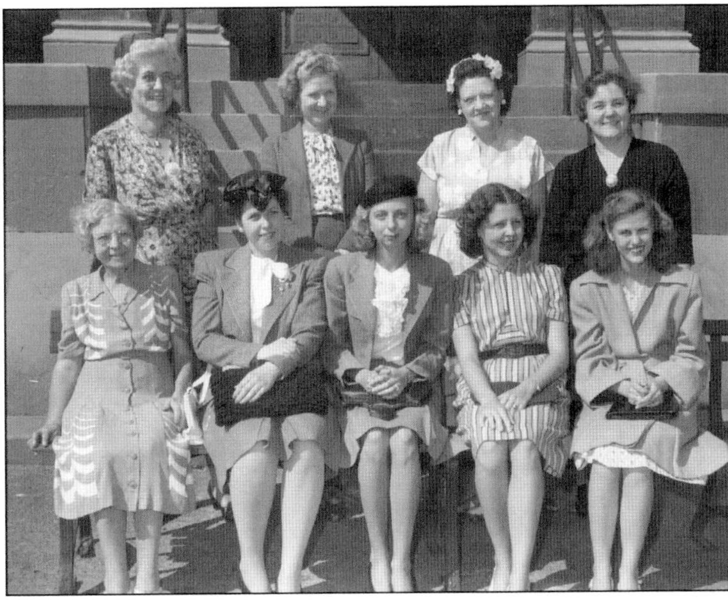

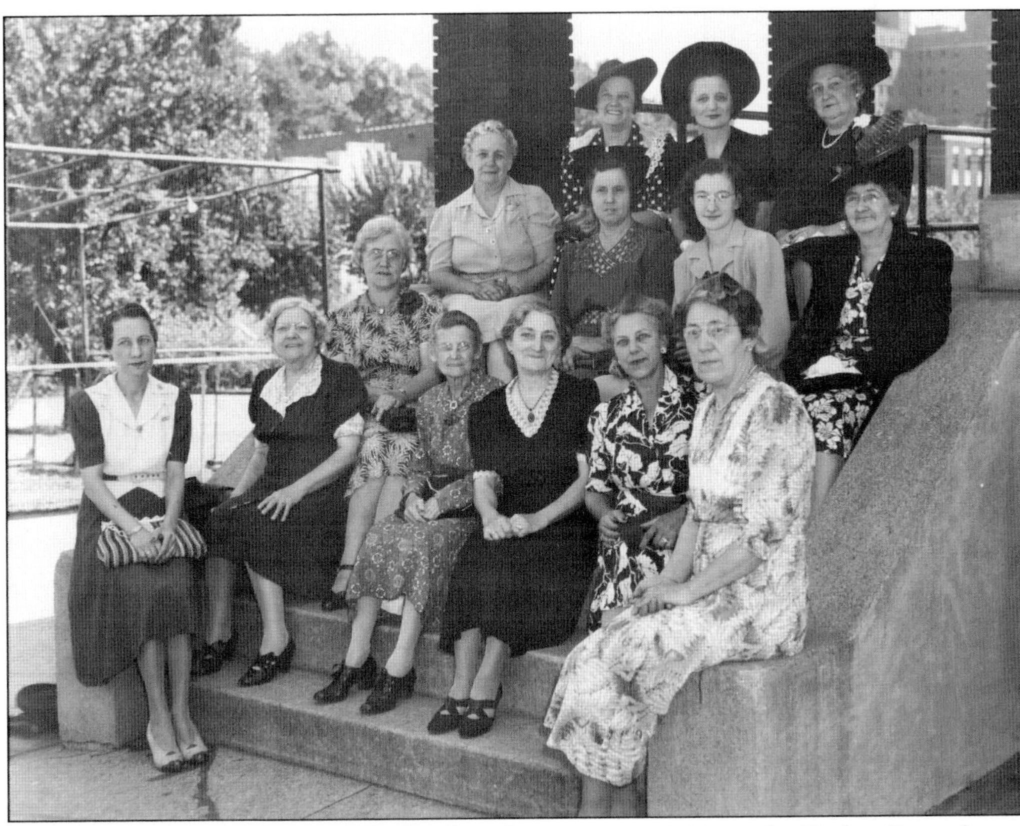

Women workers directed many of the booth and committee activities at the Orphan Feast. Among the booth chairwomen shown in this 1942 photograph are Marie Shulz, Emma Metes, Lillian Kratt, Matilda Hartenstein, May Zuccilli, Mrs. Kircker Geis, Susanna Dater, Edna Hammerlein, Mabel Muff, Mrs. A.L. Eberle, Mrs. A. Lucking, and Mrs. Louis G. Mueller.

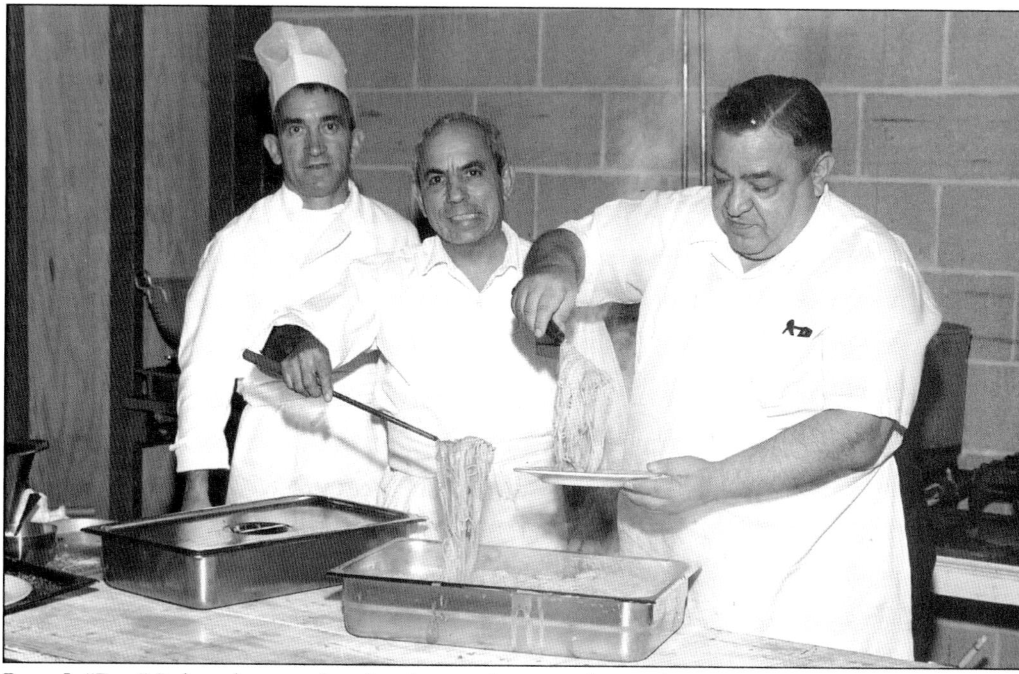

Peter J. "Pete" Palazzolo served up his famous homemade spaghetti, meat sauce, and cheese that he donated every year to the feast. Palazzolo, owner of Caproni's and the Isle of Capri restaurants, had worked 15 hours each feast day for 10 years straight. He donated his services, cooked all the spaghetti, and supplied his own equipment to prepare the delicious meal that was served in the coffee shop at the Orphan Feast. Thousands of patrons visited his very popular spaghetti booth every year.

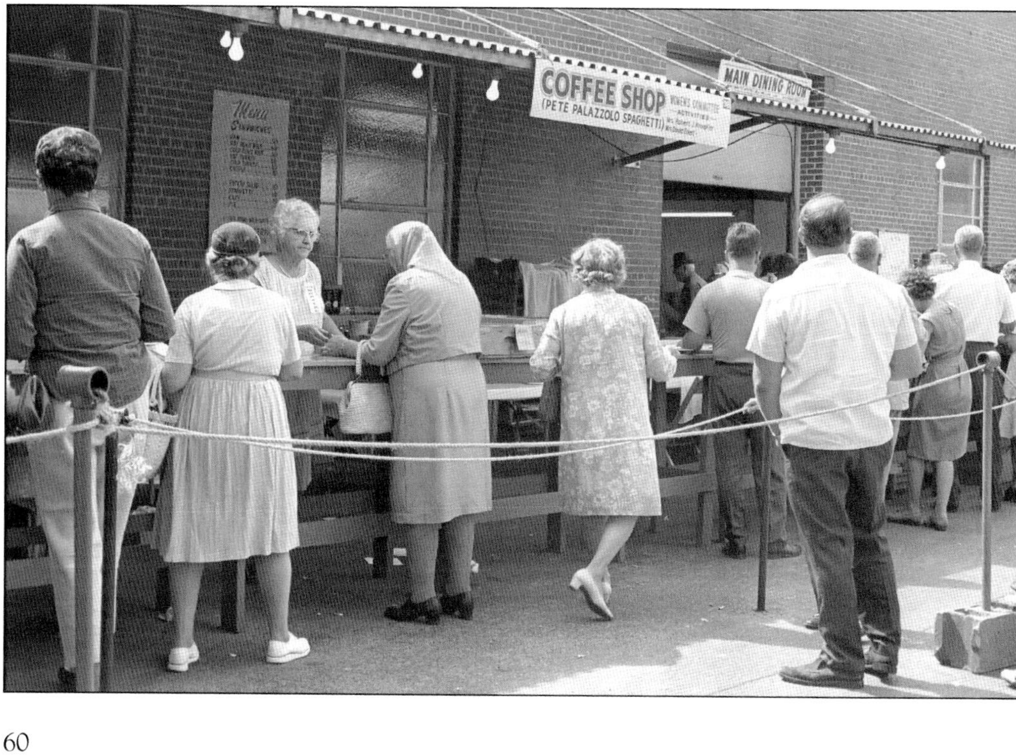

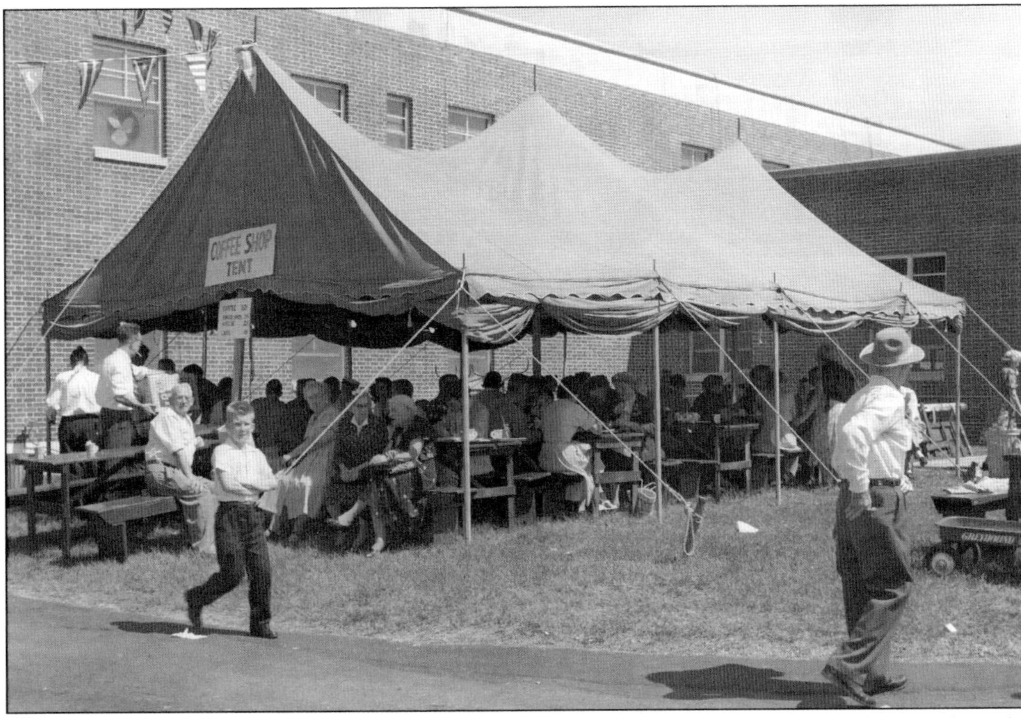

People waited in line for Pete's famous spaghetti meal. While waiting, conveniently enough at the coffee shop, they sipped homemade coffee and socialized with friends. Pete was not only famous for his homemade Italian cooking, he also served as Officer of the Day for the Orphan Feast in 1976, making him even more popular among the feast crowd.

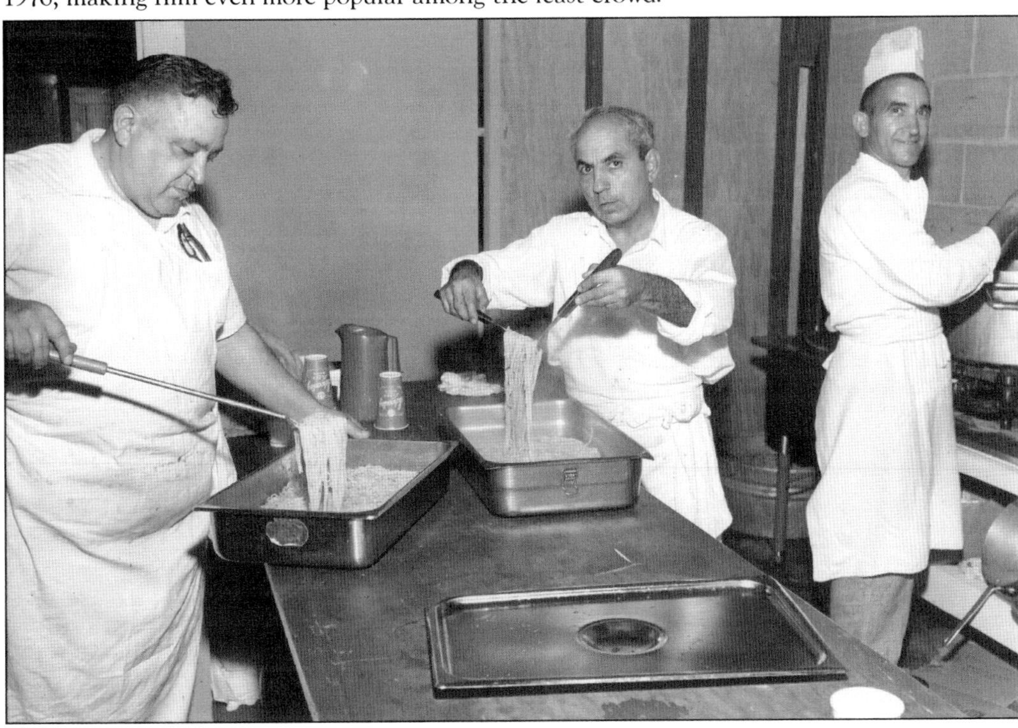

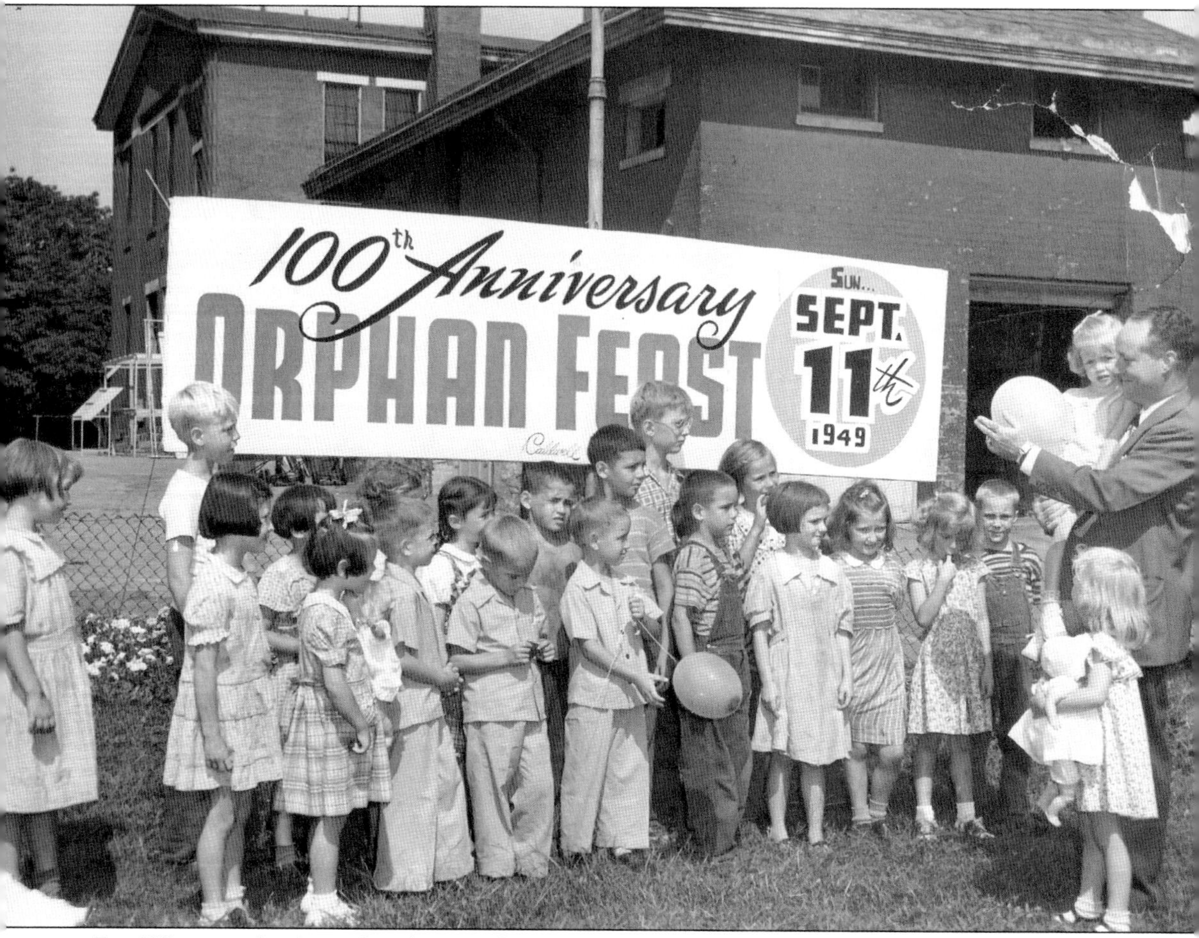

For 137 years, the feast played a significant role in the Cincinnati community and in the lives of the orphans it benefited. The 100th Orphan Feast, celebrated in 1949, was the first at the new location on Beechmont Avenue. As the needs of children in residence grew more intensive, the disruption to their routine was acutely felt. Growing competition from other forms of family entertainment and dwindling volunteer support reduced attendance and increased the amount of staff time required to coordinate the event. Gradually, its fundraising potential waned, and it became too costly to produce. The last Orphan Feast was held in 1986.

Four

Kids Being Kids

No matter the time in history, a smile on a little girl's face, laughter from a group of boys, or a song floating down the hallway all show signs of thriving children. The General Protestant Orphan Home, now known as Beech Acres Parenting Center, has always existed to help children thrive. Since 1849, it has focused on helping Greater Cincinnati's vulnerable children grow to become capable, contributing, caring, and connected adult members of society.

While the environment in which children grow up today is very different than 161 years ago, their needs have remained largely the same: food, shelter, safety, education, guidance, moral development, and, most of all, love. Beech Acres has helped children grow successfully over the decades by understanding who children are and what they need, regardless of the era, in which they experience those most impressionable and vulnerable early years.

The "work" of children is preparation for adulthood, mostly learned through play and exploration. The familiar tools of their work can be found on the following pages. From marionettes and lumberjacks to video games and action figures, changes in children's toys reflect the broader evolution of society over 161 years. They show how childhood can be a time of wonder, joy, and learning, whether living in an orphanage or a community home, as long as the adults around them ensure their safety, nurture them, and provide guidance.

From band and baseball, church and chores, to Santa, Scouts, and snow, this chapter honors the children Beech Acres has served and simply celebrates the beauty of kids being kids.

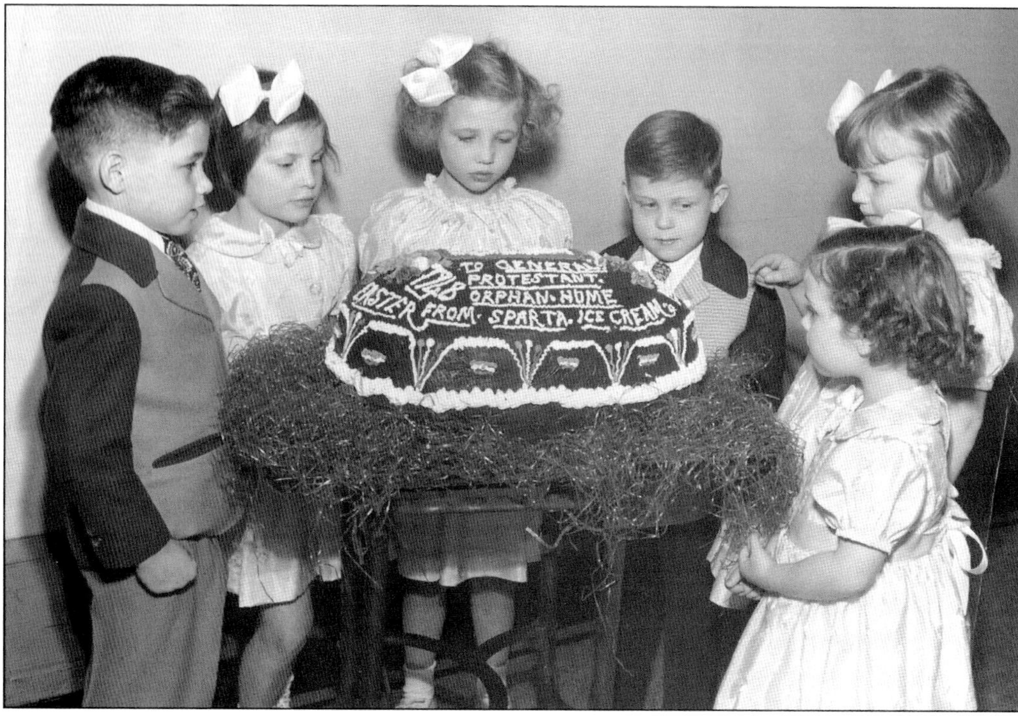

The children anticipated holidays and celebrated them with delight. Community members made special holiday donations and frequently presented fresh fruit and tasty deserts, like this Easter cake generously donated from the Sparta Ice Cream Company. Holidays provided the children with opportunities to dress in their nicest outfits and spend quality time together. Former residents share that photographs like the one above were often posed in order to provide thanks to the donor or solicit additional support from other community members.

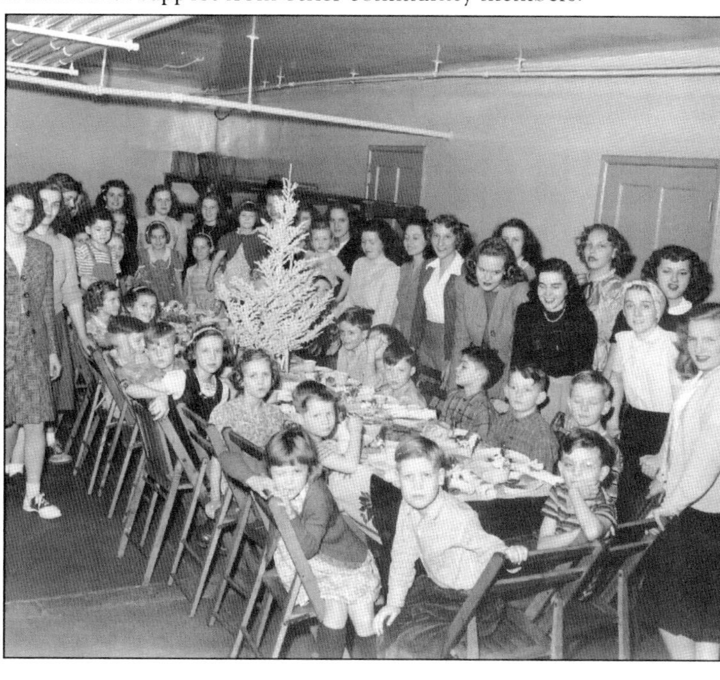

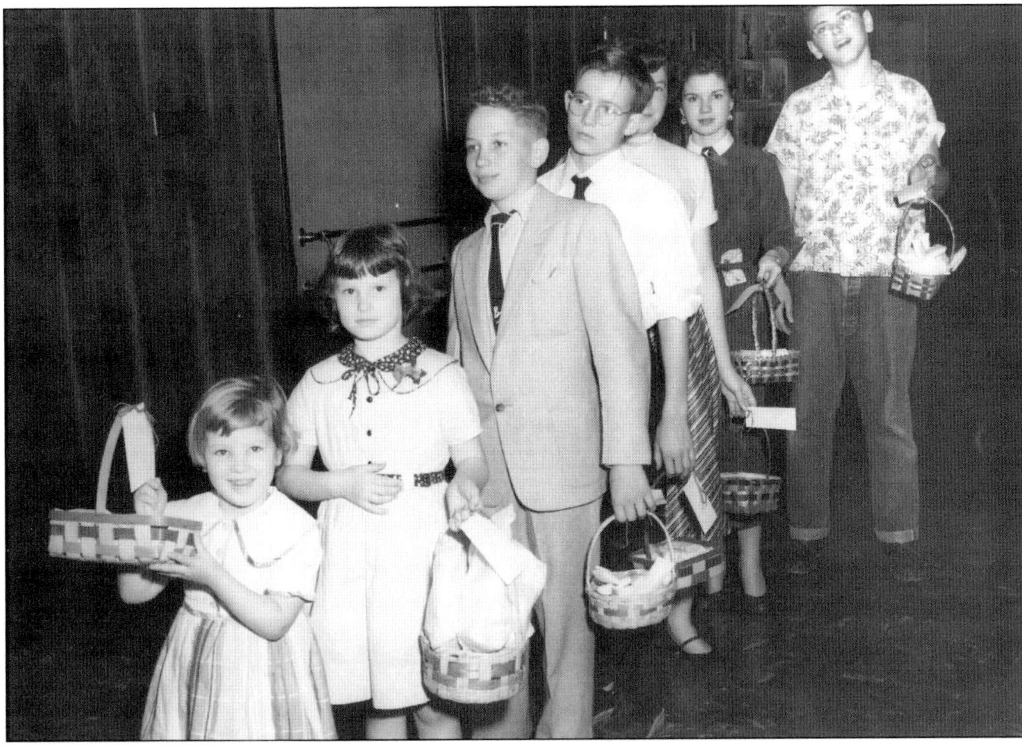

Easter was a popular holiday at the Home. Each child received his or her own basket on Easter morning and enjoyed special seating at the church for Easter services.

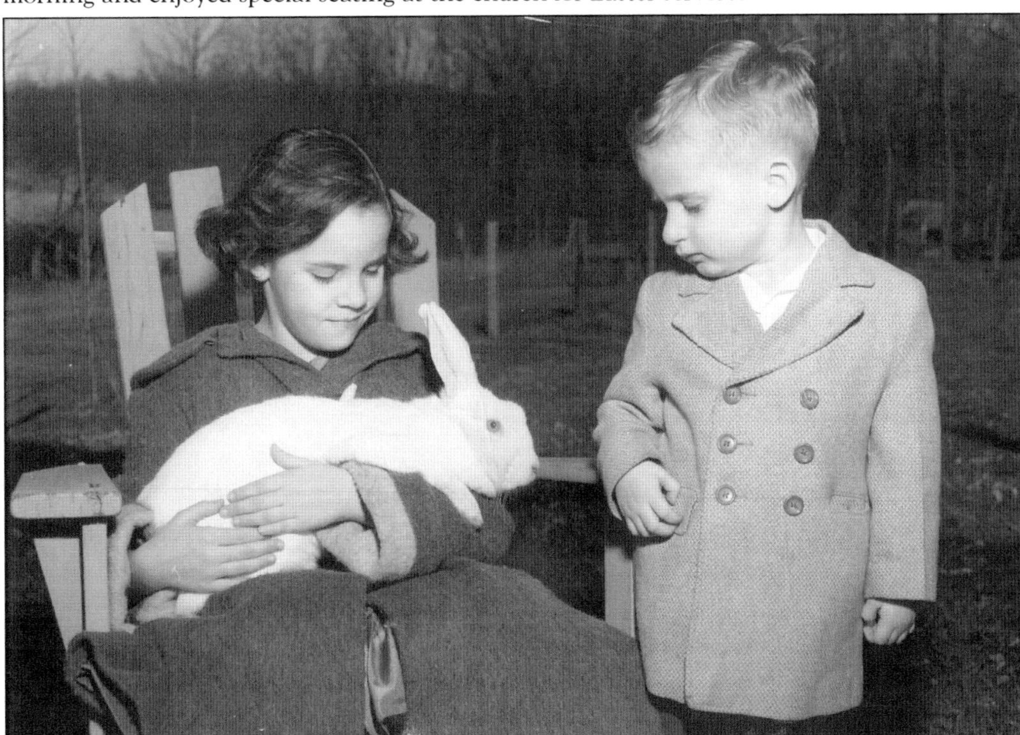

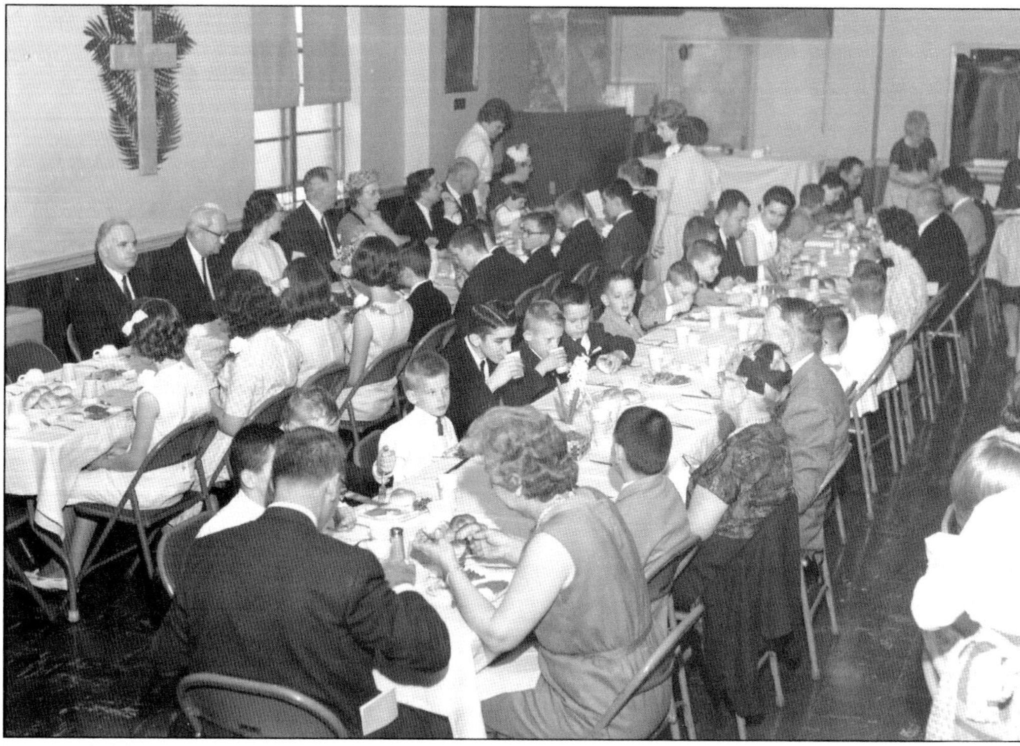

Every child living at the Home was confirmed Protestant regardless of any known family religious practice. As part of their confirmation process, every child received a Bible with his or her name imprinted in gold. The Ladies Board ensured that each child had a Bible, robe, and cross for confirmation. To this day, one known former resident wears her gold cross necklace with a small diamond.

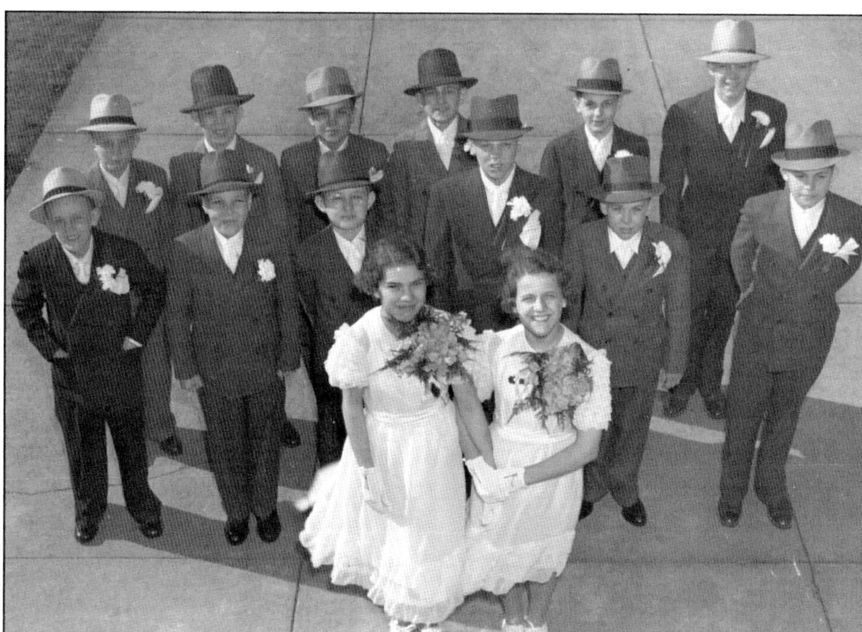

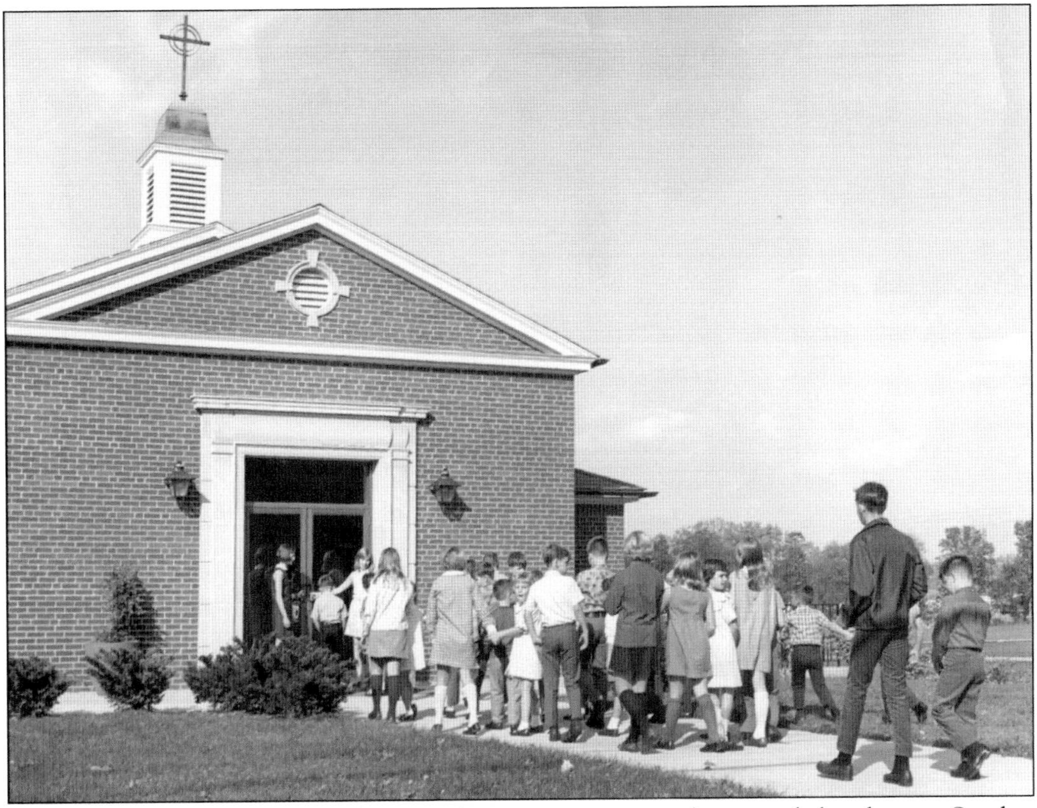

Every child, regardless of prior religious upbringing, was required to attend church every Sunday. All children walked to church to attend services. Former residents recall that they were given a penny (once confirmed they received a nickel) to place in the offertory basket at church; several have stated that they sometimes stopped to buy a dill pickle at the corner store instead. Some of the Home's property in Anderson Township, approximately 275 feet by 385 feet, was sold to the Southwest Ohio Evangelical and Reformed Church on December 31, 1953 for $500.

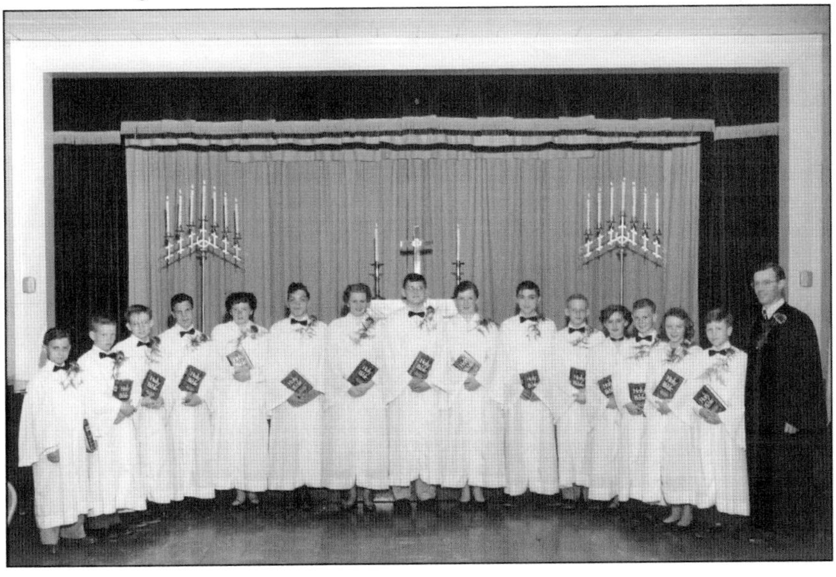

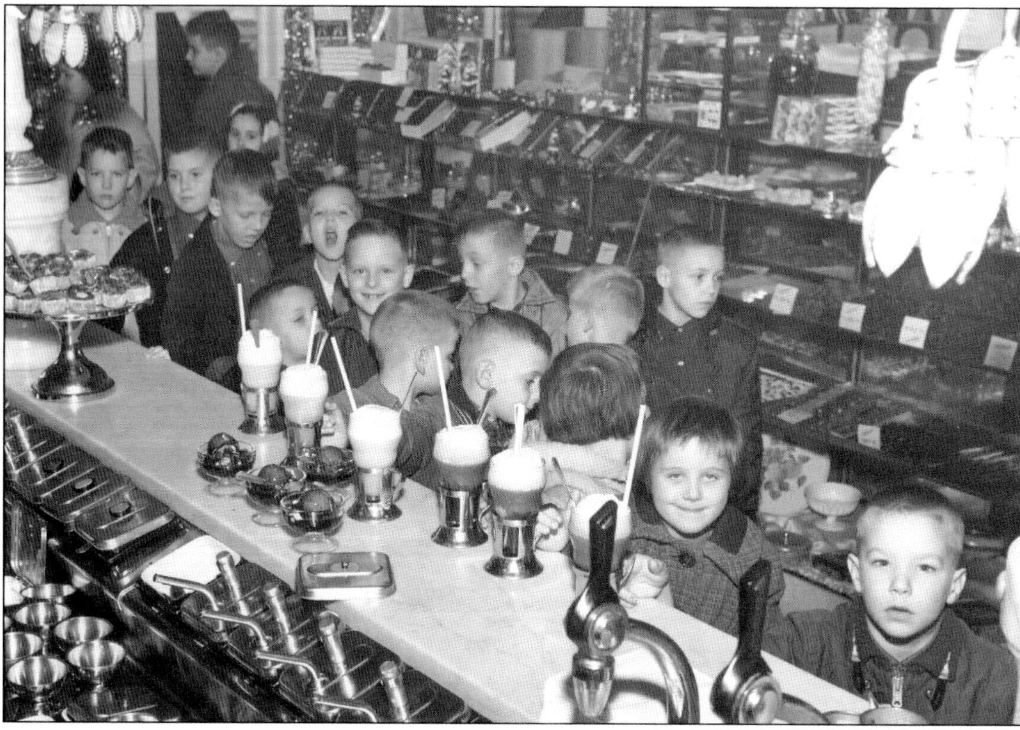

Each year the children looked forward to the holiday party at Aglamesis Brothers in Oakley Square, a local ice creamery since 1908. Mr. Aglamesis welcomed the children, stating, "Anything the kids want is on the house." Gazing at the abundance of delicious homemade candies, chocolates, and ice cream through the art deco décor that still exists today, ice cream floats and fizzy sodas were often the favorite choices.

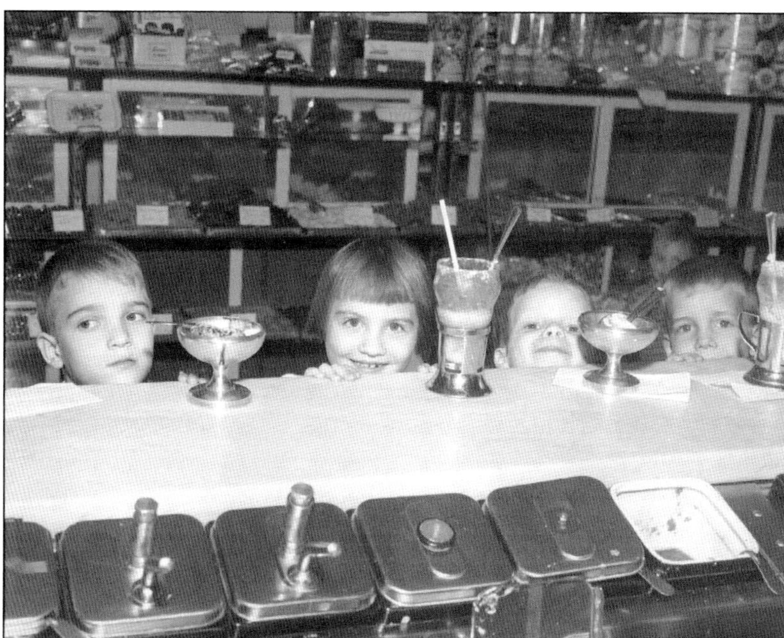

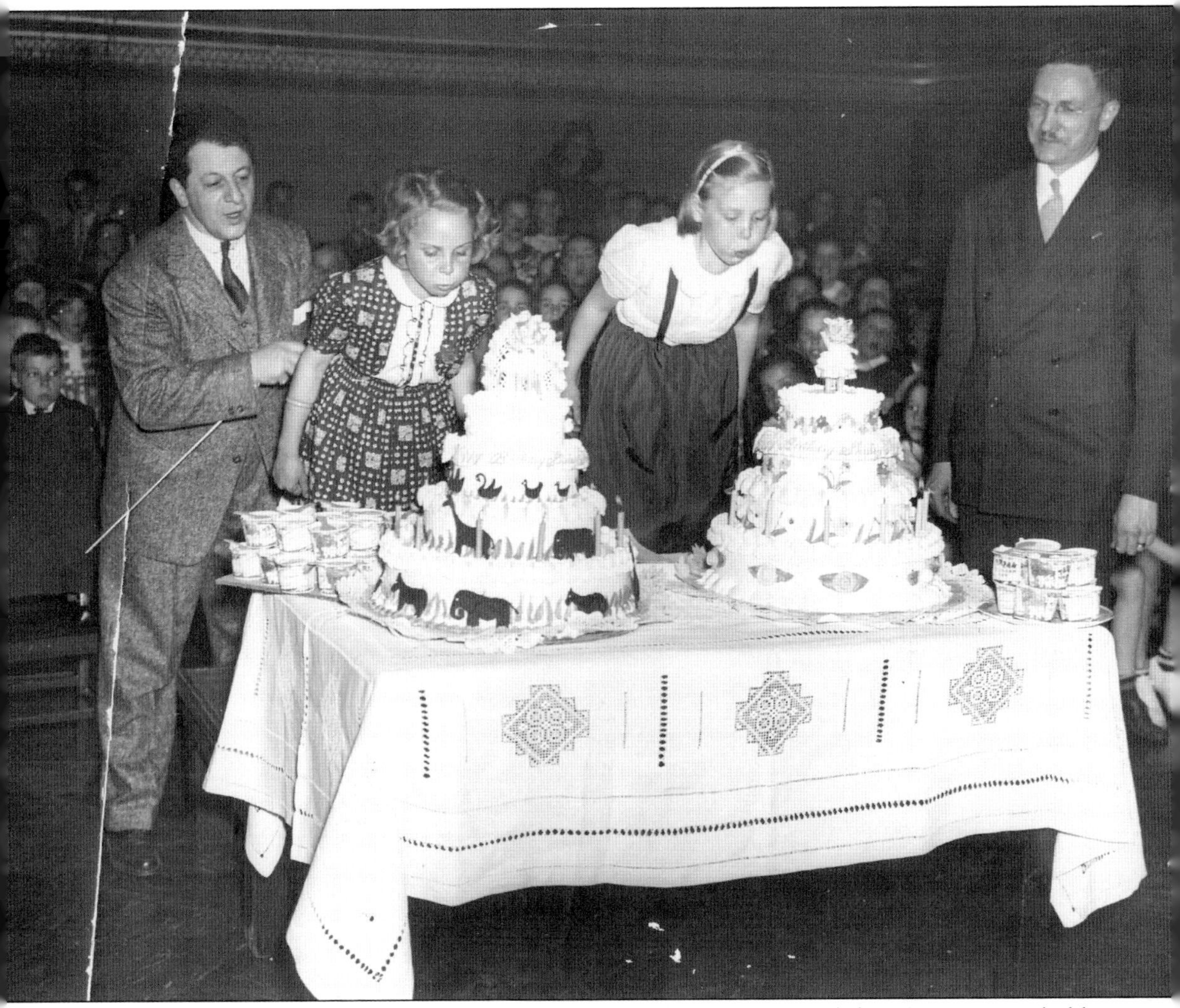

April 23, 1939, marked the celebration of Shirley Temple's 10th birthday. A party was held for the young celebrity and the children from the General Protestant Orphan Home and St. Joseph's Orphanage. Two 10-year-old children are seen blowing out the birthday cake's candles as Louis Tenner (far right), the GPOH superintendent, watches on. His temperament is remembered as genuinely kind and caring towards the children. Mary Smith of St. Joseph's and Georgia Mae See of the General Protestant Orphan Home are the lucky girls initiating the birthday party festivities.

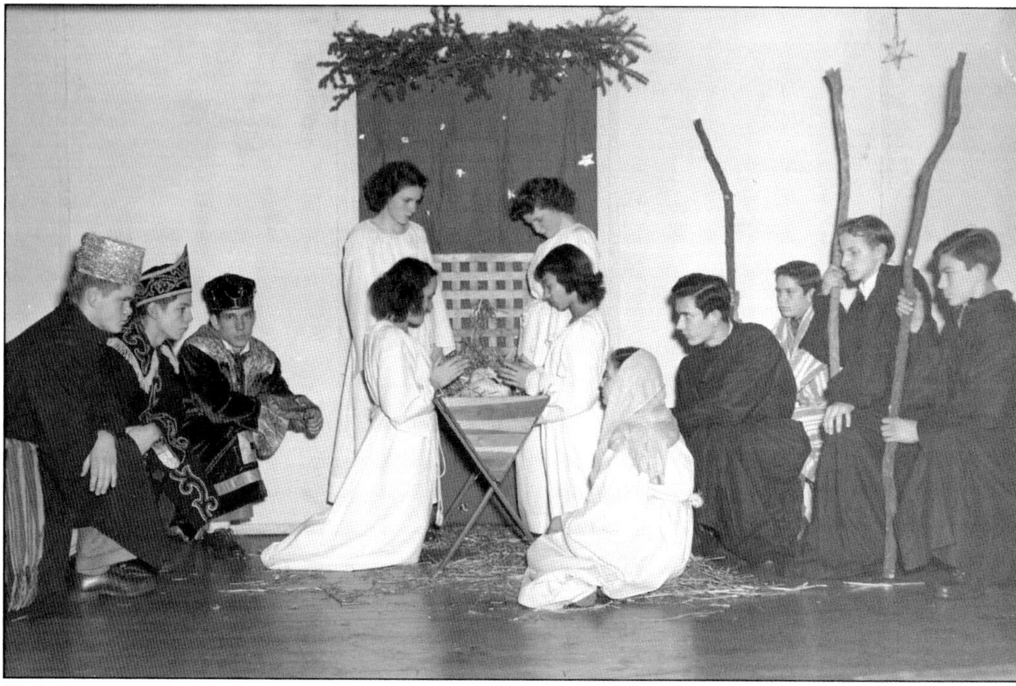

Holidays were often celebrated with performances by the children, and multiple shows were held the week of Christmas. Acting, singing, and playing instruments were important pastimes that they participated in throughout the year. Children often performed within their peer age group, whom they lived with in the separate cottages. A permanent stage was built in Townsley Auditorium, named for Everett W. Townsley. As chairman of the Building Committee, he led the move from Mount Auburn and the purchase of 62 acres on the border of Mount Washington and Anderson Township, known as the Beeches.

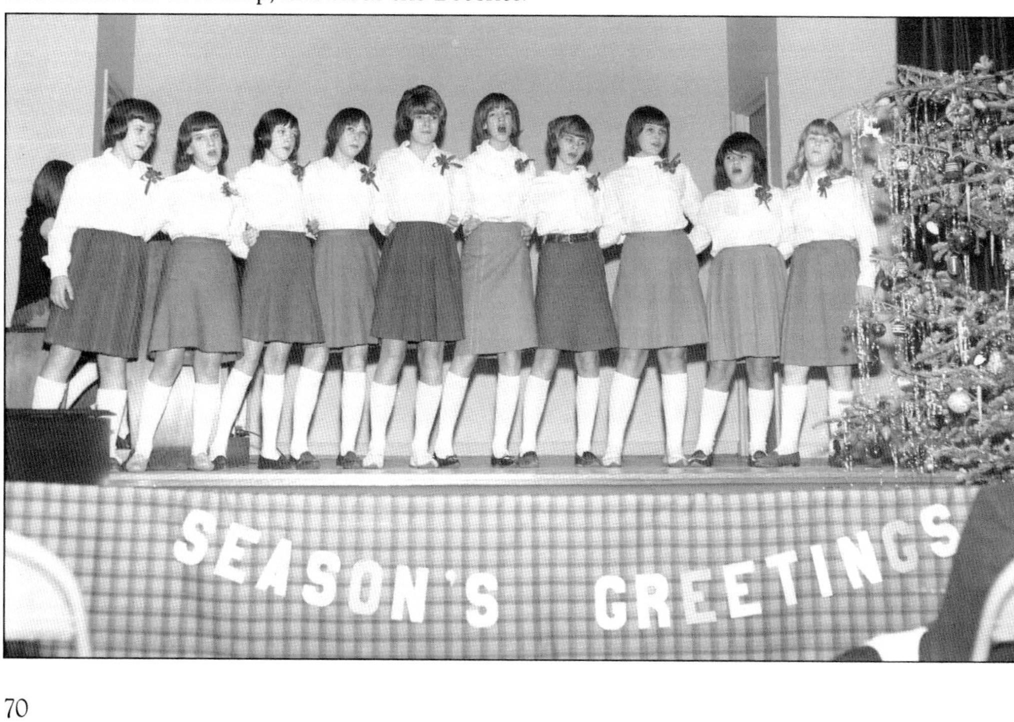

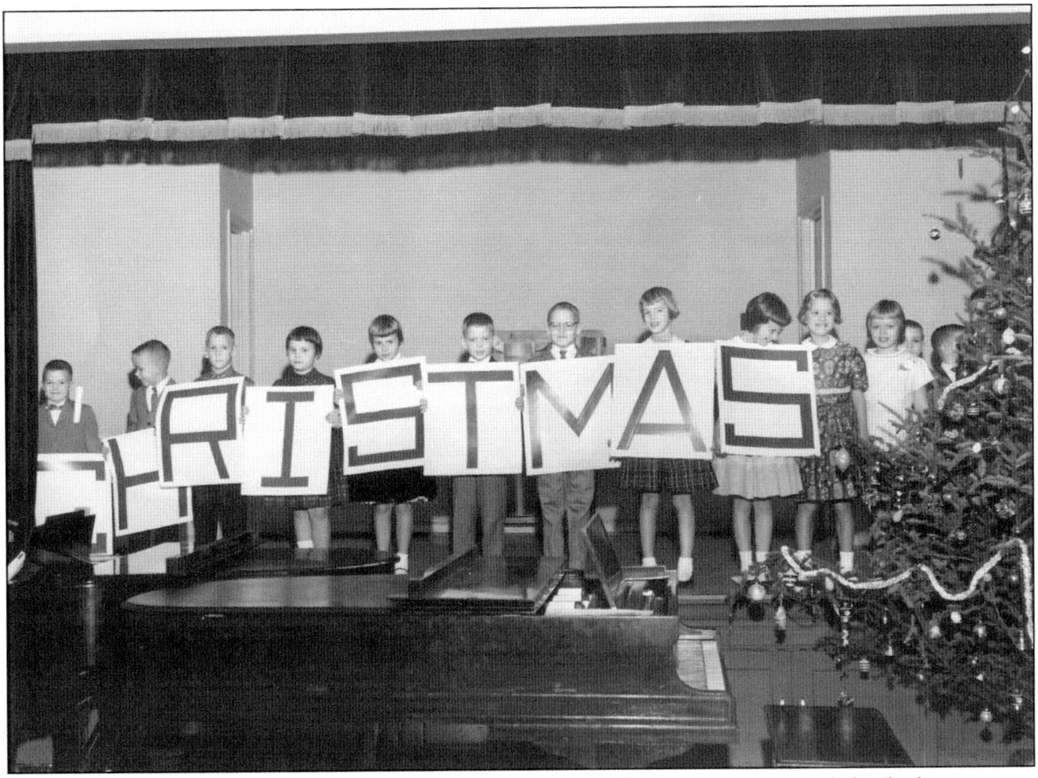

The annual Christmas play featured several choirs and a reenactment of the holy nativity. Preparation lasted for weeks, and the final performance was given on stage for the rest of the residents, staff, and friends. Songs and skits were performed by children representing each age group living at the Home.

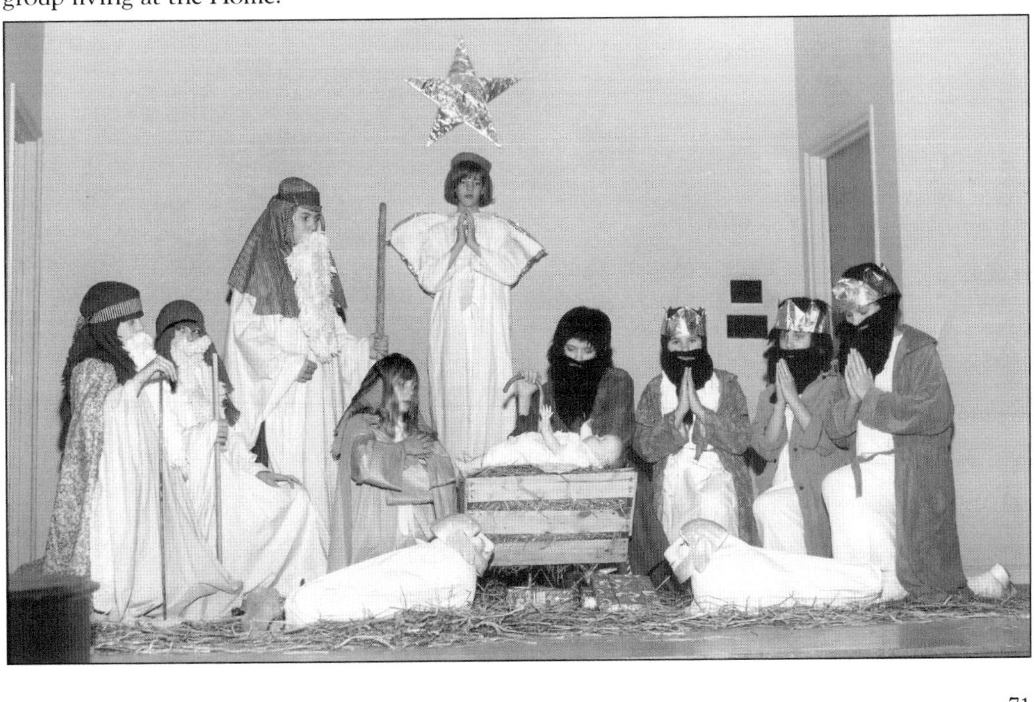

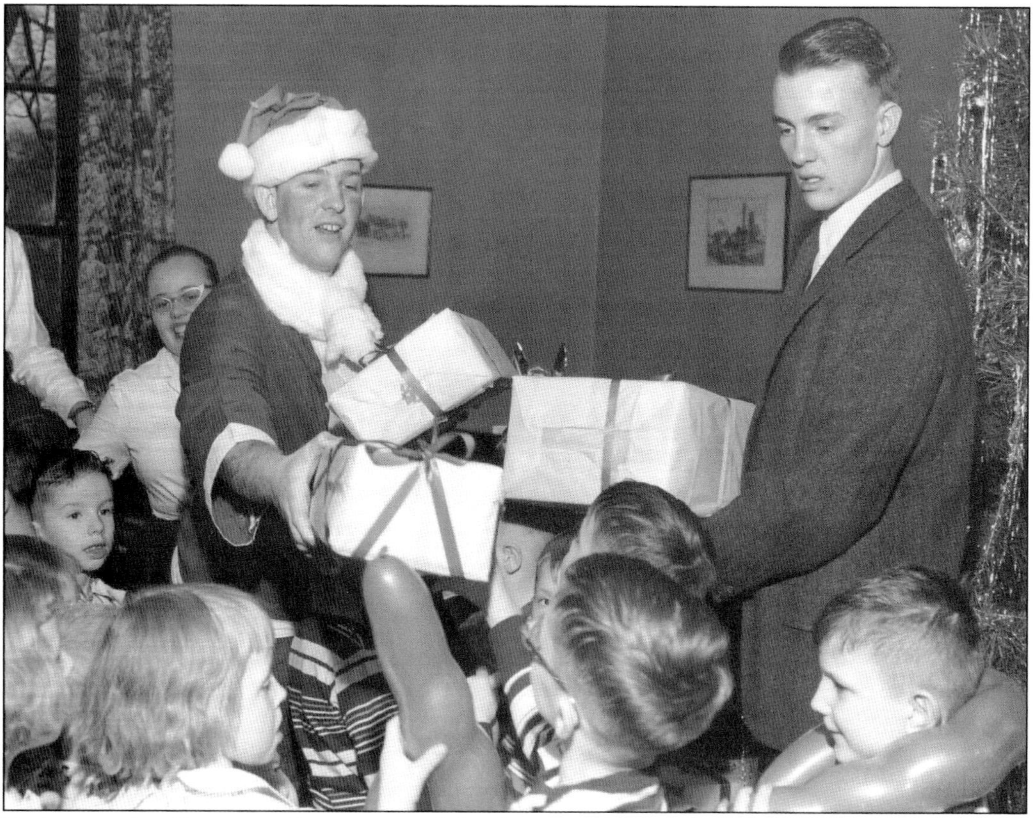

Each year, the Christmas Committee of the Cincinnati Beta Phi Theta fraternity visited the orphanage on Christmas Eve to spread some yuletide cheer. They brought gifts and candy and provided entertainment that kept the children's attention for hours. Of course it included a visit from Santa.

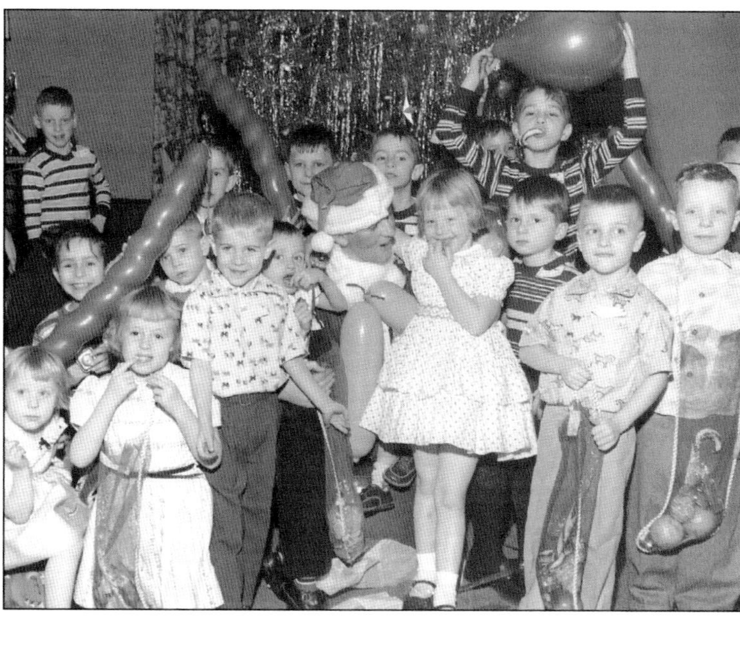

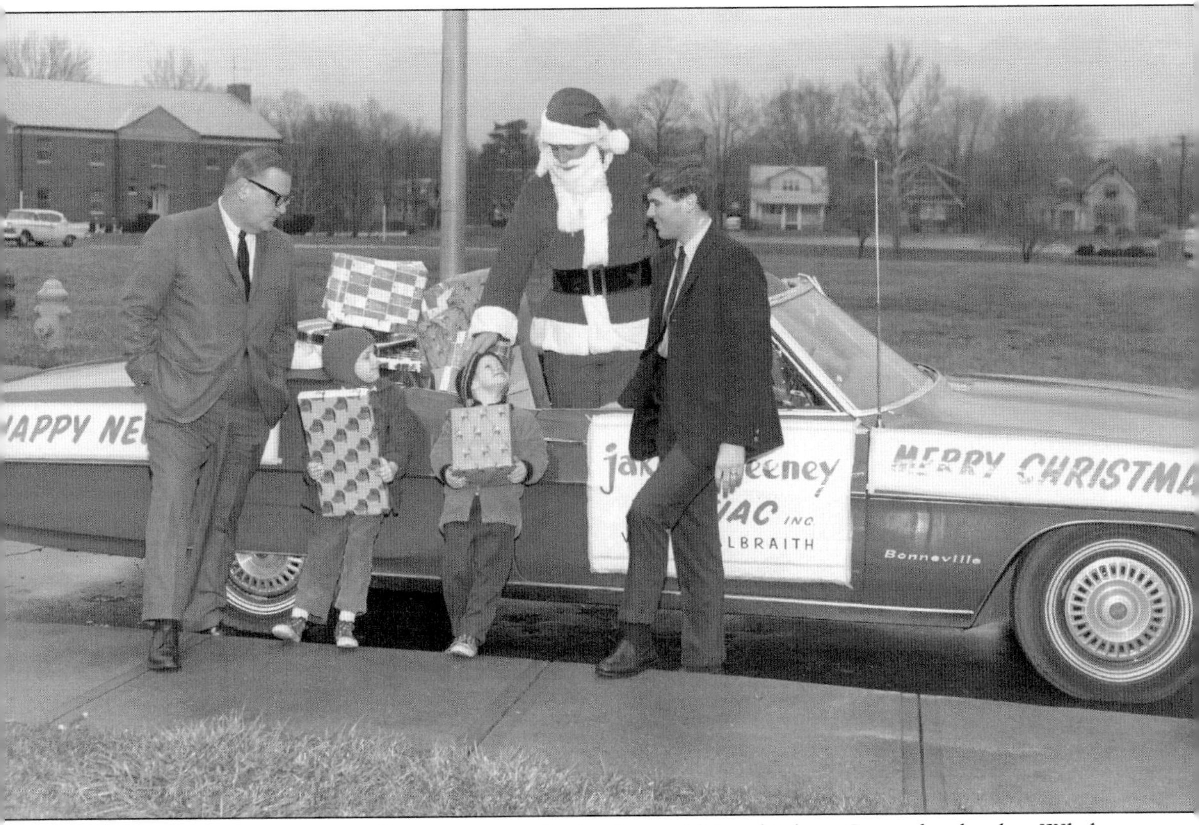

Jake Sweeney, a prominent Cincinnati car dealer, loaned his vehicle to Santa for the day. While some children know Santa to deliver their gifts by sleigh, the Santa of the General Protestant Orphan Home flew to the children in a Pontiac Bonneville. At the General Protestant Orphan Home, all the children made Santa's "nice list."

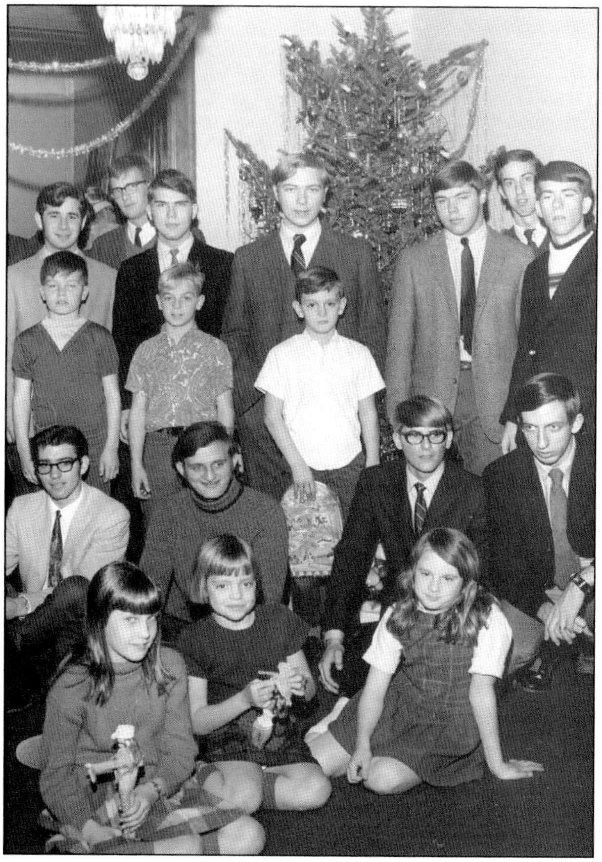

Holidays provided a chance for children from the entire Home to gather together in celebration. Throughout the decades, the Women's Committee, board members, local families, and community partners made Christmas a special time by providing each child with gifts. In the early years, many children went to stay with local families for a few days during the holidays or were invited to attend other special holiday outings. Today, the local community still supports the children Beech Acres Parenting Center and serves at Christmastime by purchasing gifts for entire families through its Adopt-a-Family program. Below, Jim Mason (far right) stands with Stacy Goldberg, Lauren Armentrout, Mike Heffernan, Mark Armentrout, and Kelly Sheppard, representing First Watch restaurant employees, as they wrap gifts they donated. Hundreds of gifts are generously donated each year by school children, local families and other community members like them.

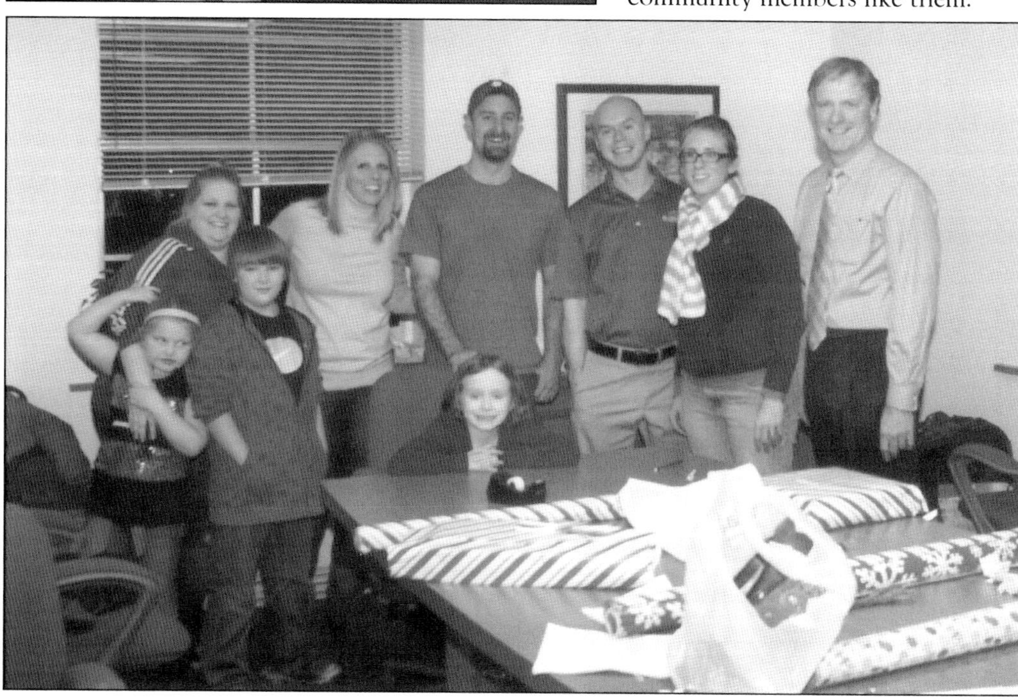

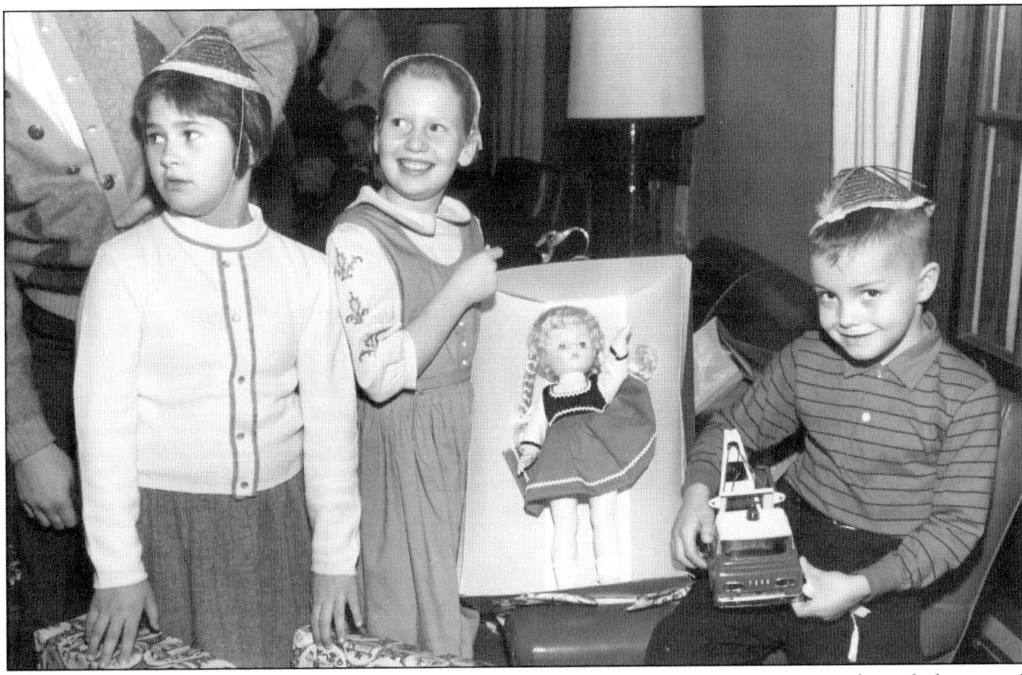

Children received gifts on Christmas morning. The Women's Committee gathered their wish lists and shopped for presents. It was always an energy-filled morning the day of Christmas as the children joyfully scavenged for the gifts with their name on them.

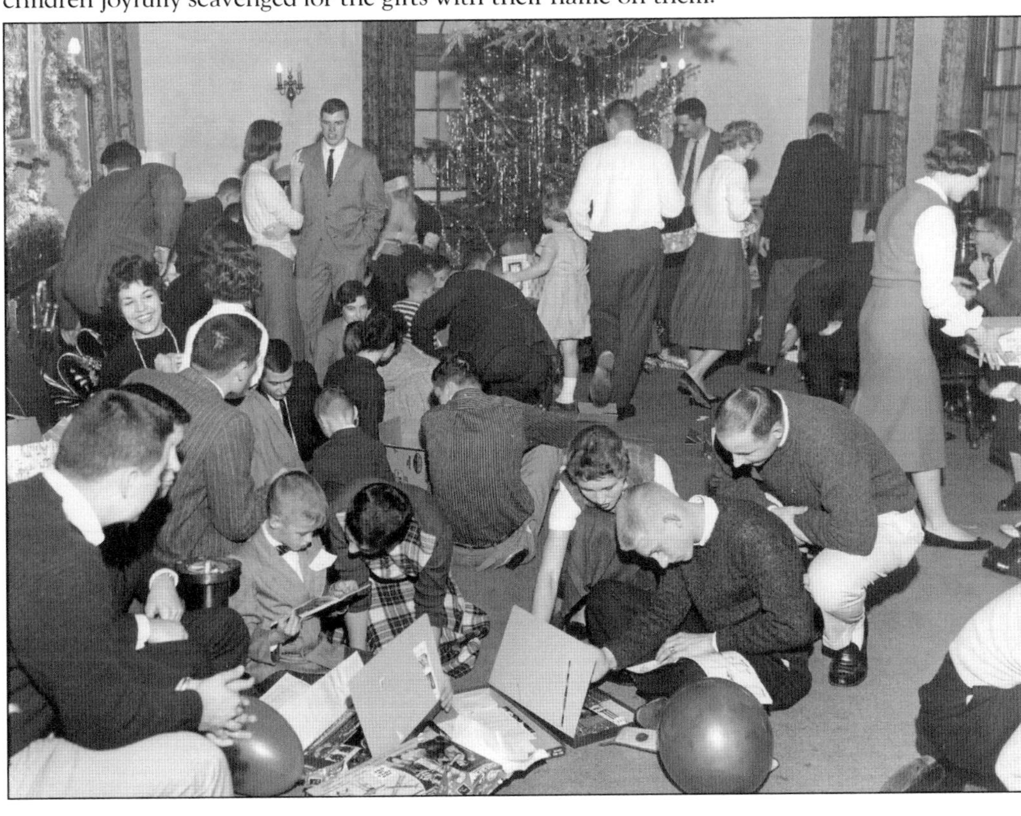

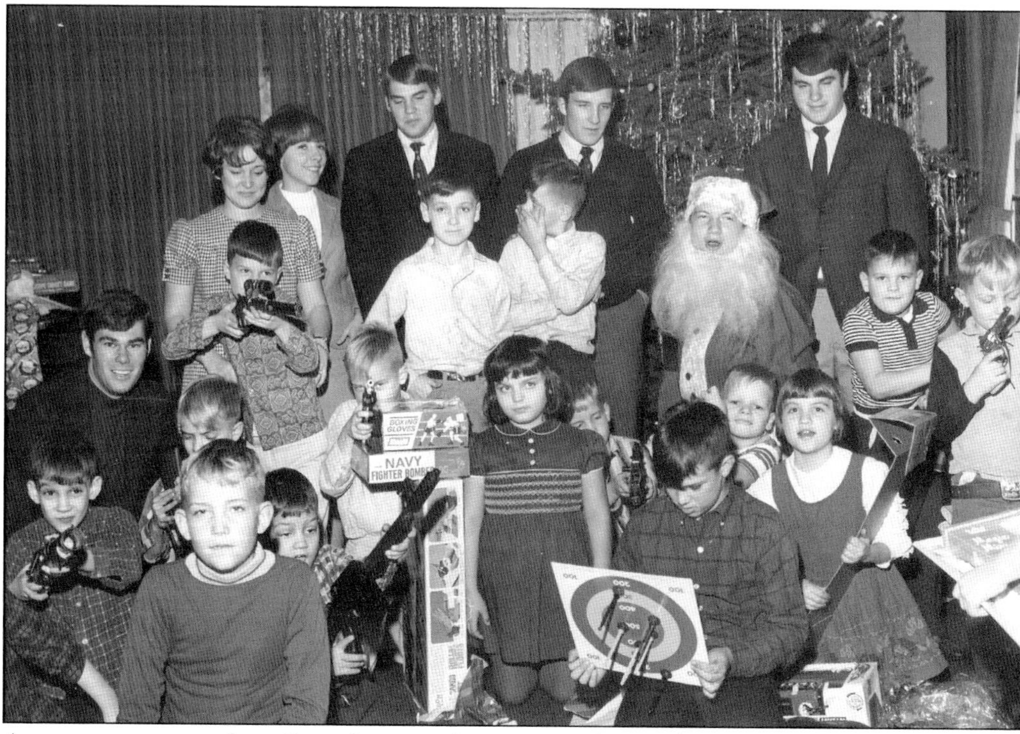

A guest appearance from Santa happened every year during the week of Christmas. Children gathered together, and gifts that had been donated from the community were distributed. There were plenty of gifts to go around, and children shared their toys with each other. This added to the collection of play items that the children could choose from during their recreation time.

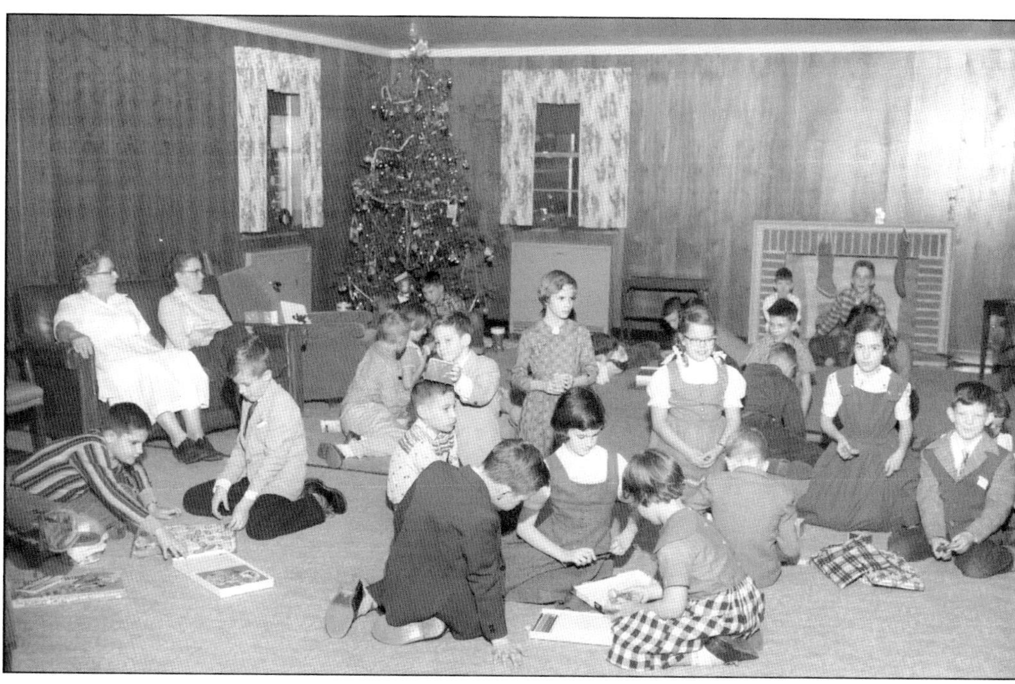

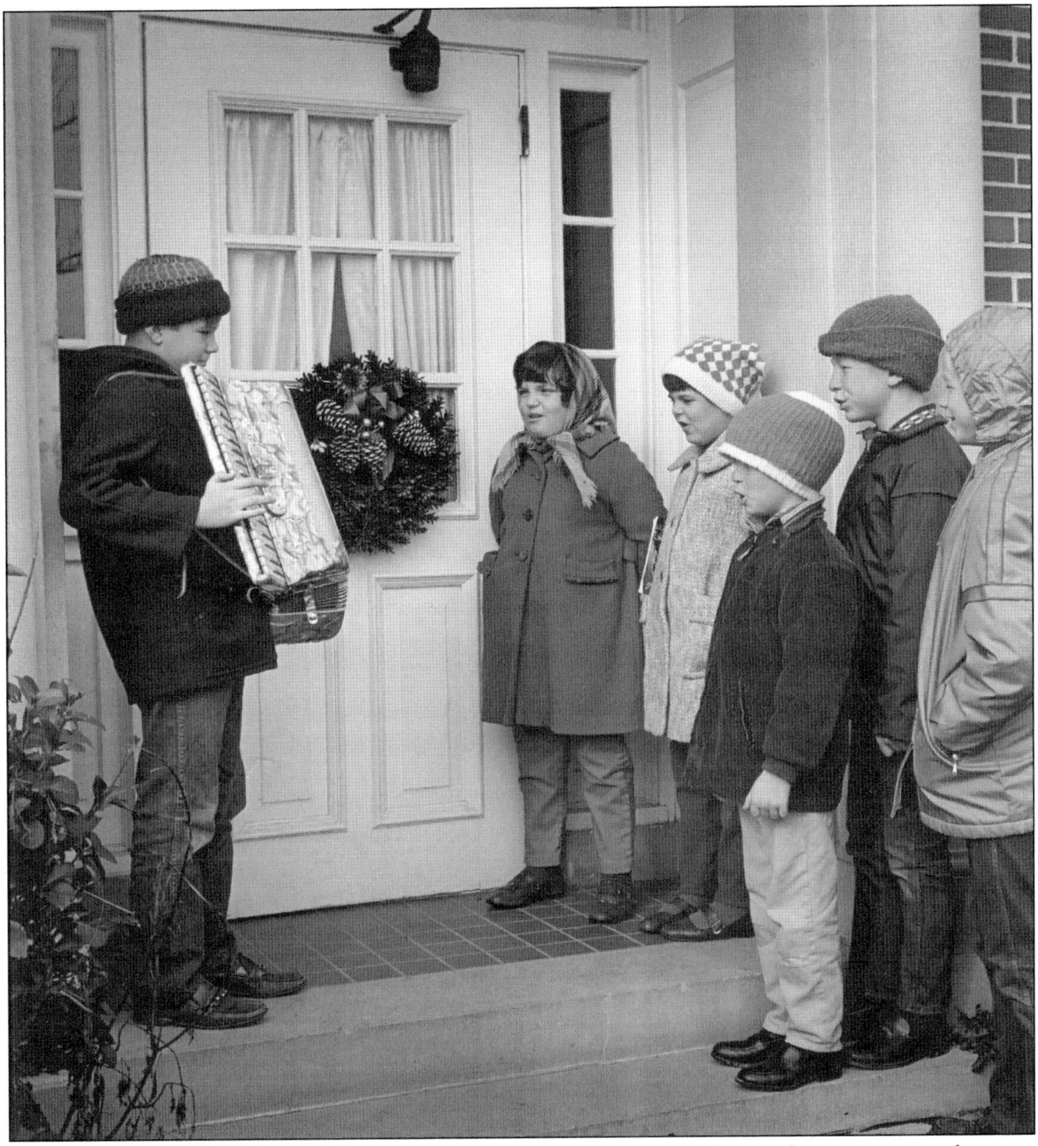

The Beech Acres—General Protestant Orphan Home's children's choir went caroling on the Sunday before Christmas, sharing songs with their neighbors in Mount Washington and Anderson. A member of the band played accordion as the choir memorably delivered their well-practiced carols.

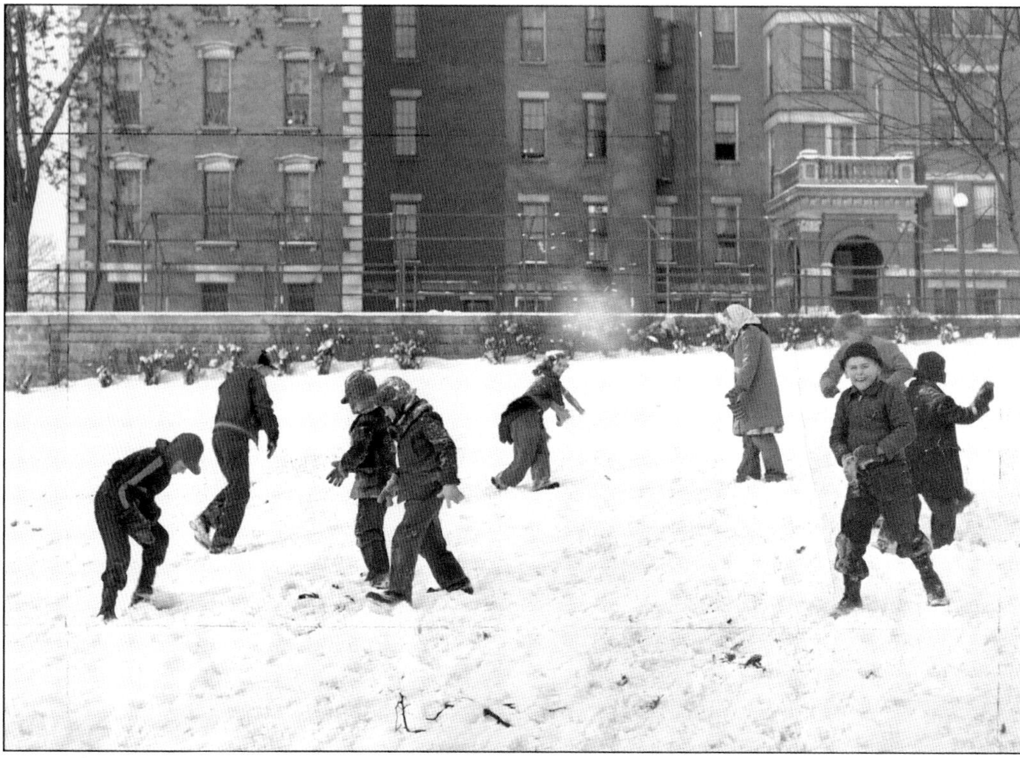

Children's love of playtime in the snow endures throughout time. Whether in Mount Auburn (above) or Mount Washington/Anderson (below), the children took great pleasure playing outside in the snow making snowballs, forts, and snowmen.

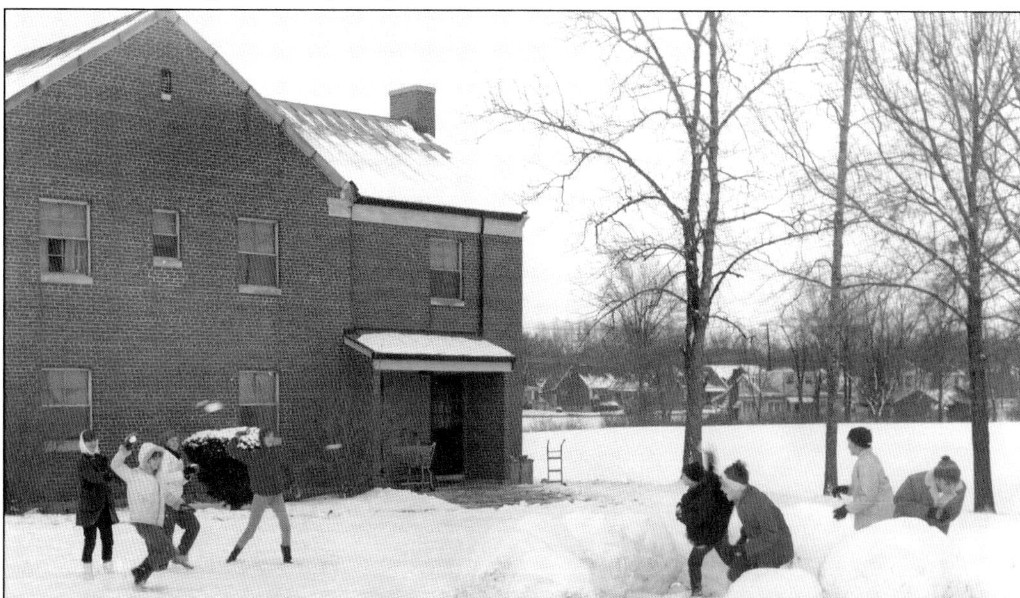

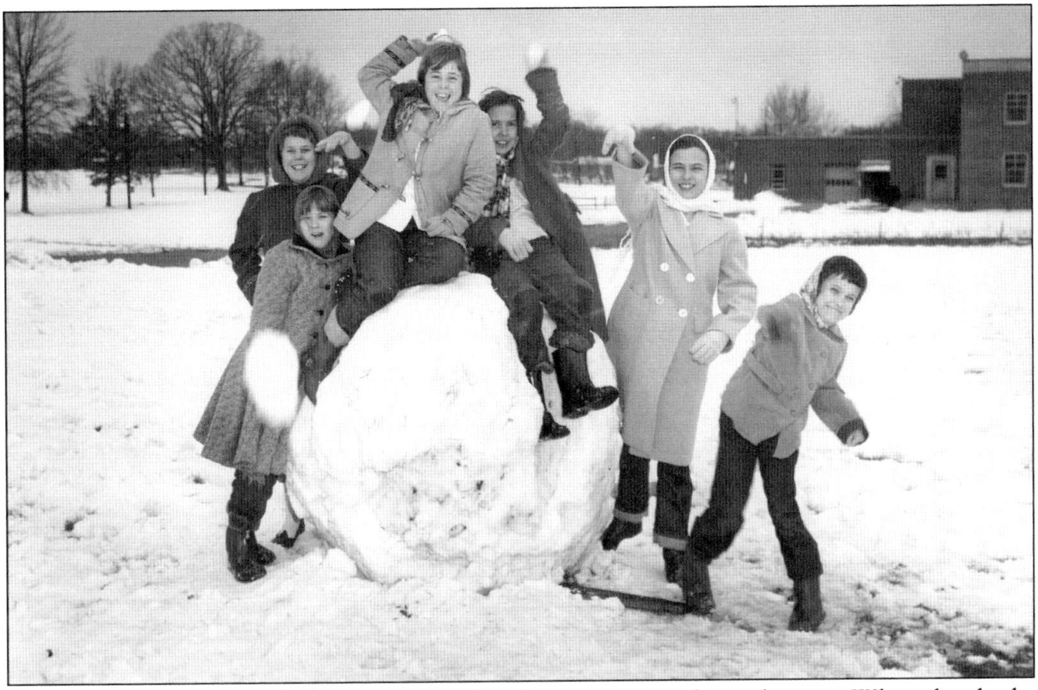

One former resident recalls that winter was her favorite time at the orphanage. When they had a snow day from school, the children were permitted to play outside for hours at a time. Typically, they had a regimented, strict schedule that did not allow for much outdoor play time, especially during the school week. So a day of outdoor activity was a special treat.

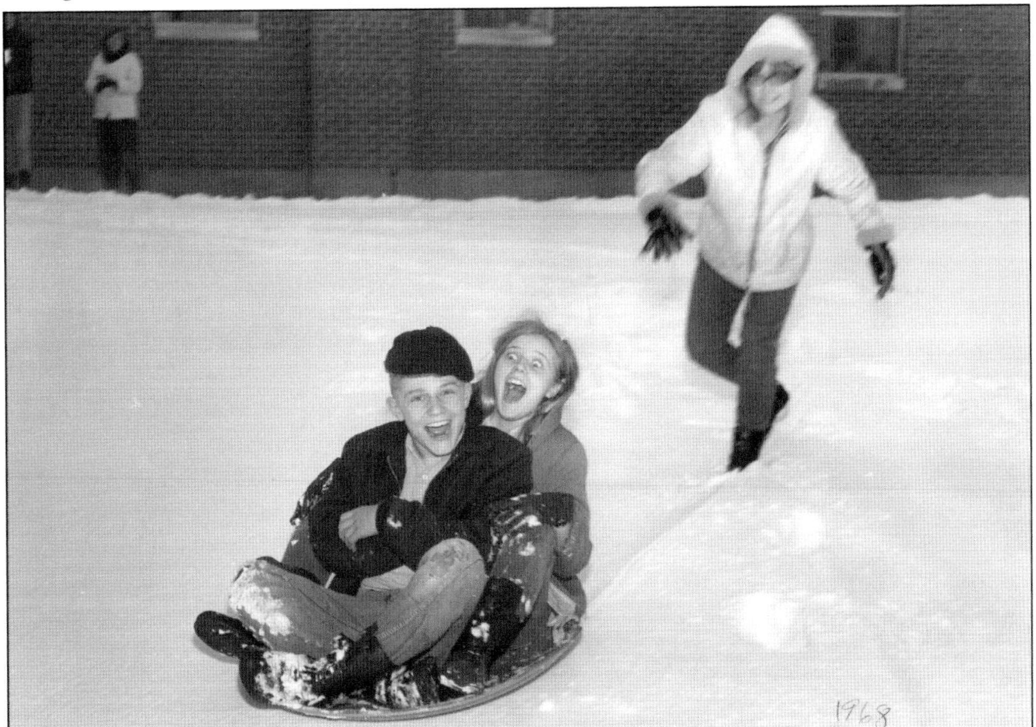

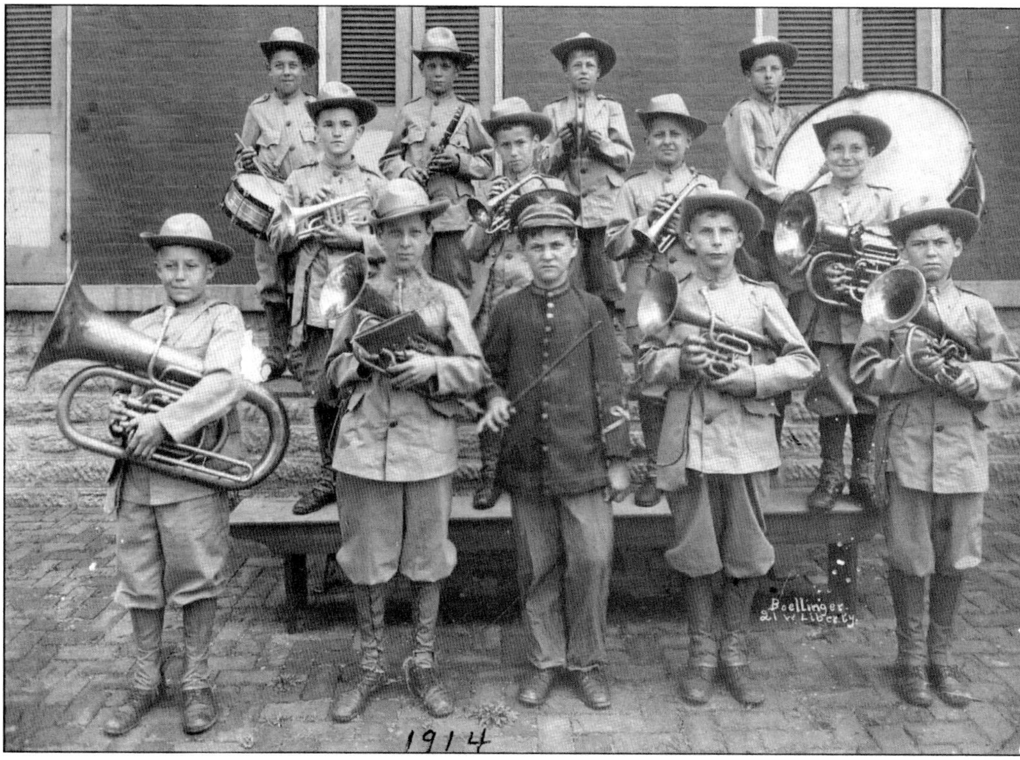

The Orphan Home band was established in 1914. The band was invited to play at various events, and the Home was usually given a donation from the event's sponsors. As the Depression began to affect every segment of life starting in the late 1920s, several generous benefactors continued to support the band, providing the children a radio from the Radio Merchants Guild and 36 capes for performances. Musical instruments provided a creative outlet. One former resident recalls after leaving the Home at the age of 18 in 1939, he returned every year until the 1950s to play in the band. Another former resident recalls that they were "the best band in Cincinnati. People asked us to play in every parade." The photograph above captures the first band in 1914. The image below was taken on Armistice Day, November 11, 1928.

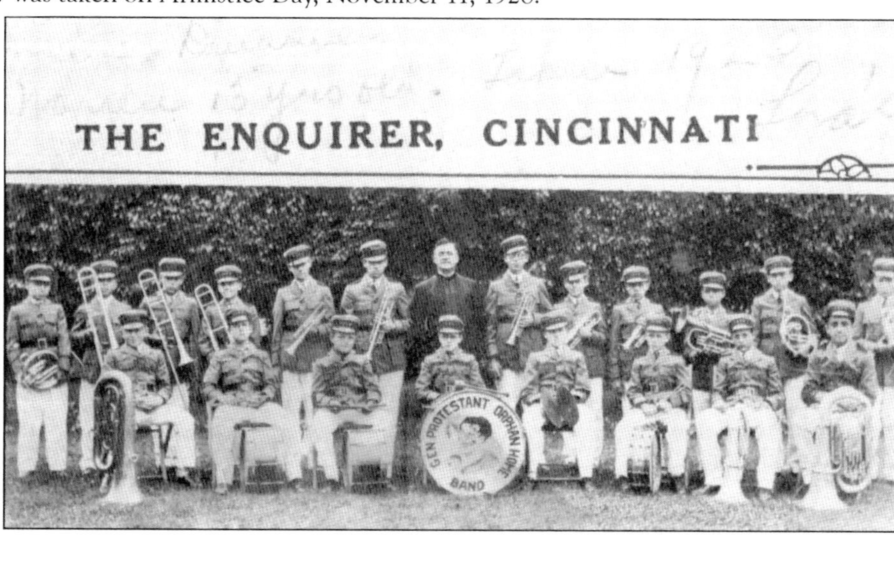

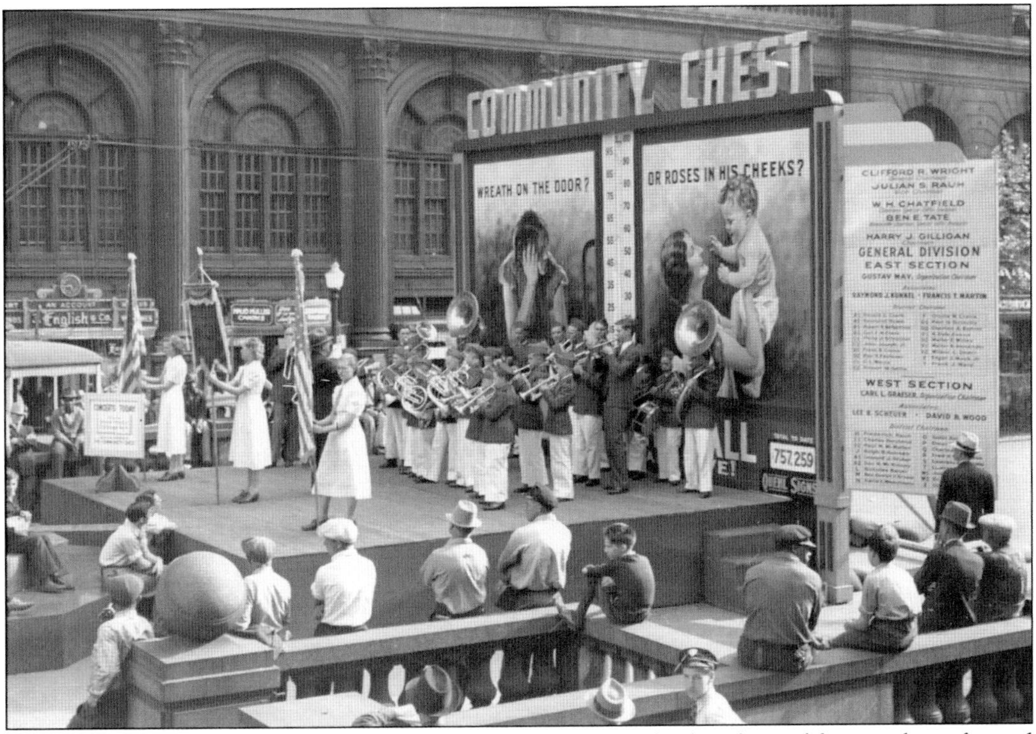

The children's band had a great reputation in the community for decades and frequently performed at community events and fundraisers. These photographs show the band playing during an early Community Chest fundraiser in downtown Cincinnati. The Community Chest raised money from local businesses and workers and distributed it to community projects. The first Community Chest was founded in 1913 in Cleveland, Ohio. The fundraising group eventually became the United Way. Today, Beech Acres Parenting Center is proudly a United Way agency partner.

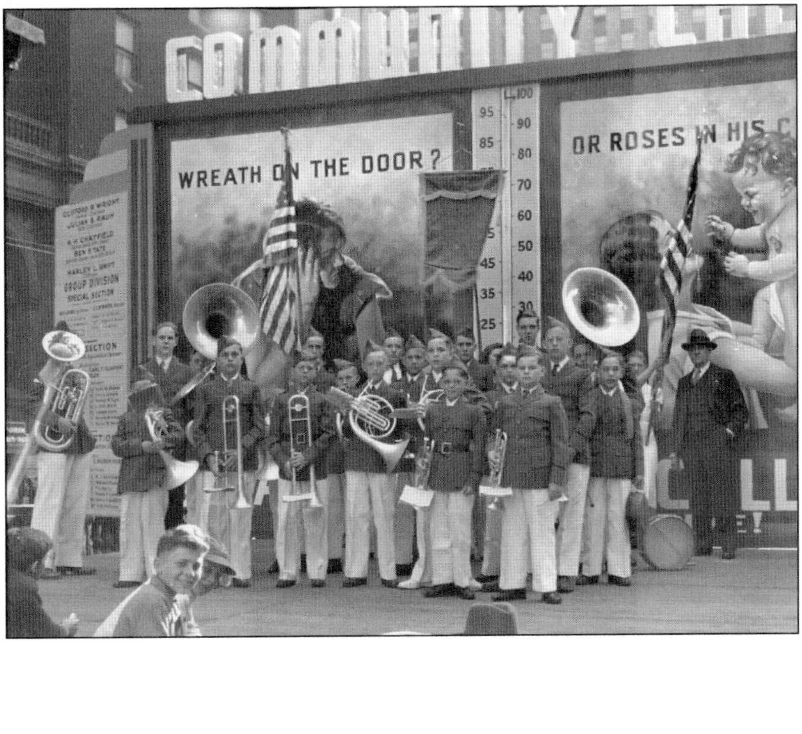

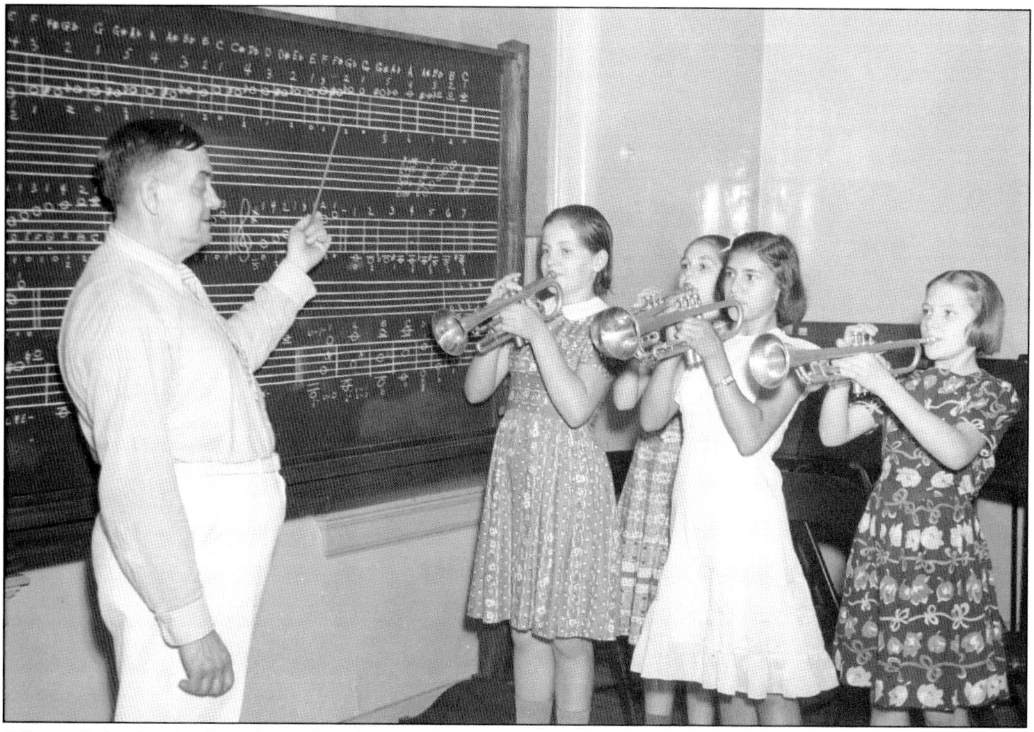

Edwin Schath, the band teacher for the children during the 1940s, leads the horn section of the girls' orchestra in practice for the 90th annual Orphan Feast. As musical director, Schath had the children practice three times a week the month before the Orphan Feast for their grand performance. The band was so popular among the community, as well as with residents, that several residents returned annually for many years after their stay at the Home to continue playing in the band for the Feast.

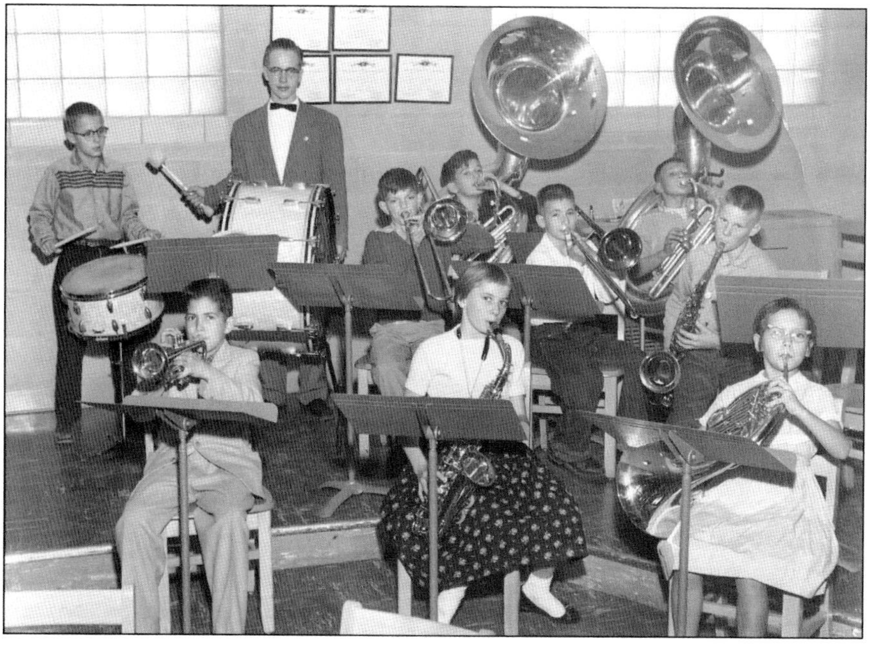

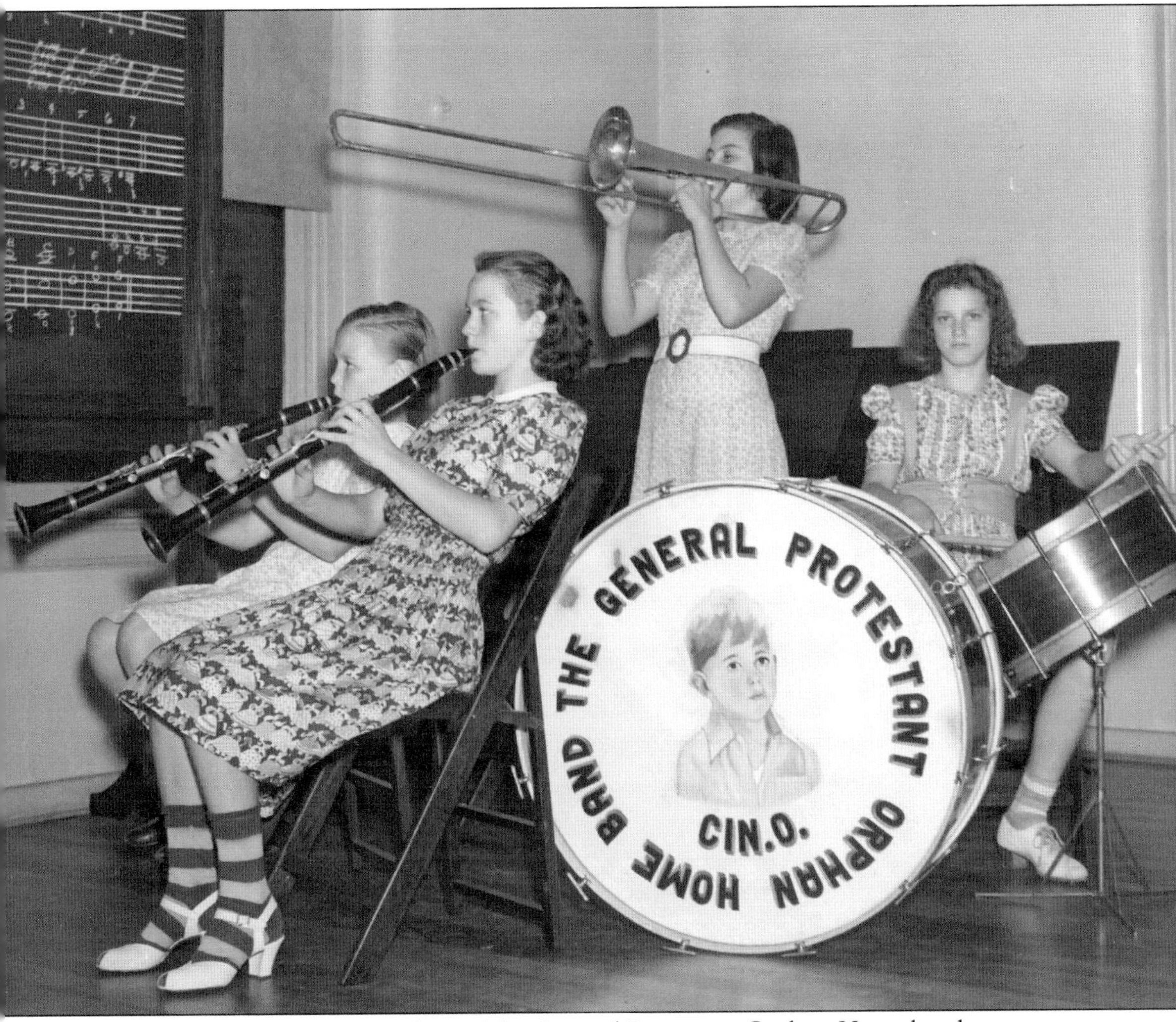

Practice makes perfect for members of the General Protestant Orphan Home band.

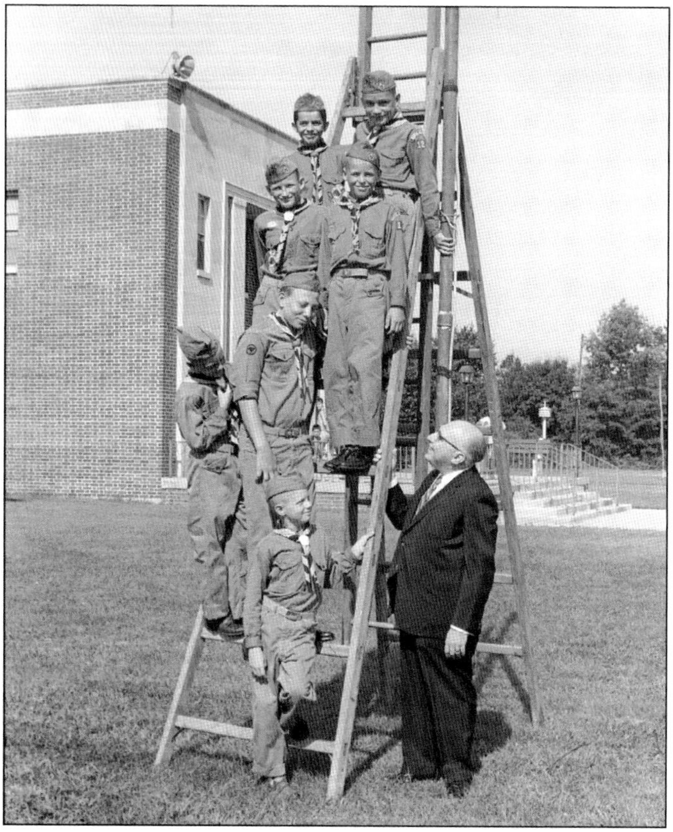

Boy Scout Troop 126 belonged to the Home. Started in the early 1900s, boys had the opportunity to join the troop, participate in activities outside the Home, and earn merit badges in accordance with Boy Scout Law. Many residents joined the Boy Scout troop to enjoy the camaraderie, achieve badges, learn new skills, and participate in outdoor education.

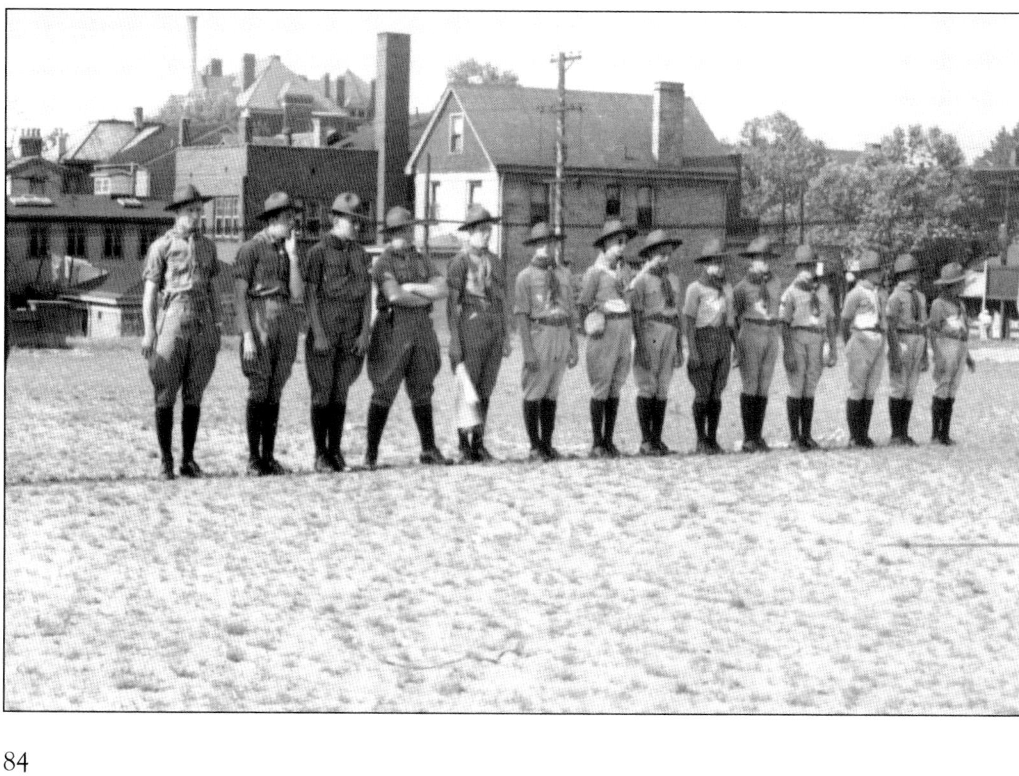

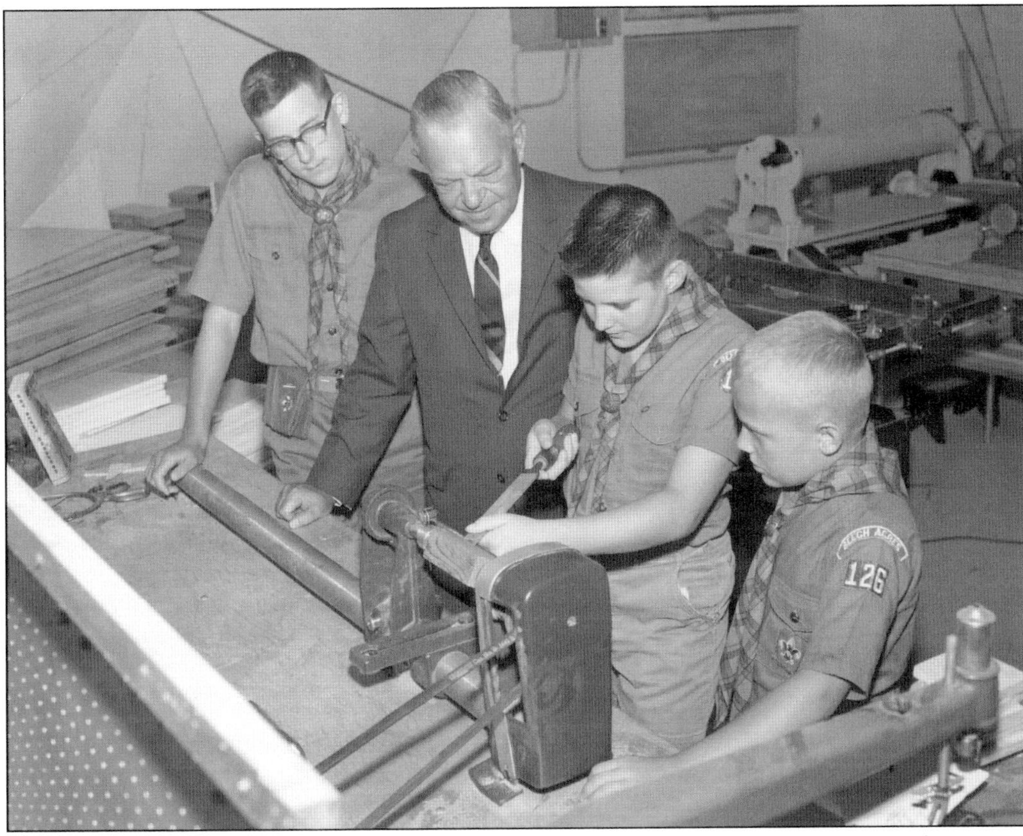

The Boy Scouts at the Home had several types of projects; one was to whittle wood into lampposts. As seen above, the Boy Scouts learned the trade of woodworking and contributed their skills to making homemade lamps for the Home.

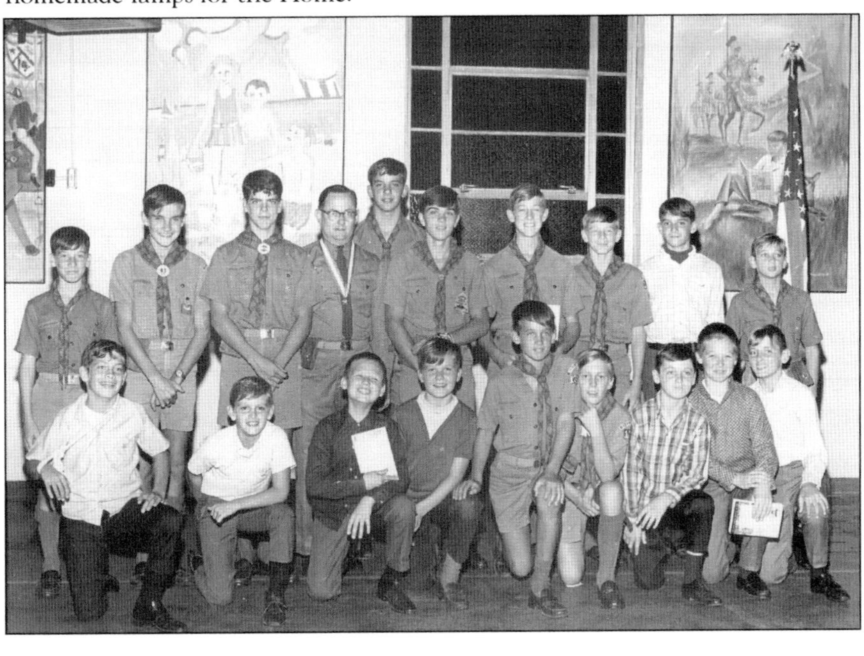

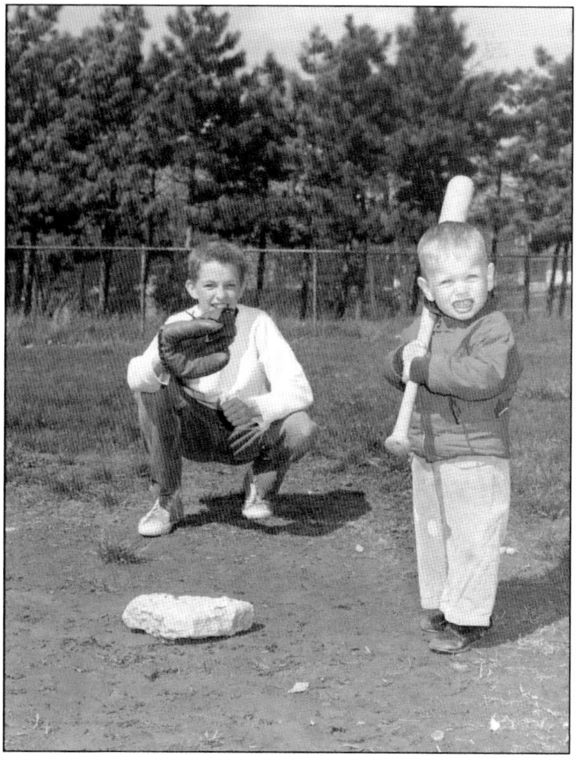

Children were involved in many types of extracurricular activities. Sports always played an important role in the lives of many of the Home's children. In the early years, teams were formed, and they played teams from other orphanages in the area. Later, children joined teams at their community schools. To this day, former residents who participated on Beech Acres' sports teams hold fond memories of the practices and games of 50 years ago.

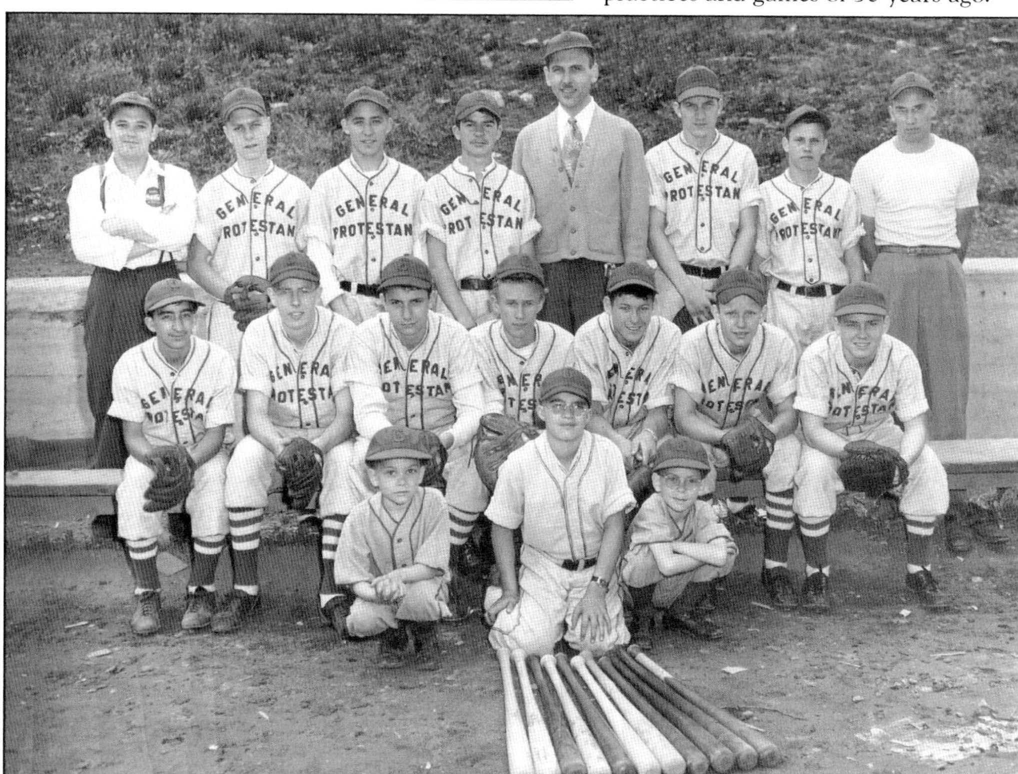

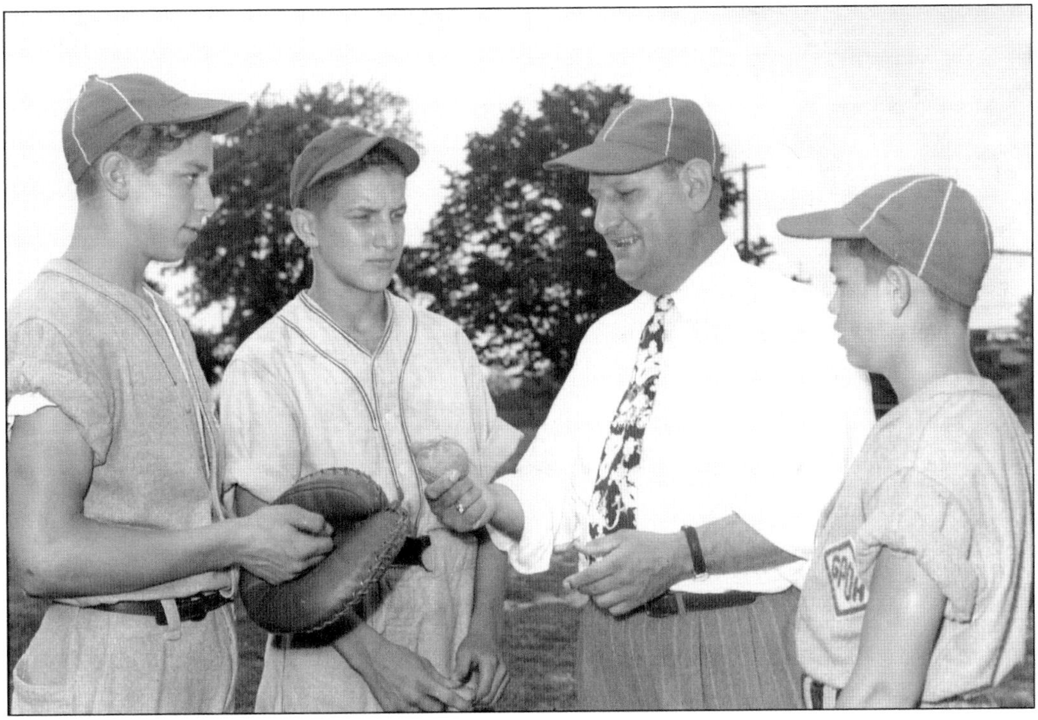

Above, a well-dressed coach offers some pitching instruction. Below, the stacked bats reflect the Home and team's commitment to orderliness and discipline.

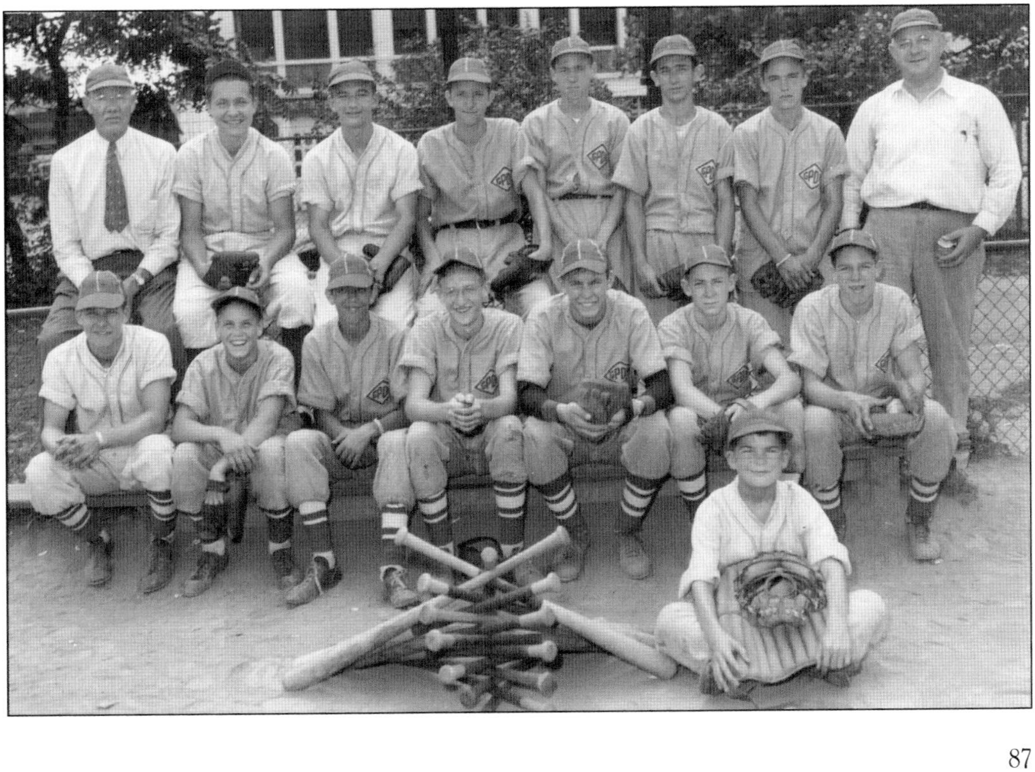

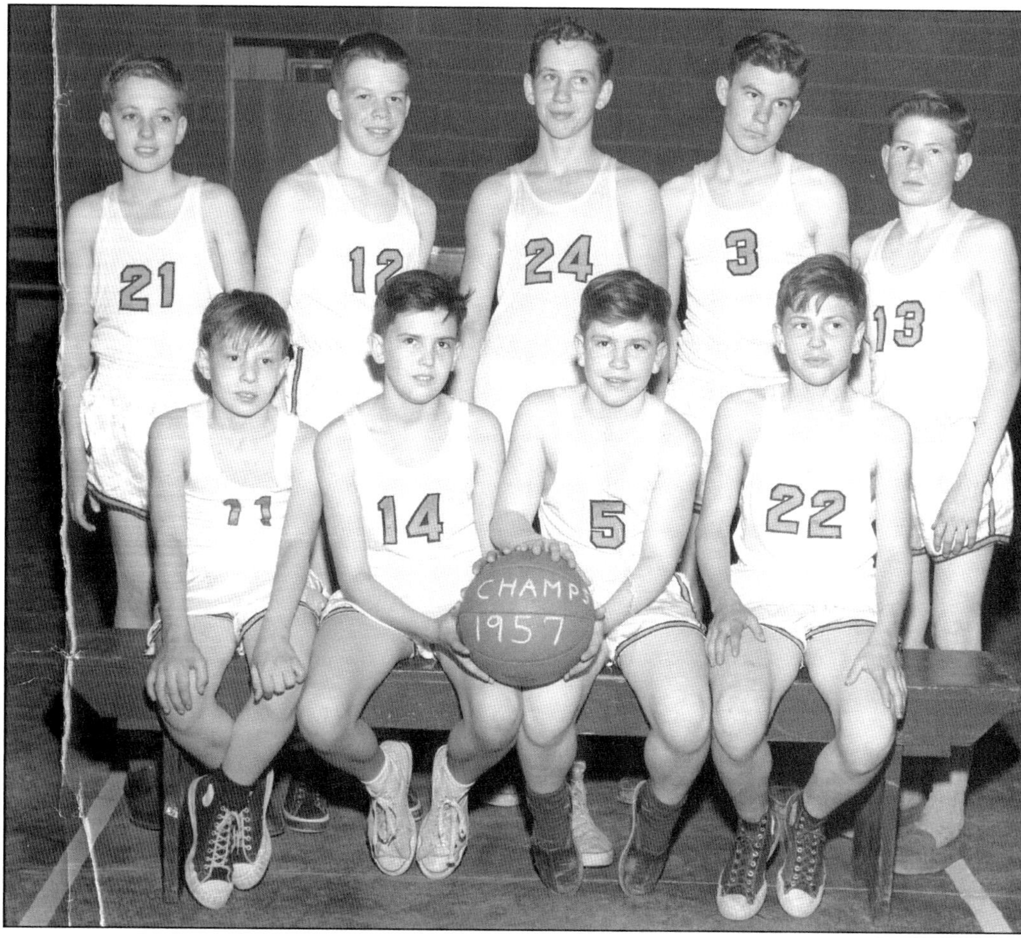

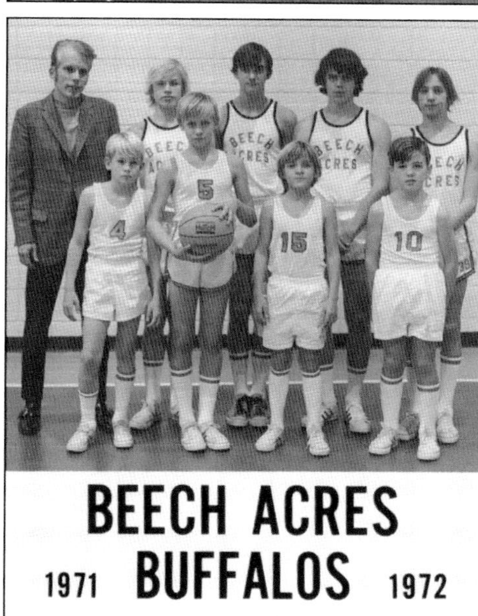

The stigma of being an orphan persisted over time, as the need for such homes transitioned with society's needs. Children at Beech Acres attended the local public schools in Anderson Township, Hamilton County. Although attending public school, most orphans participated in sports provided by Beech Acres and not those in the schools. This was intended to keep the children guarded from prejudice and allowed the children to remain with their friends from the Home.

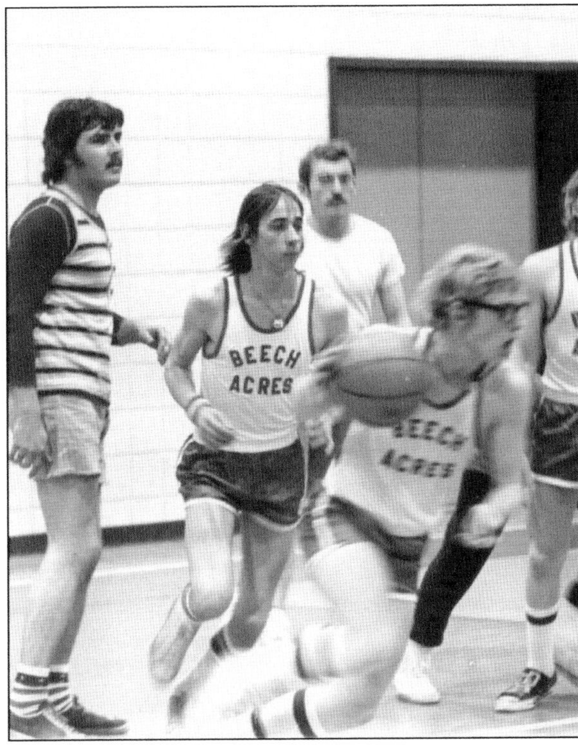

Beech Acres' basketball team competed against Cincinnati's other orphanages in a league of their own. The Children's Home and St. Joseph's Orphanage were among the teams against which Beech Acres played.

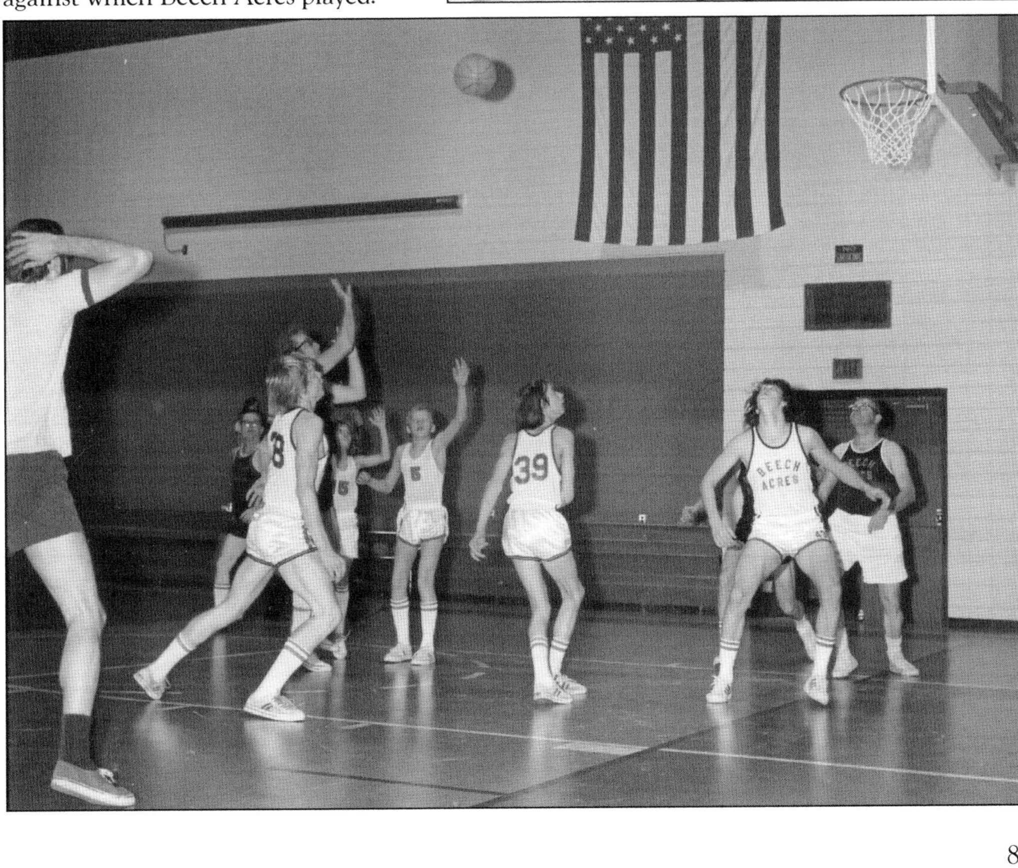

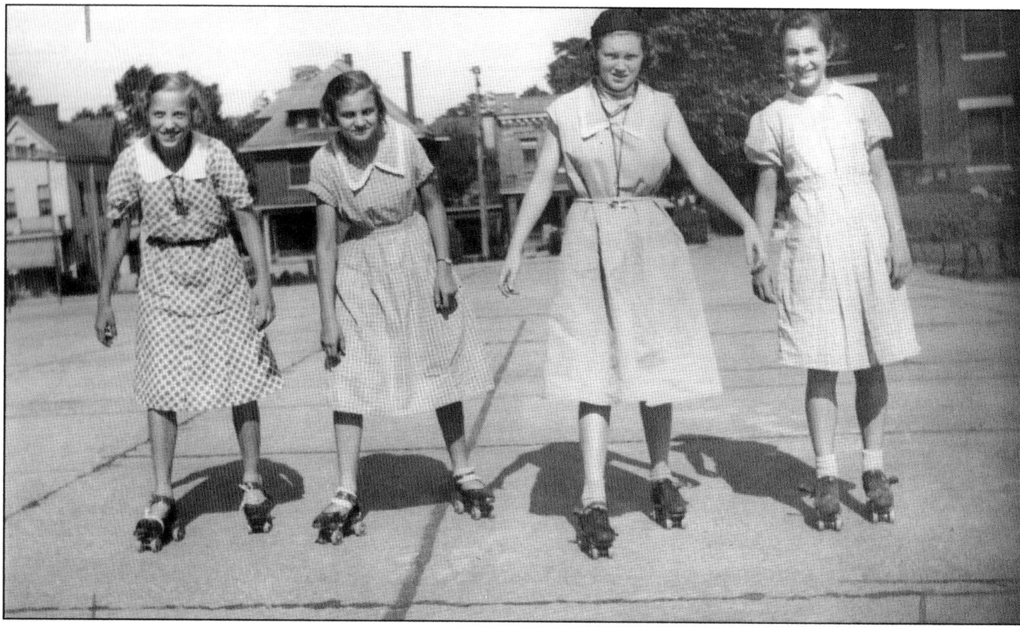

Roller-skating became a popular outdoor activity on the playground at the Mount Auburn location. The Girl Scouts and other clubs provided additional activities for girls to participate in.

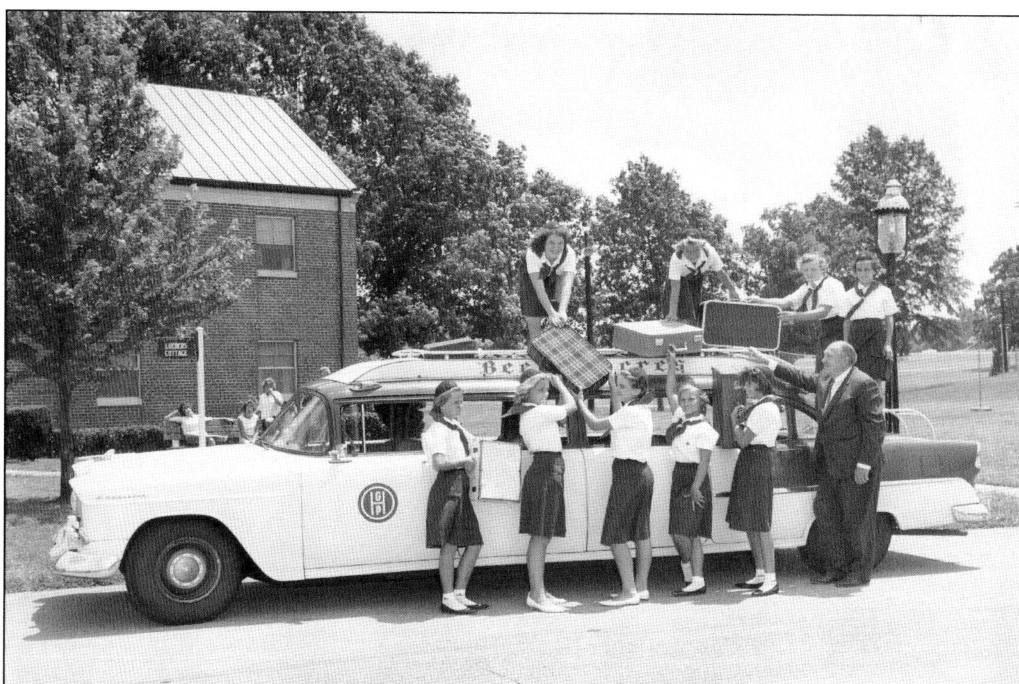

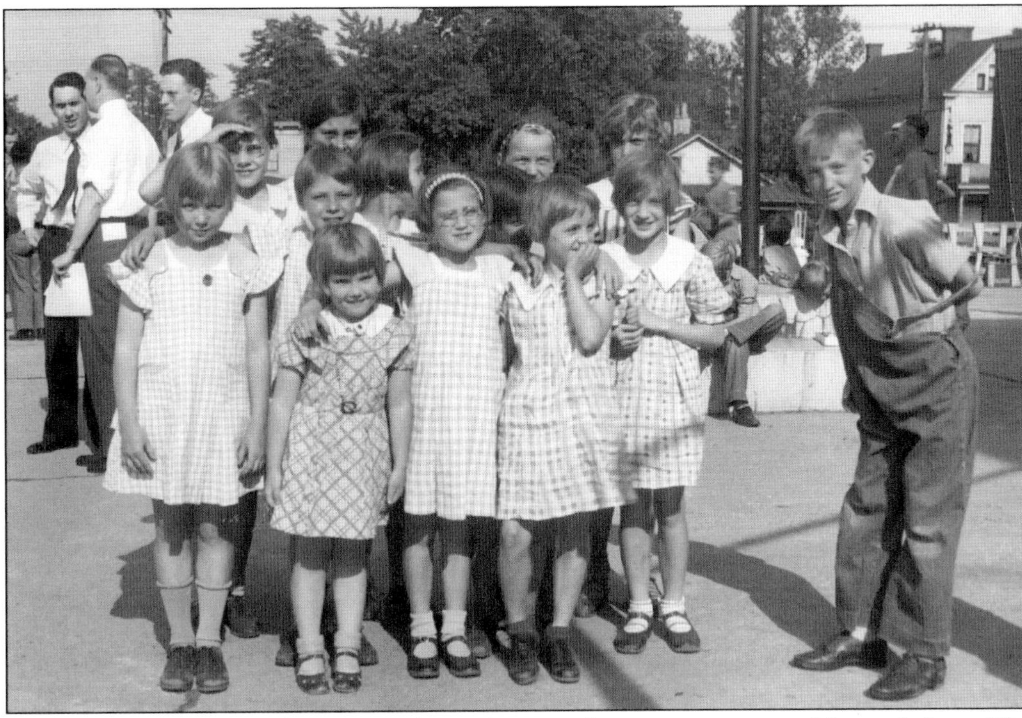

In the early years, the orphanage was located in an urban environment in Mount Auburn. The children played on cement playgrounds and had little opportunity to spend time in the great outdoors. During the 1940s, summer camping trips to the "country" began for elementary and high school children. In contrast to the large brick building and shared sleeping quarters they were accustomed to, the children slept under the stars on cots in screened tents. Children were able to stay on the land, known as the Beeches, for up to two weeks. Former residents fondly reminisce about this time with fun memories of fishing, camping, and playing outdoor games including hide-and-seek; several remember just running around freely. The camping property was eventually purchased, and the orphanage left Mount Auburn after being in that location for 100 years.

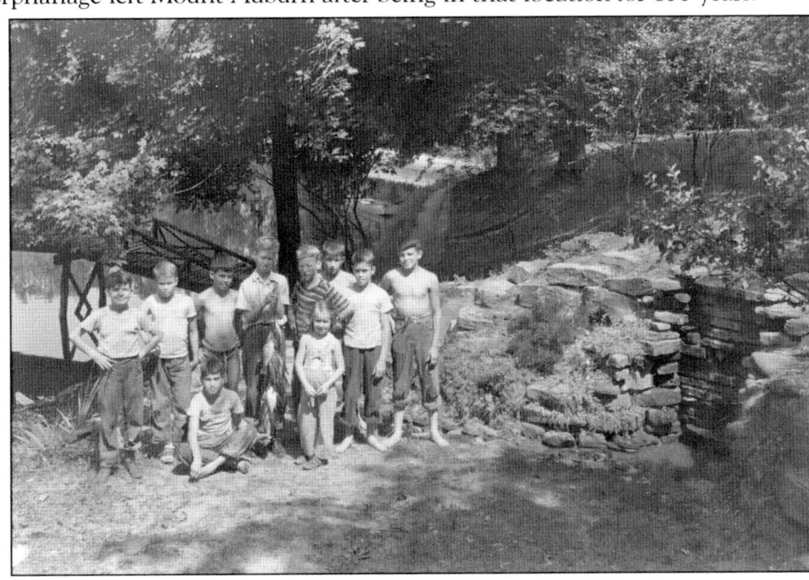

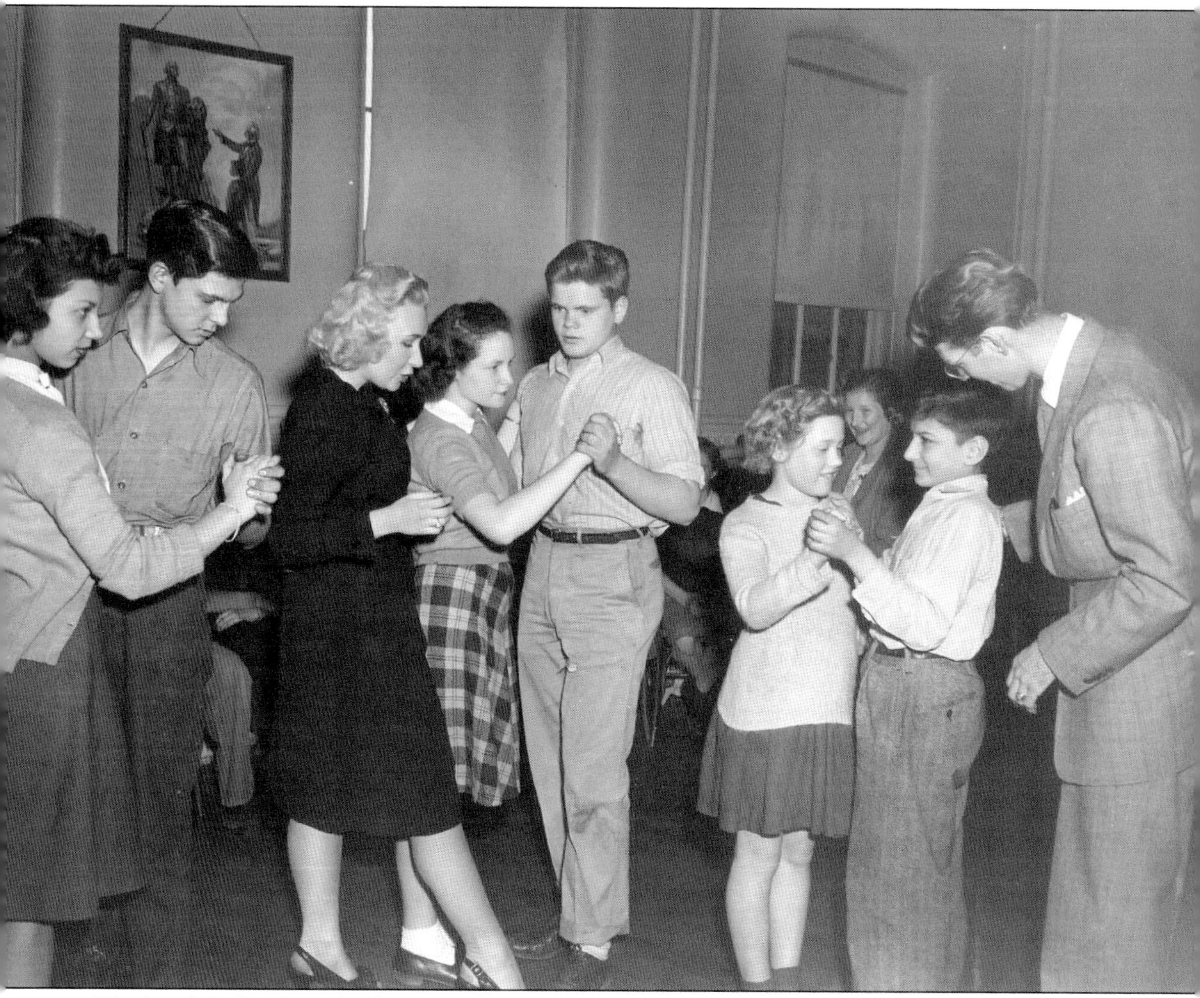

The local Arthur Murphy dance studio provided free dance instruction to the children of GPOH. These lessons were exciting to the children, as they learned the etiquette and manners necessary on the dance floor while swaying with their partner. Several of these children later became professional dancers as well as life partners.

A large pond used to exist on the property near Beechmont Avenue. Children spent hours at the pond fishing and enjoying other activities such as the ropes course the boys are climbing on in the 1954 photograph at right. Several former residents of the Home recall that children were allowed to spend time together outside unsupervised if they had no disciplinary action for a week. Local community residents recall enjoying the pond and surrounding property for their own recreation as well.

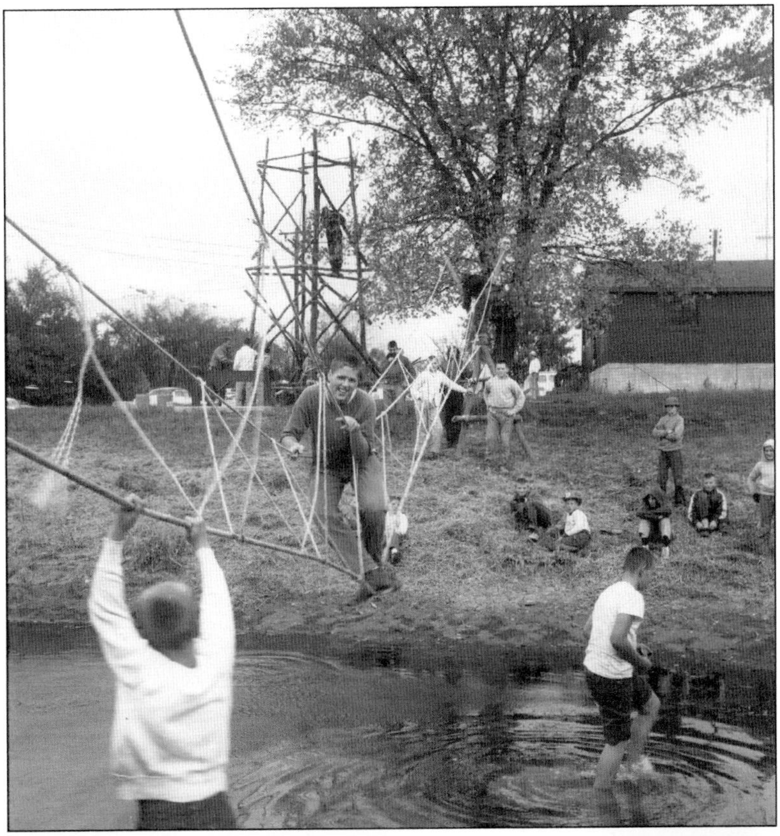

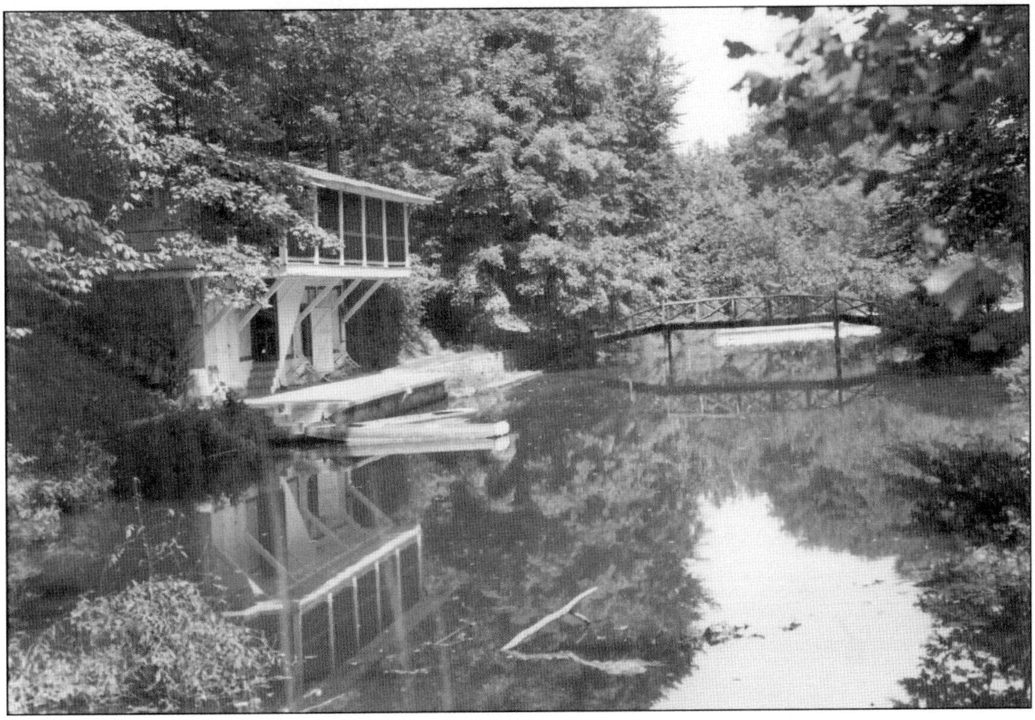

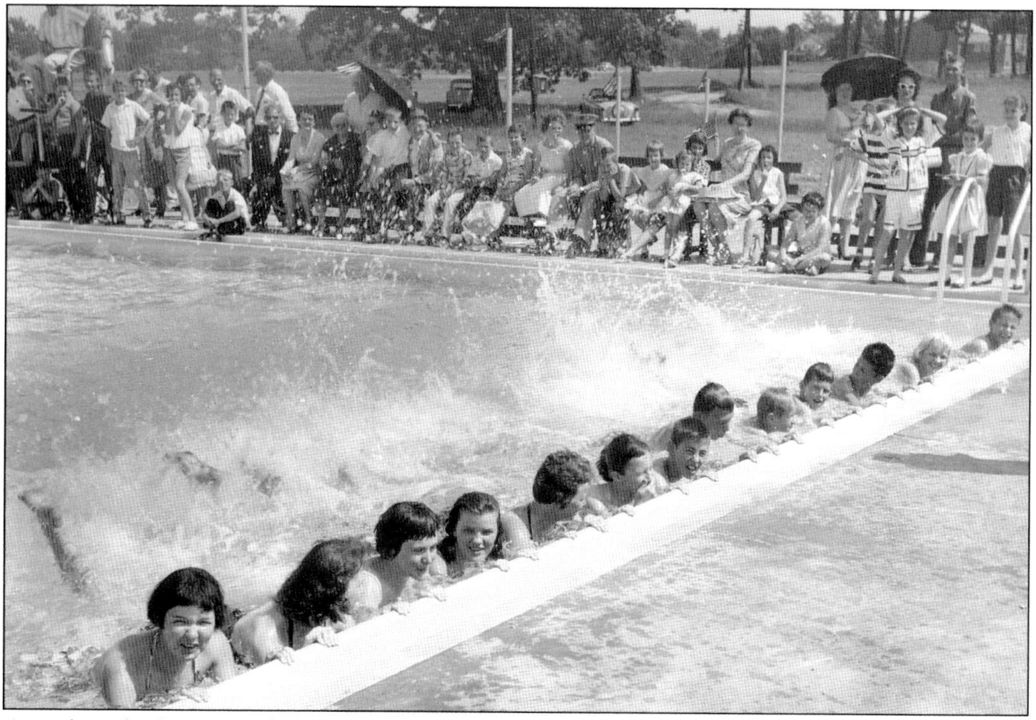

A pool was built next to the Geiger Activity Center on the Beechmont campus and was dedicated on June 5, 1960. Each resident was required to take swimming lessons and participate in the Red Cross lifesaving certification process. The pool provided an opportunity for all of the children to learn how to swim. One former resident remembers having fun in the pool and recalls being appreciative at the time for the chance to learn how to swim.

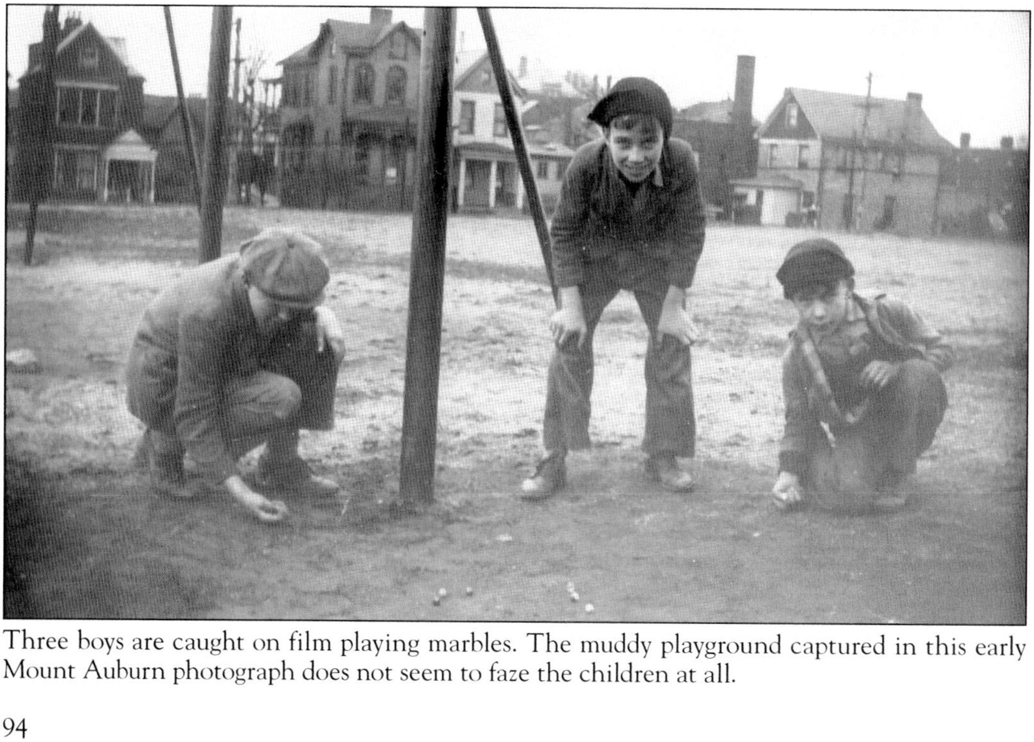

Three boys are caught on film playing marbles. The muddy playground captured in this early Mount Auburn photograph does not seem to faze the children at all.

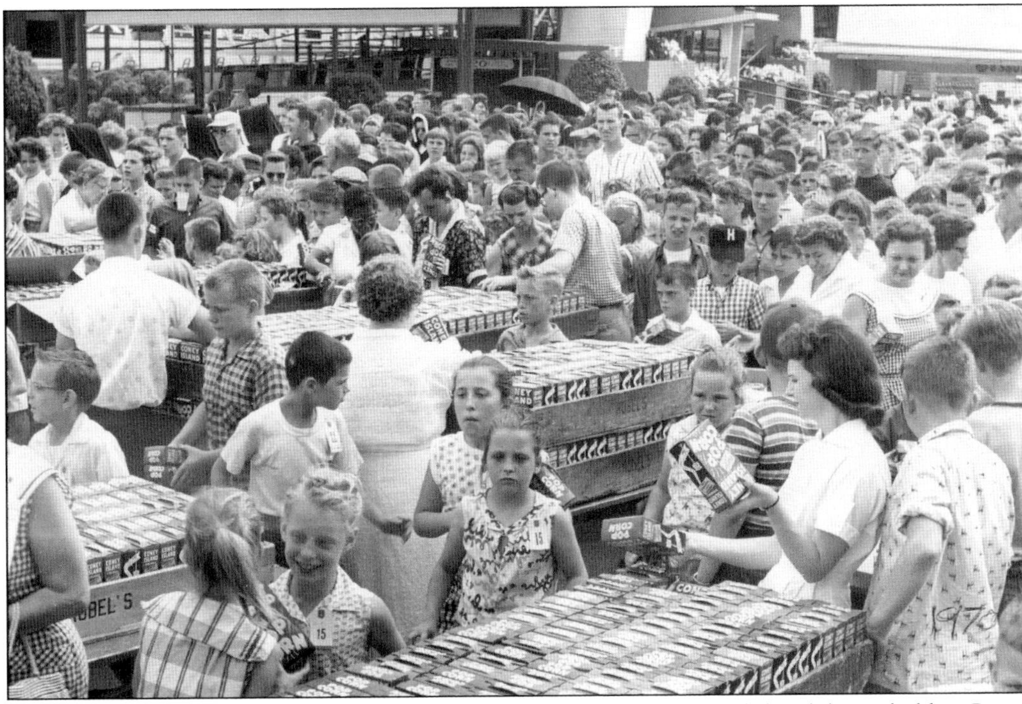

In 1933, the 26th-annual Orphans' Outing of the Cincinnati Automobile Club was held at Coney Island. George F. Schott, a friend to all children, hosted the outing. Refreshments and rides were available to all of Greater Cincinnati's orphans thanks to the generosity of the auto club and Coney Island management. Bus rides were provided thanks to donations from generous citizens. The AAA Allied Group remains a good friend and supporter of Beech Acres Parenting Center to this day.

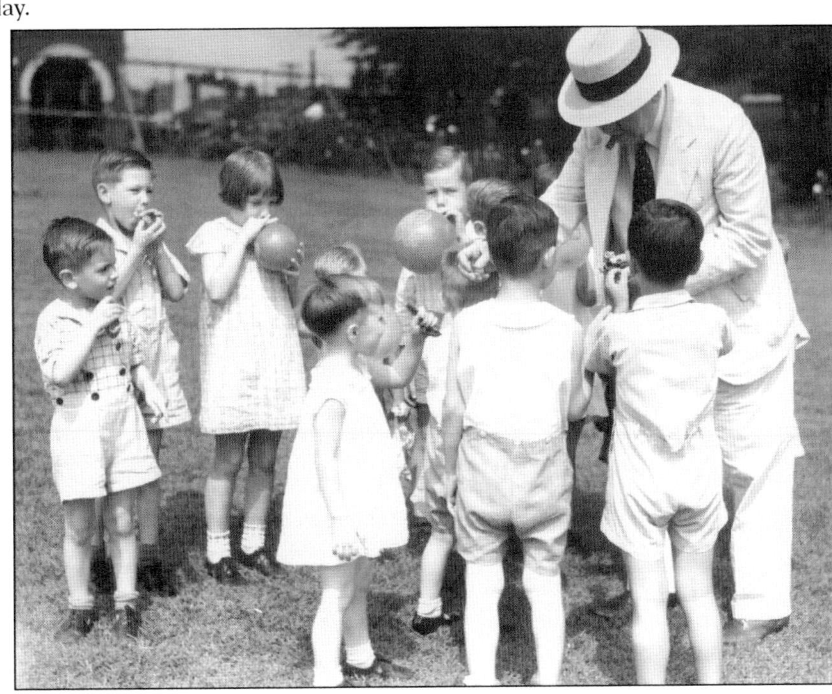

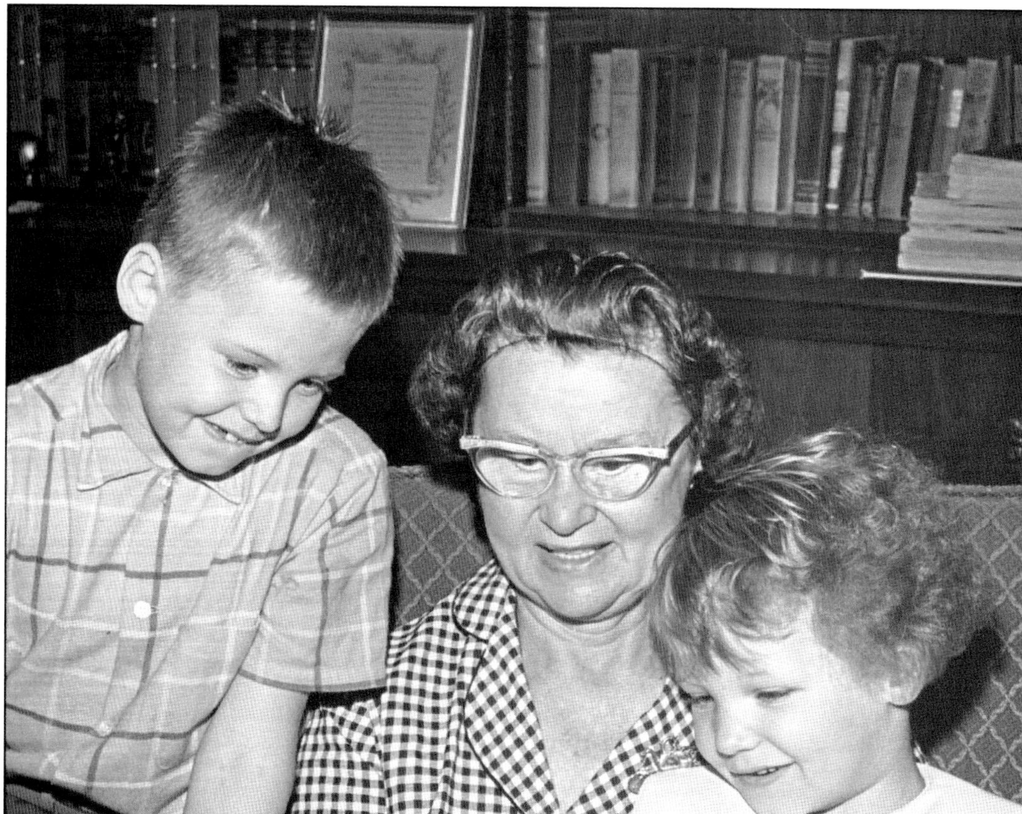

A housemother takes time to read a book entitled *A House For Everyone*.

Five

The Orphans Get a New Home

The General Protestant Orphan Home (GPOH) was originally located on four acres in Mount Auburn, purchased in 1849 from Judge Burnet. The parcel was roughly bordered by the streets now known as Martin Luther King Jr. Drive, Burnet Avenue, East University Avenue, and Highland Avenue. In the mid-20th century, with the growing pressures of city life on its land-locked Mount Auburn campus, the board of directors increasingly sought opportunities to take the children to the country. A 60-acre farm bordering Mount Washington and Anderson became an attractive summertime destination. Time spent on the farm was of great benefit to the children and a wonderful reward for good behavior. Camping, fishing, and hiking became favorite activities.

The Building Committee of the General Protestant Orphan Home's board of directors, chaired by Everett W. Townsley, recommended purchasing the farm, known as the Beeches, from the Provident Savings Bank & Company. Townsley generously donated one third the purchase price of the land in honor of his wife, Minnie, and daughter, Kathryn. Over time, residents and friends nicknamed the new home "Beech Acres" in respect for the beech trees growing on the property.

Plans were made for a permanent move of the orphanage to the country. Living quarters would be transitioned from a large institutional dormitory style to smaller, individual cottages designed to provide the children with a more home-like setting. Each cottage housed up to 16 children, based on age and gender. Siblings were often split, as the cottages were age based. Housemothers lived with the children. Often older and widowed themselves, they were split among three shifts: days, nights, and weekends. All housemothers received room, board, and a small stipend. Nine housemothers could care for 72 orphans.

After many months of planning and building, moving day finally arrived. According to an article in the *Cincinnati Post*, "Clutching baby dolls and teddy bears and waving small American flags, 104 excited orphans move to their new home in Mount Washington, Tuesday, August 15, 1950." With a police escort, the children were transported in a cavalcade of shiny new autos, loaned by the Chevrolet dealers of Cincinnati.

The children attended the Anderson Township schools. Home superintendent Joseph Quick stated that the new Home provided "a closer home life atmosphere and our staff will have better opportunities to teach the children the right way of living and respect for each other."

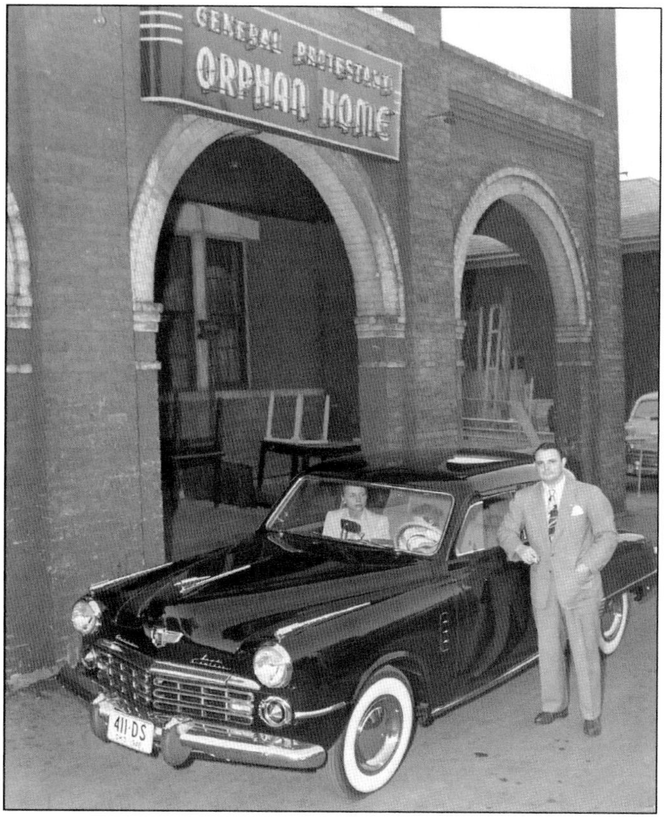

The new orphanage was located on Beechmont Avenue on the line between Mount Washington and Anderson Township. On moving day, the 104 orphans were escorted from Mount Auburn to their new home in shiny new Chevrolets donated for the day. Below is a 1949 picture of Beechmont Avenue.

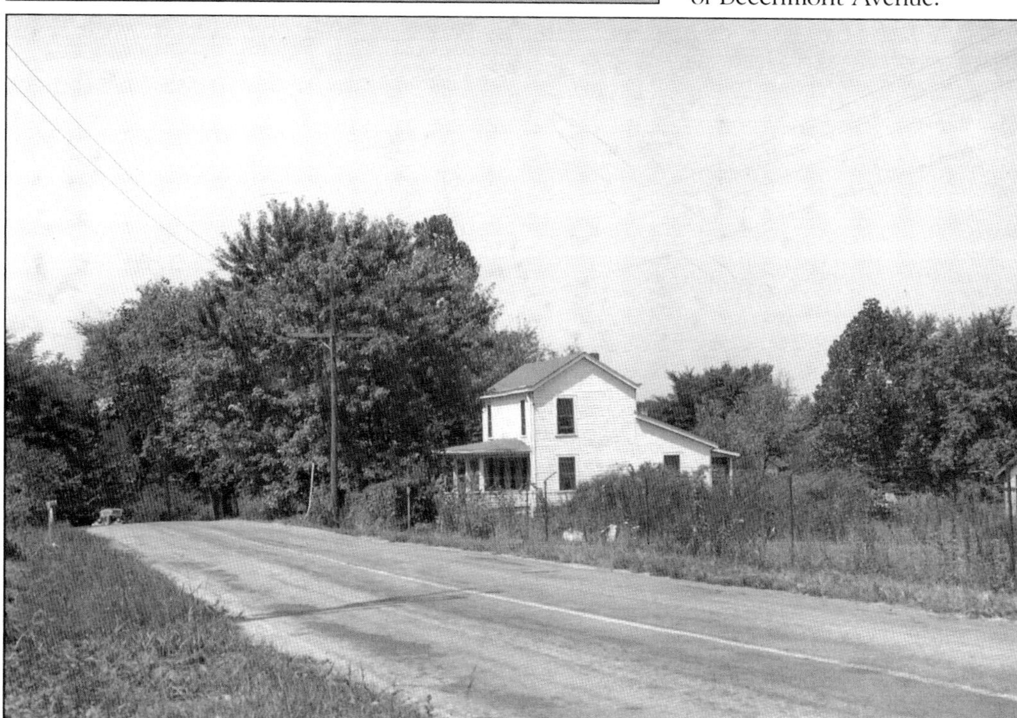

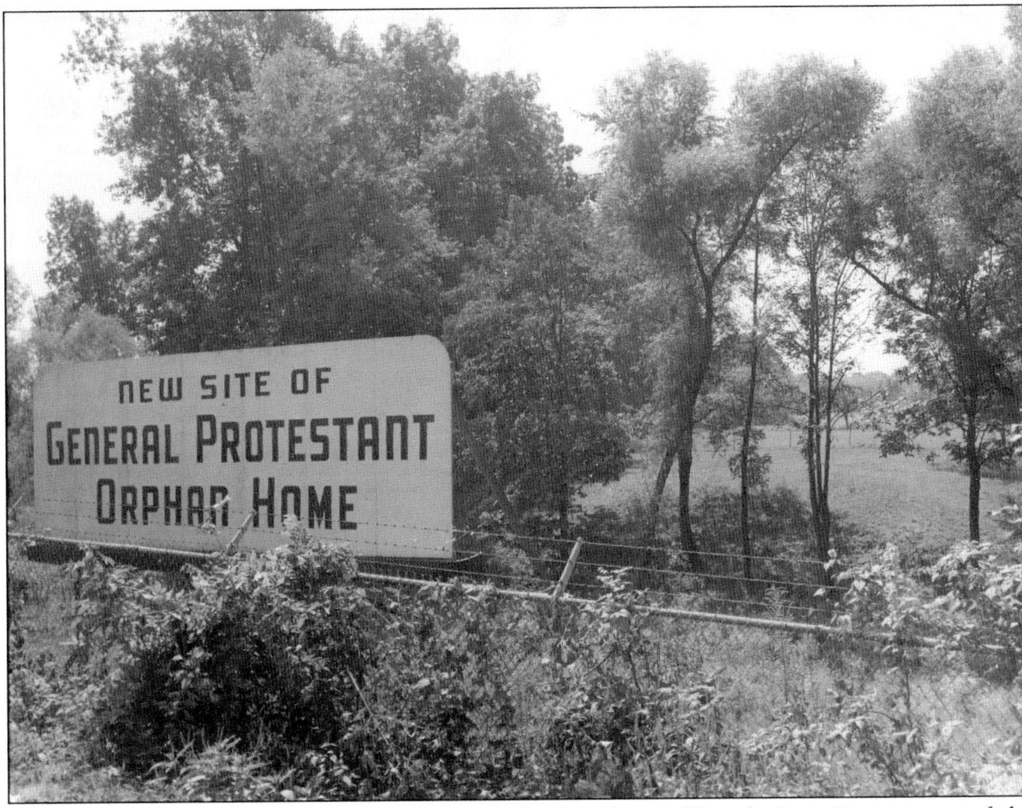

Over time, residents and friends nicknamed the new home "Beech Acres" in respect of the acres of beech trees growing on the property. The trees lined the area that the children played in and served as a symbol of the new home. As the "orphan" stigma increased, and the agency transitioned from orphanage to community-based social service provider, the name transitioned as well; first to Beech Acres—The General Protestant Orphan Home and then officially to Beech Acres in 1990.

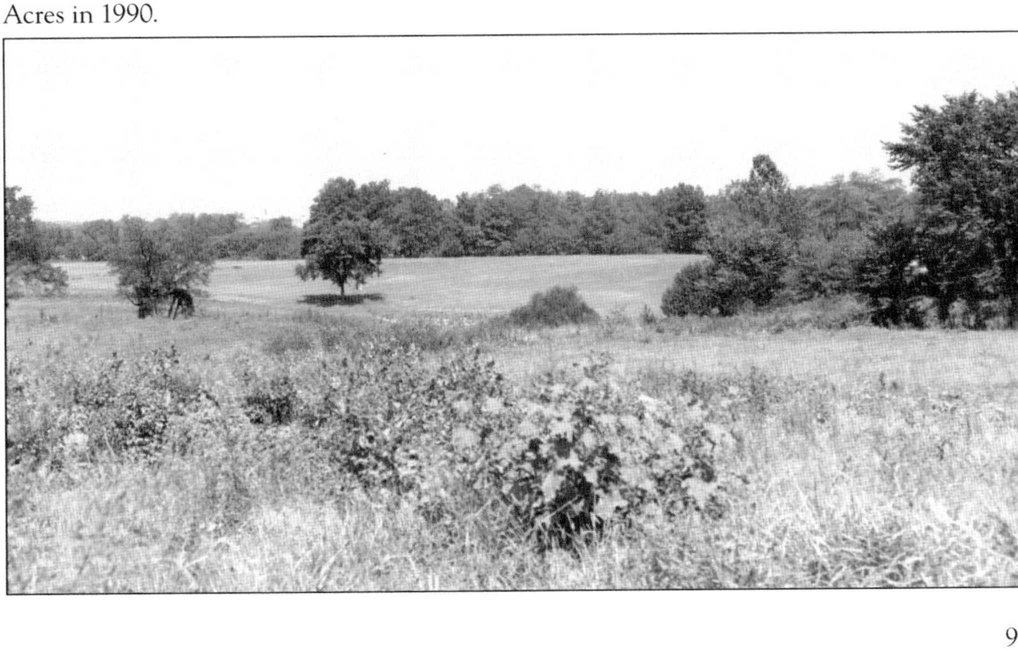

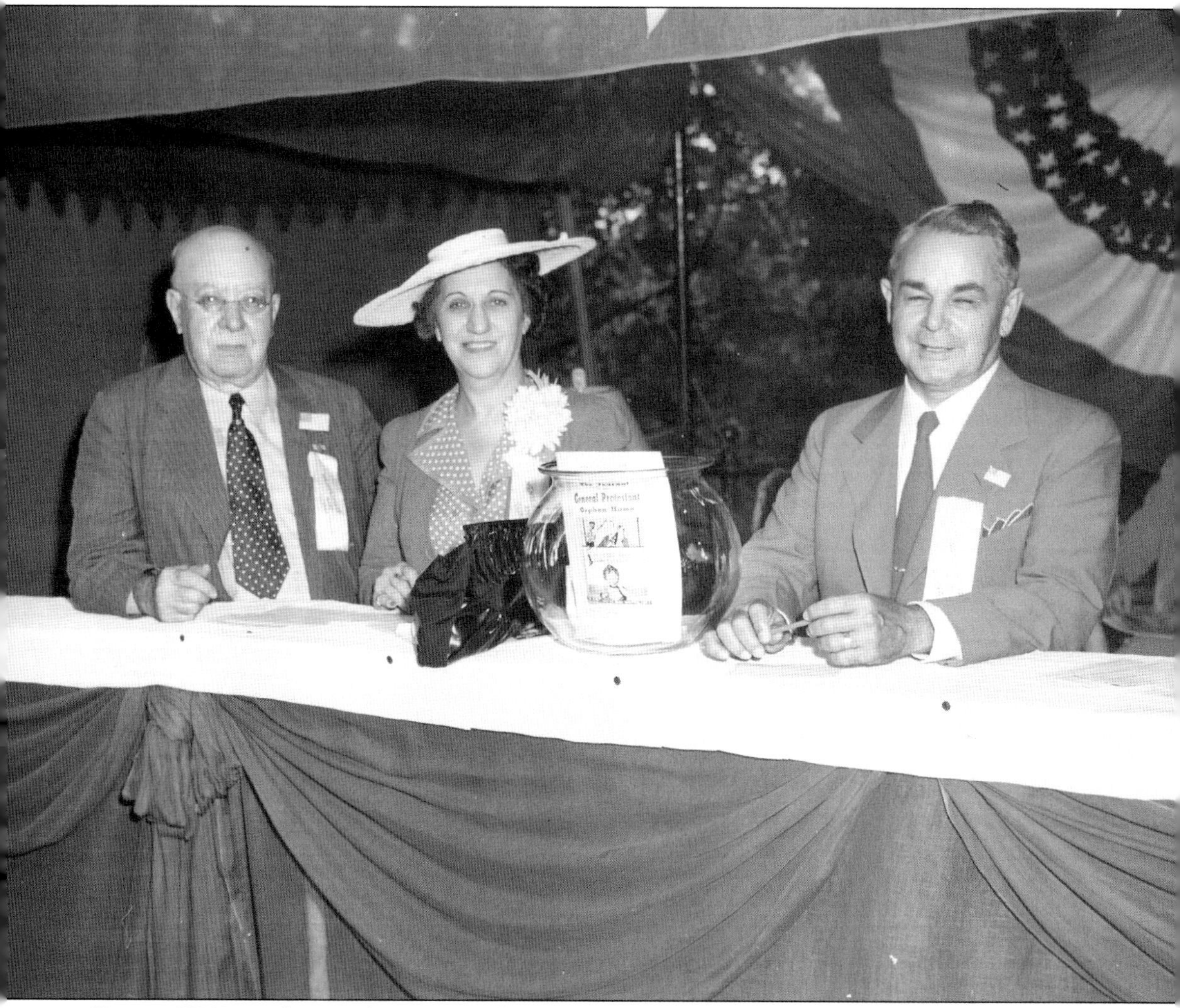

Everett W. Townsley was born December 26, 1877, in New Richmond, Ohio. Upon returning from service in the Spanish American War, he became a prominent businessman in Cincinnati. Townsley joined the board of the General Protestant Orphan Home in the 1930s. As chairman of its Building Committee, he led the Home's purchase of 62 acres of property in Mount Washington, known as the Beeches. It was to become the new home of GPOH, and the first children moved in on August 15, 1950. Townsley generously donated one third of the price of the new property. His service also included membership on the Music & Exhibition and Recreation Committees. He was Officer of the Day at the Orphan Feast in 1941 and 1942 and was a longtime member of the Orphan Feast Executive Committee.

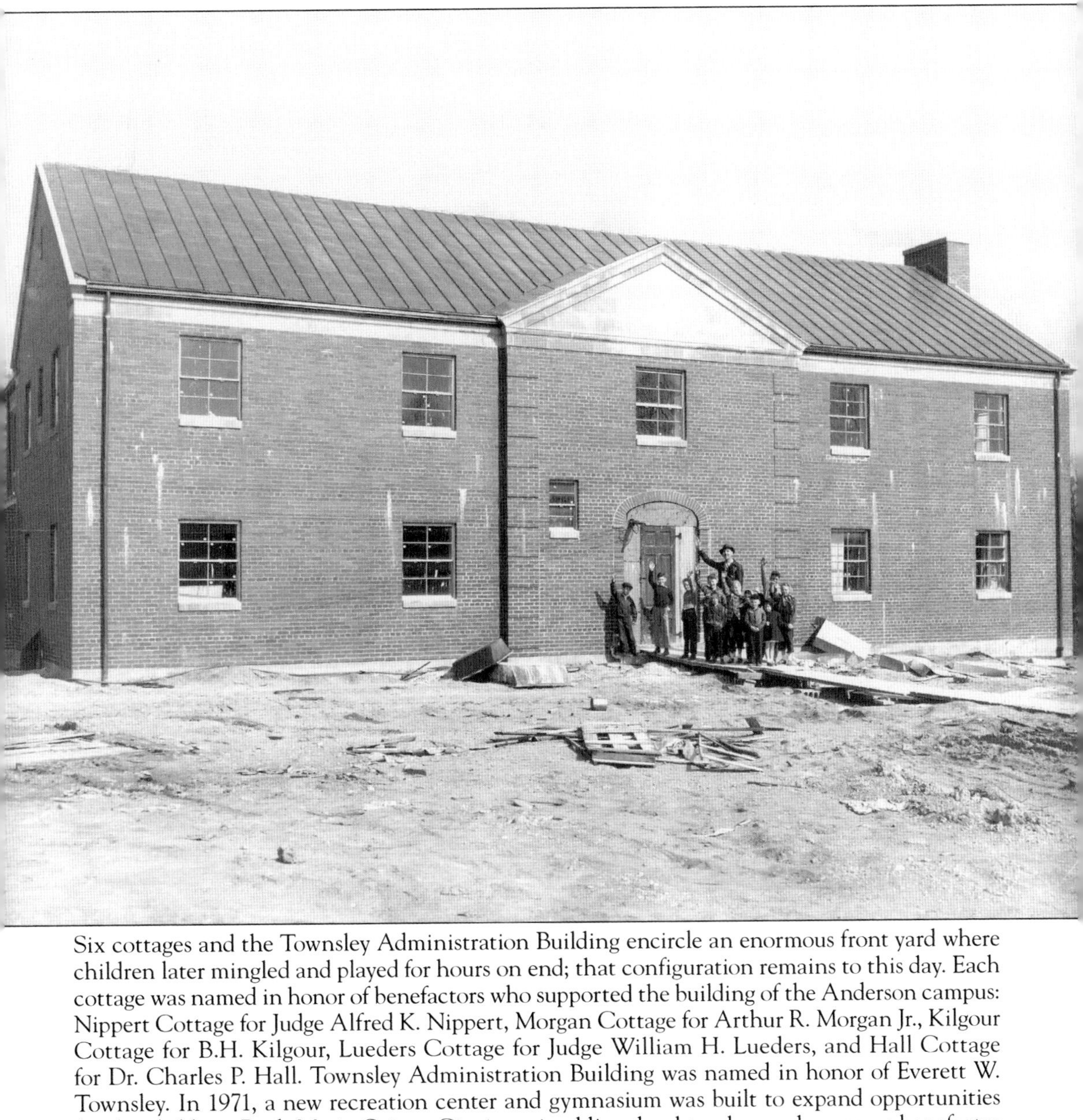

Six cottages and the Townsley Administration Building encircle an enormous front yard where children later mingled and played for hours on end; that configuration remains to this day. Each cottage was named in honor of benefactors who supported the building of the Anderson campus: Nippert Cottage for Judge Alfred K. Nippert, Morgan Cottage for Arthur R. Morgan Jr., Kilgour Cottage for B.H. Kilgour, Lueders Cottage for Judge William H. Lueders, and Hall Cottage for Dr. Charles P. Hall. Townsley Administration Building was named in honor of Everett W. Townsley. In 1971, a new recreation center and gymnasium was built to expand opportunities for the children. Ruth Marie Geiger, Cincinnati public school teacher and generous benefactor of the Home, named the Geiger Activity Center in honor of her parents, Charles Albert Geiger and Katherine Hauenstein Geiger.

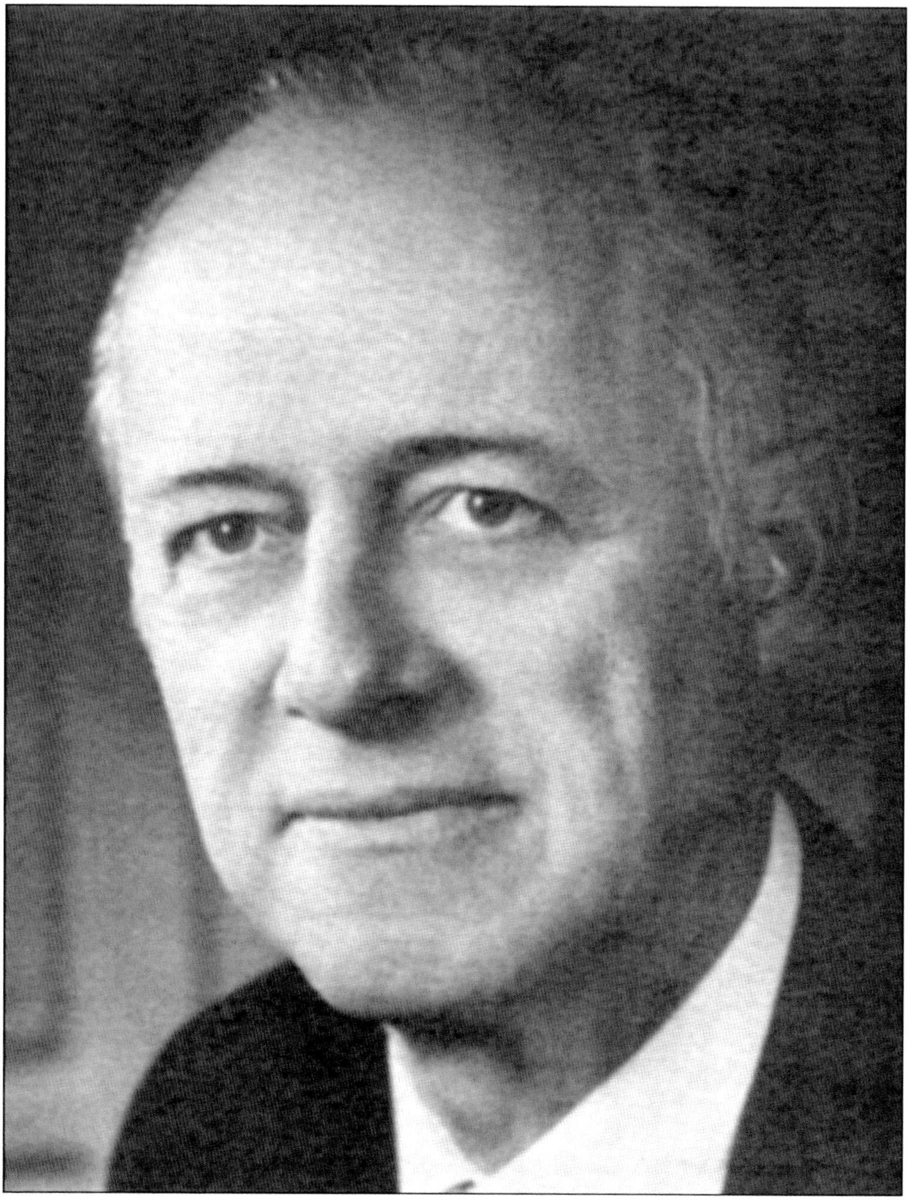

Carson "Ross" Whiting's involvement with the Home began when his father-in-law, Everett W. Townsley, died while board president in 1956. Ross was appointed to succeed him on the GPOH Board of Directors. He remained on the board until 1977 and served as its president from 1965 to 1972. Ross was Orphan Feast Officer of the Day in 1978. One of his noted accomplishments was the construction of the Geiger Activity Center, which was built to accommodate the children's need for year-round physical activities. The building was dedicated on the Fourth of July, 1971—exactly 120 years after the cornerstone had been placed at the Mount Auburn location when the orphan home was founded. Upon his resignation from the board (after 21 years of service), Ross was succeeded by his son Richard T. Whiting. Dick served from 1977 to 1990, including a term as board president from 1985 to 1988 during a time of significant shift in GPOH's services from restorative to preventive. The Townsley/Whiting family is another shining example of several generations of families contributing significantly to the organization's progress across eras.

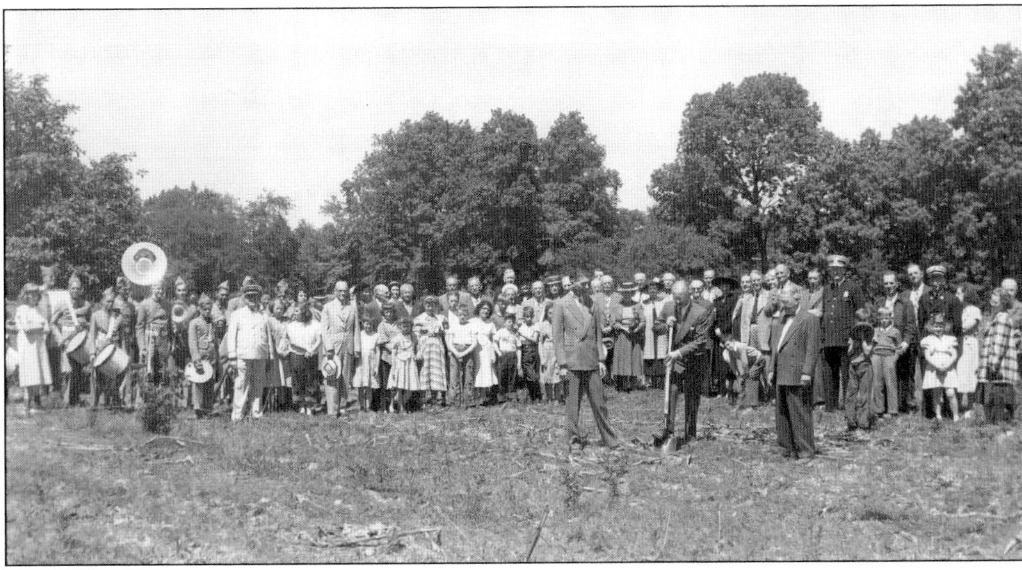

Arthur H. Heitz, president of the General Protestant Orphan Home Board of Directors from 1939 to 1949, is seen presiding over a cornerstone ceremony for the new Home to be built in Mount Washington.

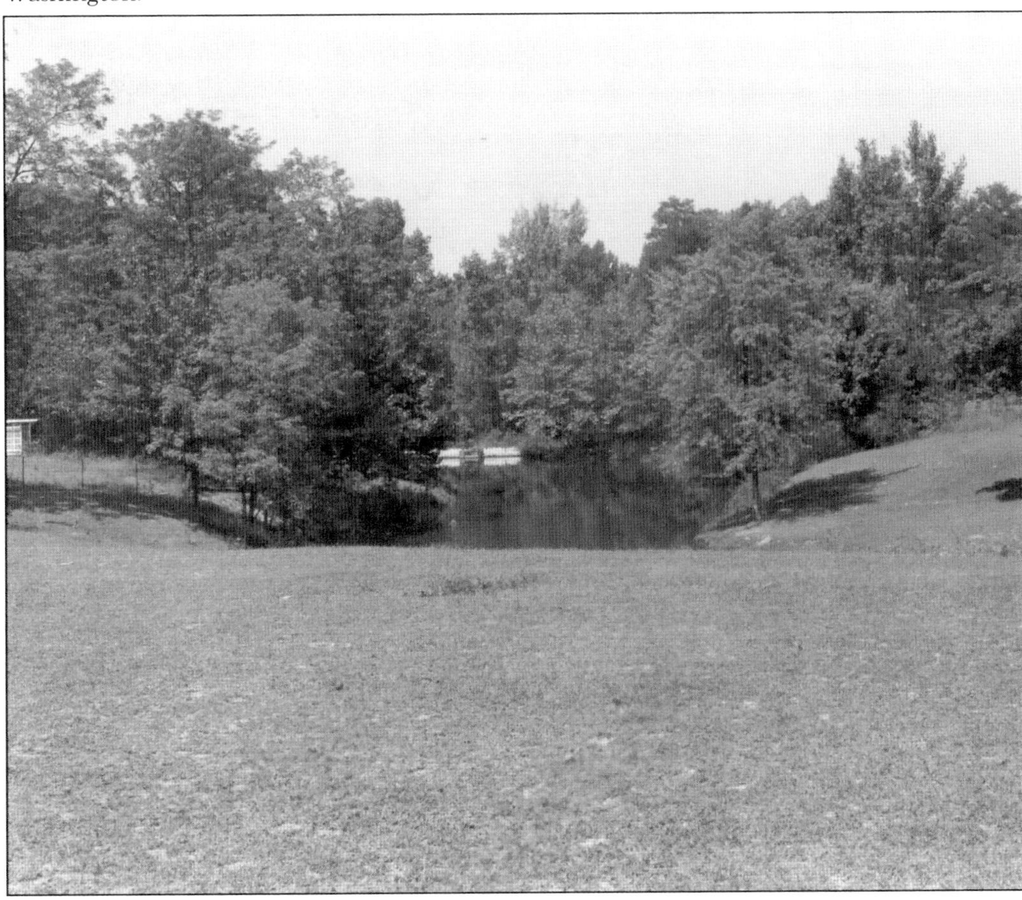

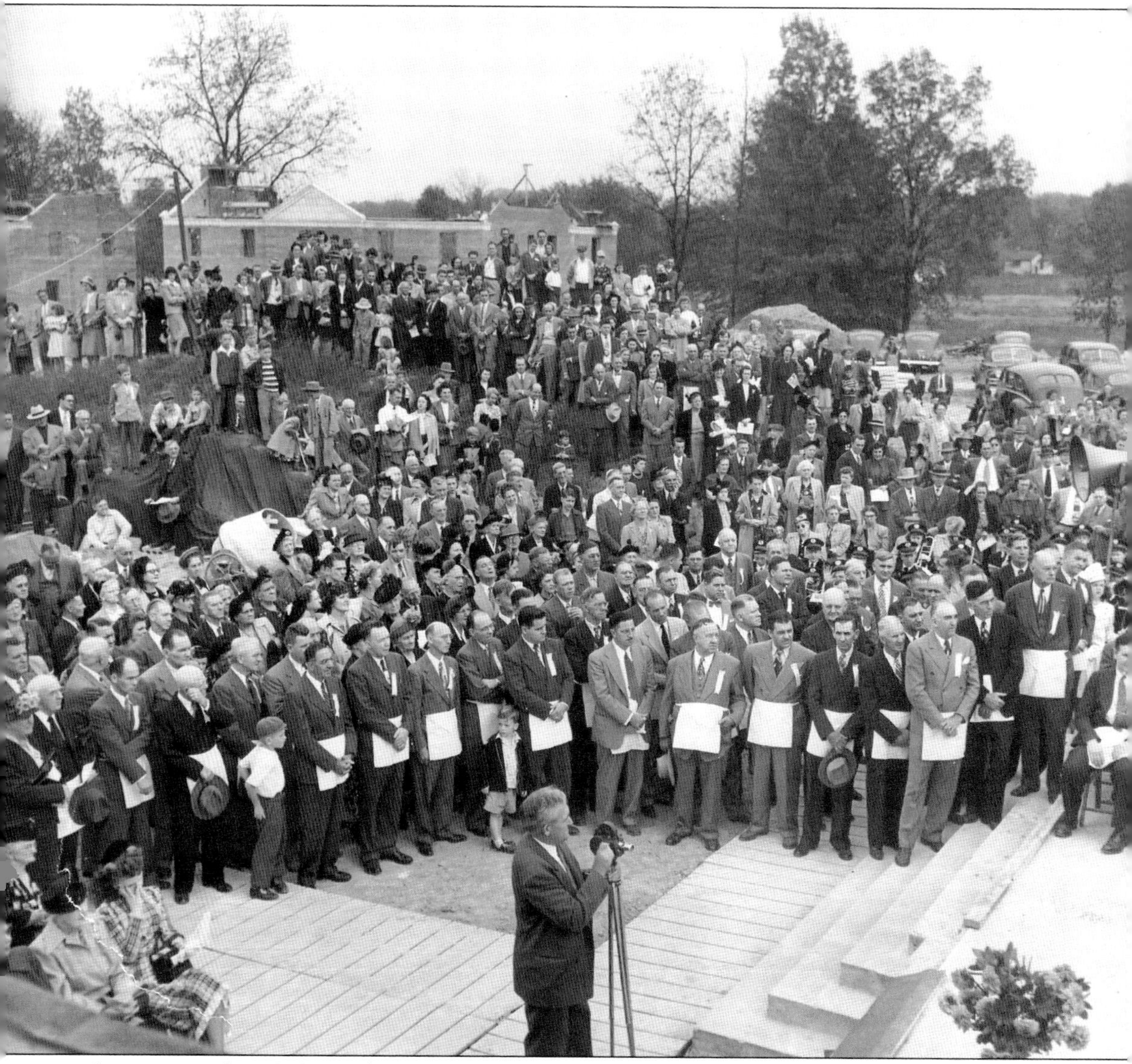

Approximately 1,000 people were present on Sunday, October 14, 1949, at the cornerstone dedication. As part of the ceremony, corn was scattered over the stone as a symbol of plenty, wine was poured over it signifying joy and gladness, and oil was poured over the stone as a symbol of peace. The cornerstone still remains as part of the Townsley Administration Building at Beech Acres.

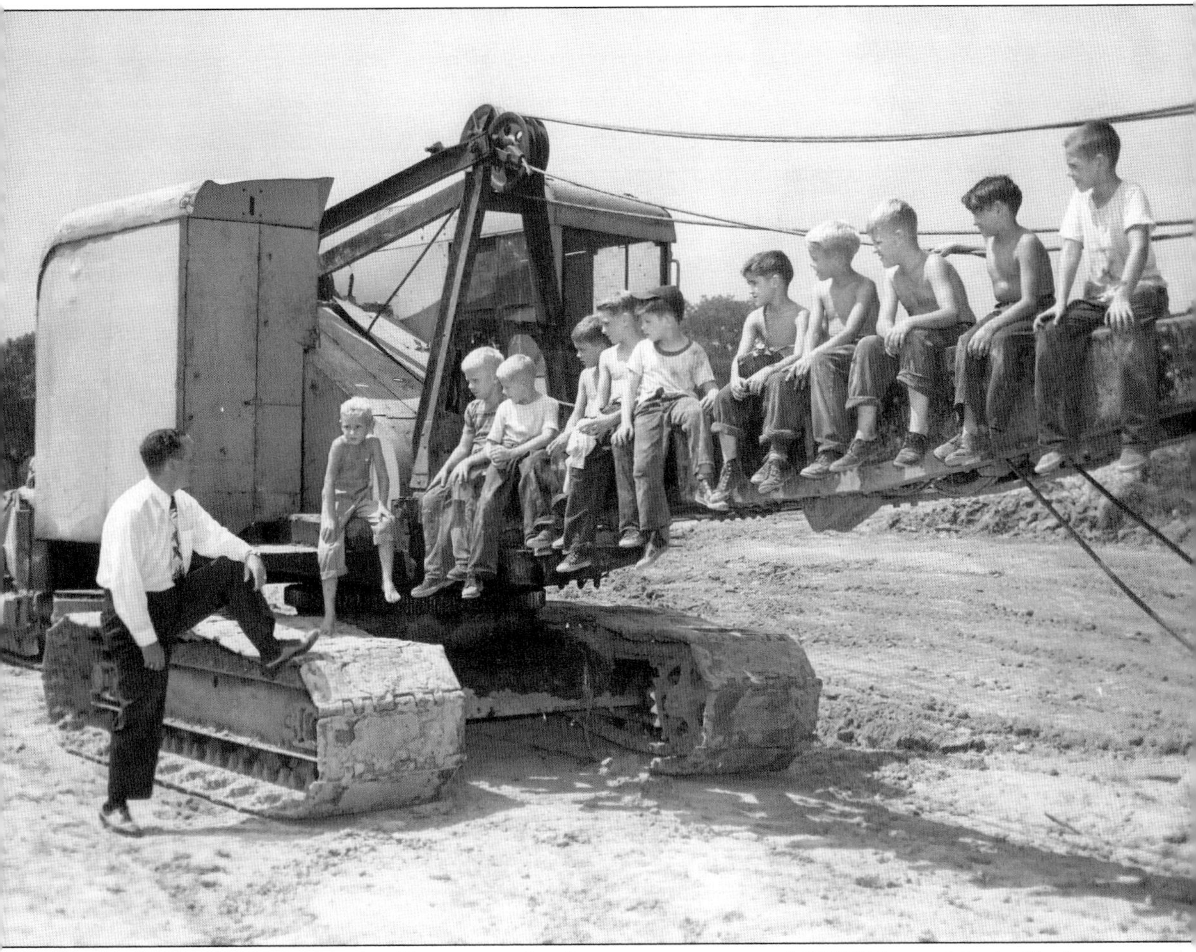

Adopting huge excavators and booms as playthings gave a group of GPOH boys a big thrill when they came to visit the building site of their new Home.

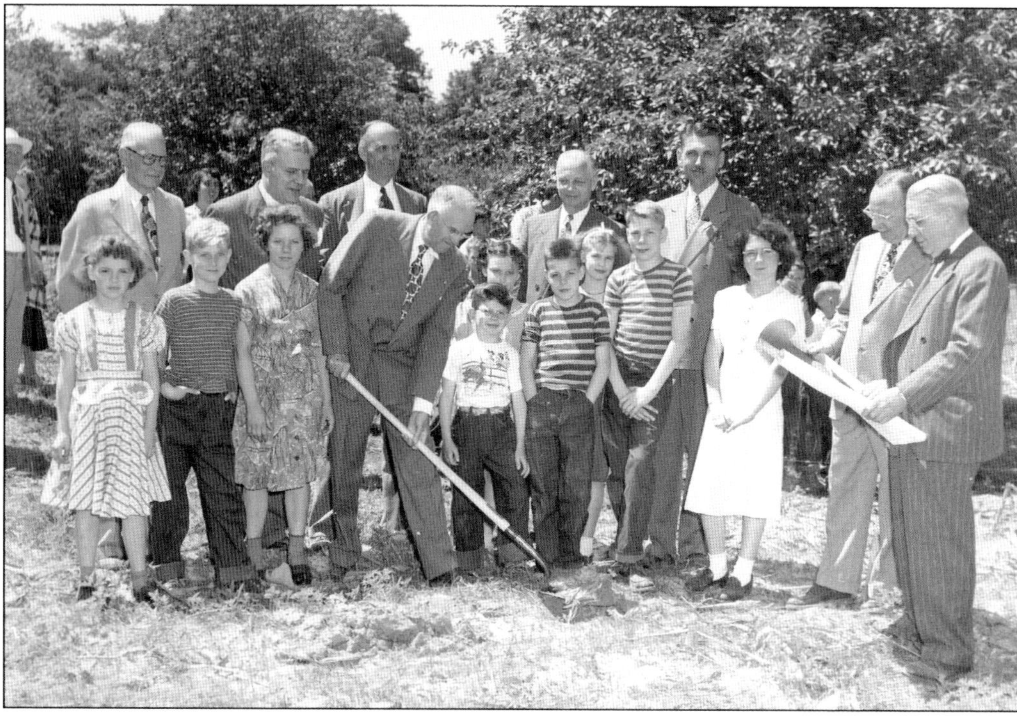

The dedication of the land and the buildings in honor of the many donors and supporters is seen here.

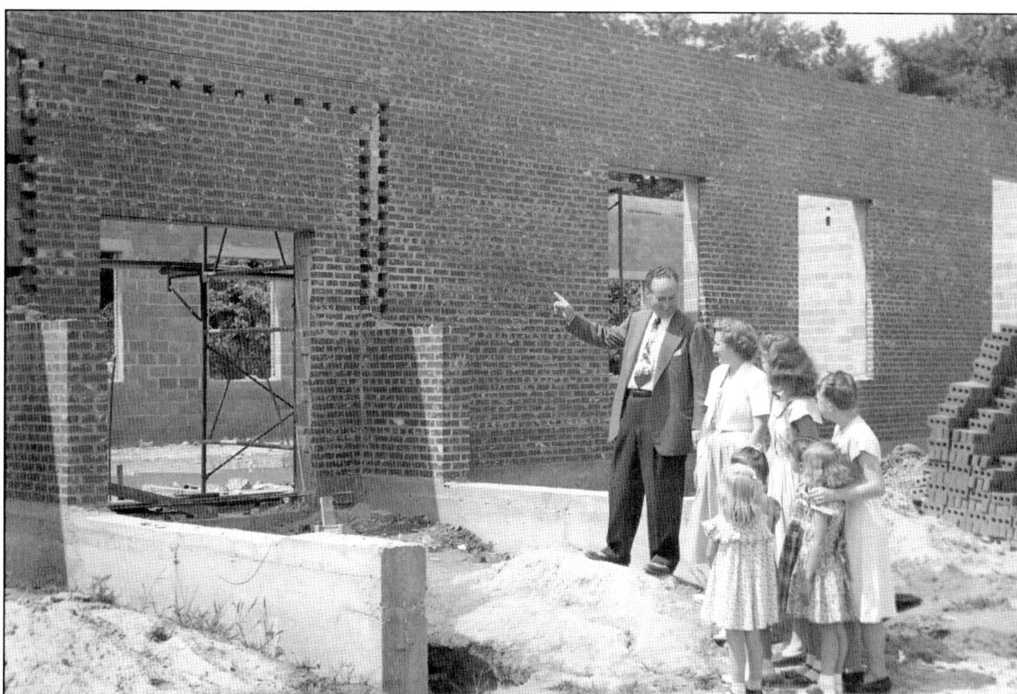

Board members show a new building of the General Protestant Orphan Home in Mount Washington to a group of children from the Home.

The Geiger Activity Center, used by the residents for physical activities, was dedicated on the Fourth of July, 1971, exactly 120 years after the cornerstone had been placed at the Mount Auburn location when the orphan home was founded. The time capsule placed in the cornerstone (right) included a list of residents, staff, board members, committee members, and other friends of Beech Acres. Board member Andrew Hopple (below, far right) speaks at the dedication. Board members Herman Guckenberger, Phil Berghausen and wife Alma, executive director Bob Stephens, and board president C. Ross Whiting attended.

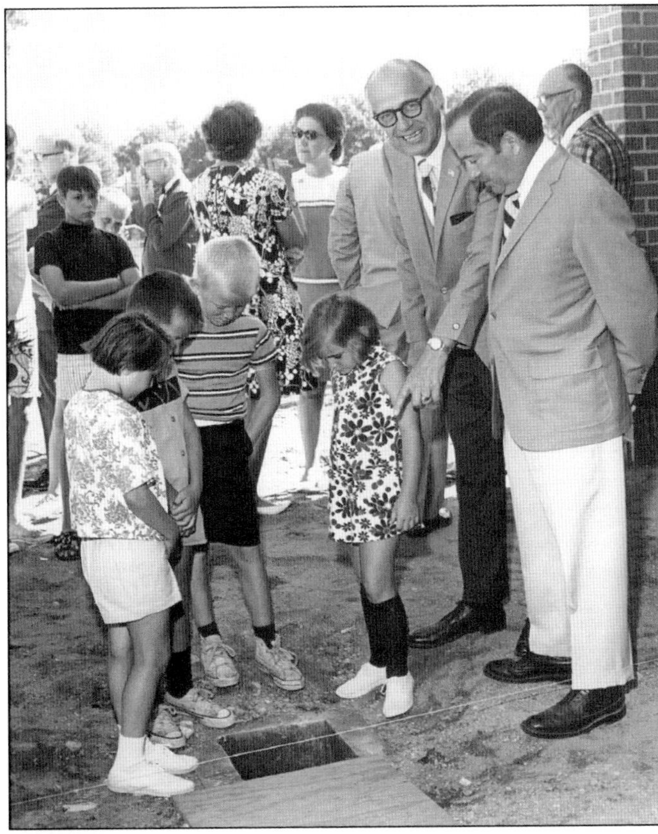

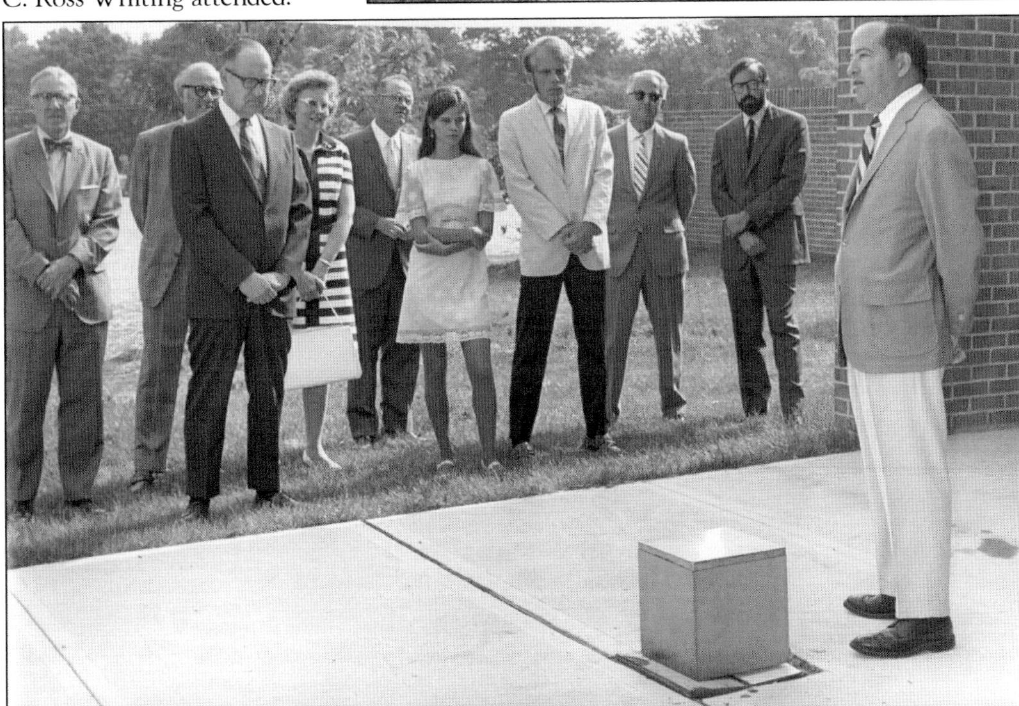

Board of Directors Presidents

Thousands of dedicated men and women have served as members of the Beech Acres Board of Directors over its 161 years. The agency's ability to shift from an orphanage, to a social services agency, to a parenting center in response to changing times is due to the mission-driven and visionary approach these volunteers have taken to their stewardship responsibility. Listed are the names of the presidents and chairs of the board of directors since 1850. Behind each has been a dedicated and hardworking group that has truly cared about the well-being of the community's children.

Weitzel, Louis	1850
Ballauf, Louis	1851–1854
Reiss, C.	1855
Ficke, Herman	1856–1857
Weitzel, Louis	1858
Klotter, George	1859
Mehner, Louis	1860–1861
Bramsche, G.F.	1862
Boss, C.	1863–1865
Wuest, Jacob	1866–1867
Kistner, E.	1868
Baker, David	1869–1870
Unnewehr, Fred	1871–1872
Kallendorf, Friedrich	1873–1874
Stegner, Henry	1875–1877
Spreen, C.F.	1878–1880
Bramsche, G.F.	1881
Gottfried, Roth	1882
Moser, J.F.	1883–1884
Koch, H. W.	1885
Kattenhorn, J.H.	1886
Kreimer, Henry	1887–1888
Gramp, Michael	1889–1890
Langhorn, Louis	1891–1892
Muth, Charles	1893–1895
Guckenberger, Charles	1896–1900
Mueller, Herman	1901–1903
Pape, H.A.	1904–1905
Ritter, Philip J.	1906–1907
Leeker, Bernard H.	1908–1909
Steinkamp, August	1910–1913
Schriefer, Edward G.	1914
Cherdon, Daniel	1915–1917
Heitz, Henry E.	1918–1936
Noell, George	1937–1938
Heitz, Arthur H.	1939–1949
Schille, Fred L.	1950–1955
Townsley, Everett W.	1956
Hammerlein, George R.	1956–1964
Whiting, Carson R.	1965–1972
Baetz, William G.	1973–1975
Guckenberger, Herman J. Jr.	1976–1979
Lishawa, Allen C.	1980
Landen, Joseph D.	1981–1984
Myers, Russell C.	1985
Whiting, Richard T.	1985–1988
Smith, Linda	1989–1990
Scoggins, Samuel	1990–1991
Hesser, Grant V.	1992–1993
Bruestle, Eric G.	1994–1995
Richards, Margaret K.	1996–1998
Uible, Woodrow H.	1999–January 2001
Berghausen, Eleanor	January 2001–June 2003
Hathaway, David	June 2003–June 2005
Bloomstrom, John C.	June 2005–June 2007
Cassady, Thomas D.	June 2007–June 2009
Morris, Ph.D., Barry H.	June 2009–

Six

The Social Service Era

By its 125th anniversary in 1974, the population of residents in the Home consisted of children whose parents were living but unable to care for them at the time. The children arriving at its doors were increasingly affected by problems brought on by modern society. In the late 1970s, orphanages nationwide started to feel the need to modernize in response to growing problems faced by the modern family. Proudly, Beech Acres became a leader in this movement.

In 1978, the first Beech Acres resident was placed in a foster home, because she did not need the intense level of oversight provided in the Home. Gradually, more children began to live with Beech Acres' foster parents in community homes. Today, the agency serves more children, more effectively, each year in well-trained foster homes than it once did when the orphanage flourished.

In the 1980s and 1990s, Beech Acres' board and staff made many courageous decisions to transform the orphanage into a social services agency. Staff leaders, in partnership with executive director Robert A. Stephens (1974–1989) and board president Joseph D. "Jake" Landen (1981–1984), advocated a shift from restorative to preventive services. Landen's steadfast belief that educating parents was central to preventing abuse and neglect and improving positive childhood outcomes led to the establishment of The Aring Institute (1982) and Cincinnati Family Center (1984). Creation of the modern Beech Acres social services agency was underway.

By 1989, Beech Acres was serving over 7,000 children and their families each year in contrast to the few hundred children that the orphanage once served. With the success of its family-focused and community-based programs, the decision was made to close the organization's 140-year-old orphanage. Board presidents Dick Whiting (grandson of Everett Townsley and son of Carson Whiting, 1985–1988) and Linda Smith (1989–1990) presided as the organization closed its historic residential dormitories and converted its programs to family- and community-based alternatives. Passionate and innovative staff members adapted the organization's excellent child-caring skills into services that would strengthen their families, thus preventing the need for placement outside their homes.

During the 1990s, all children faced increased challenges as society grew more complex. More children were showing more severe problems than ever. Beech Acres moved deeper into the social services sector under the strong leadership of board presidents Sam Scoggins (1990–1991), Grant Hesser (1992–1993), Eric Bruestle (1994–1995), Margy Richards (1996–1998), and Woody Uible (1999–2001). Innovations such as Emergency Treatment Foster Care (1991), Ujima Partial Hospitalization (1994), Creative Connections Managed Wraparound Care (1998), and the purchase of Psych Systems partial hospitalization and counseling (1998) represent a segment of the agency's immersion in community-wide efforts to prevent the growing number of at-risk children from needing more intensive and costly treatment services.

New services were created to respond to issues such as divorce and single parenting, children's behavioral health issues in schools, and child abuse and neglect. Many programs were designed to intervene earlier in a child's life, before the onset of traumatic life experiences, with the hope of preventing or delaying the need for more intensive services or a child's removal from the family.

The agency's purpose of helping children thrive remained the same, but annually thousands more children and families were served in more relevant and cost-effective ways.

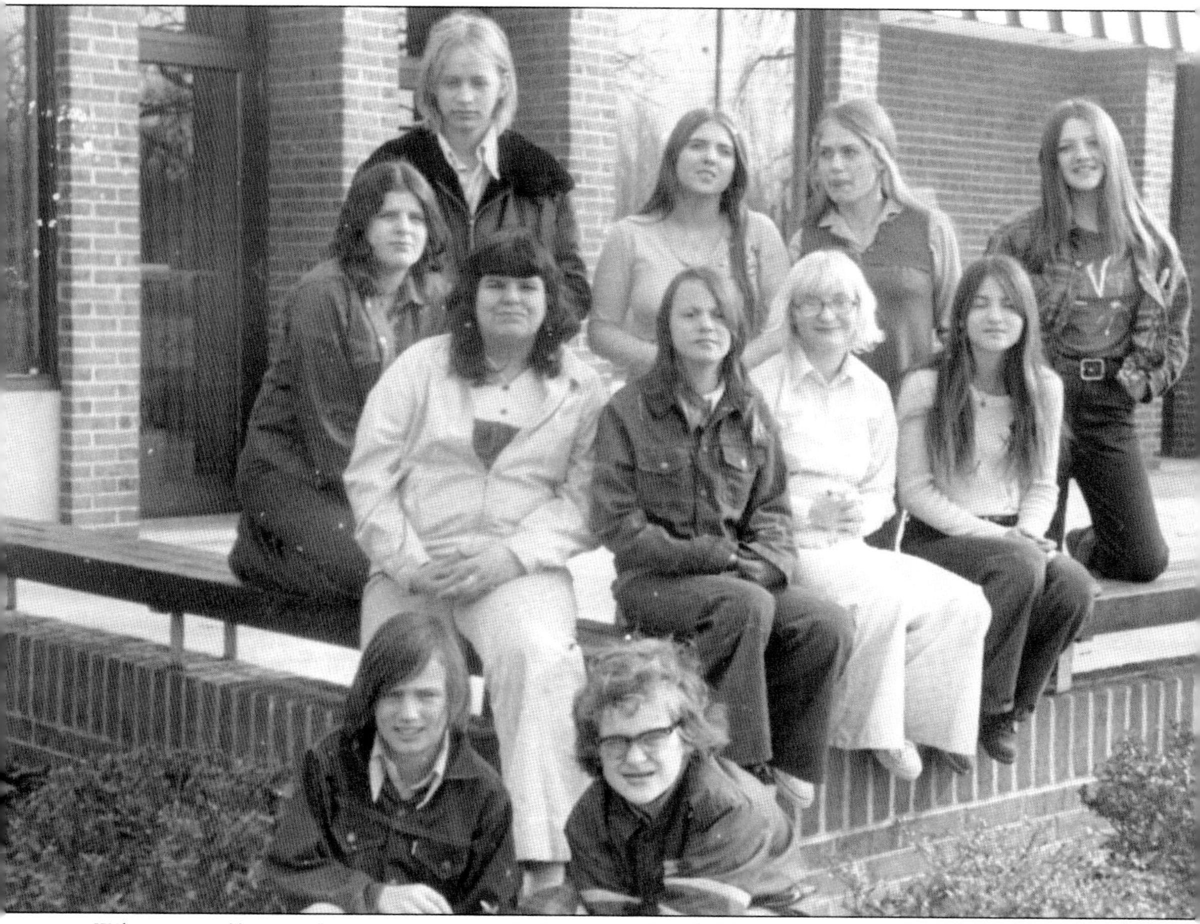

When out-of-home placement was needed, a more family-like, community-based alternative to the orphanage was sought. Foster care was the answer. It began in 1979 with the placement of two sisters who were living in the Home. A compassionate and creative social work employee of Beech Acres knew that institutional care was not what the sisters needed. She took it upon herself to recruit, license, and train a family in the community as foster parents. The girls adjusted very well to leaving the orphanage. Since then, hundreds of at-risk children have successfully been served by Beech Acres' foster parents. It has proven to be better for the children's care and treatment and a much more cost-effective use of the agency's resources than placement in the orphanage. Today, Beech Acres Parenting Center continues to provide high-quality foster-care and family-reunification services in southwest Ohio.

Joseph D. Landen, known to his friends as Jake, was board president from 1981 to 1984. He believed that to be most effective in helping families, Beech Acres should commit itself to building preventive services. Under his leadership, the organization established a goal to shift the orphanage by creating a continuum of services of which at least 50 percent would be considered preventive in nature. Jake was a driving force behind the organization's emphasis on preventive services in helping to educate families early as a means of preventing larger problems later. At right, he poses with his wife, Betty, who always appreciated Jake's innovative leadership and who remains supportive of Beech Acres Parenting Center today. Louise "Pat" Landen, inspired by her late brother Jake, continues the family legacy of involvement and support for Beech Acres Parenting Center's new innovations, such as parent-to-parent mentoring.

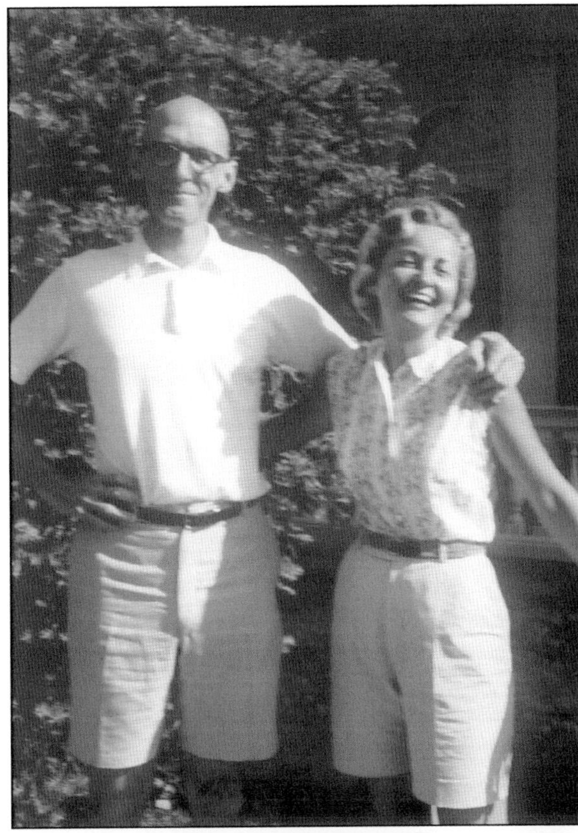

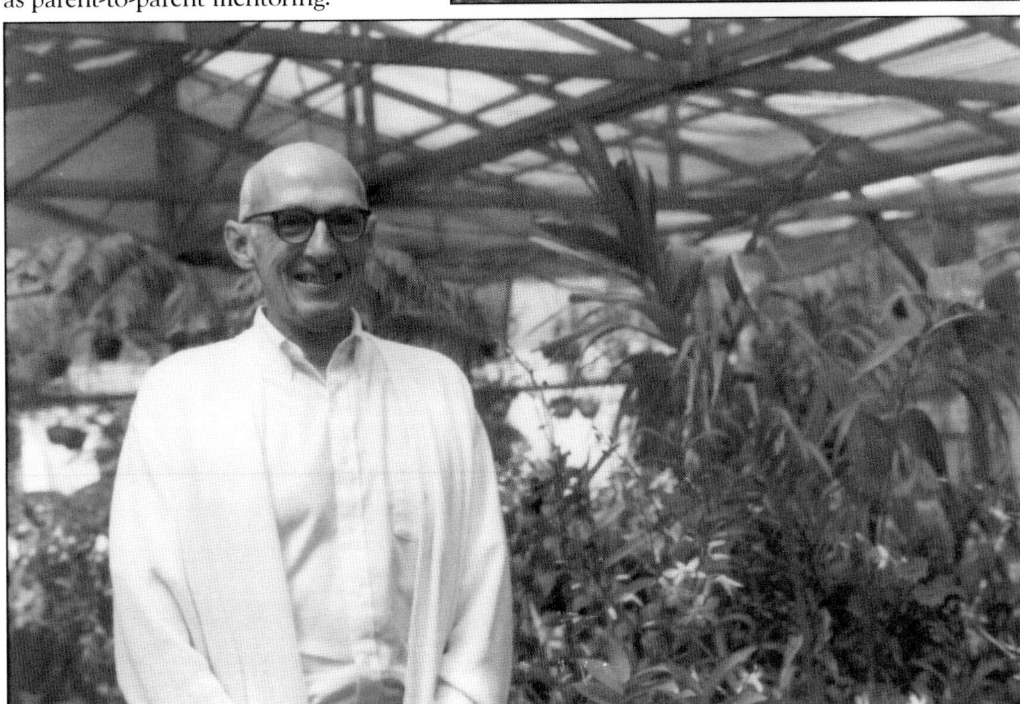

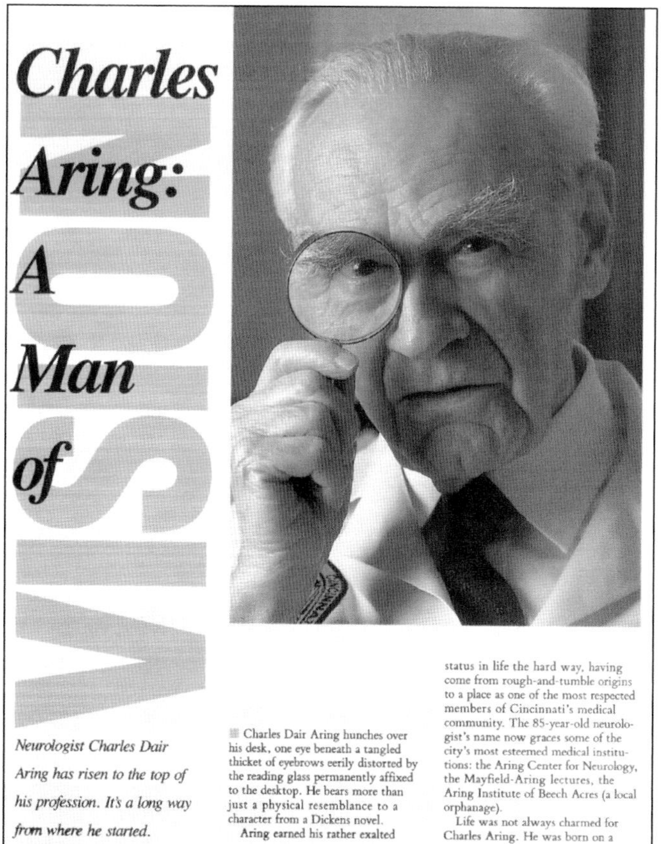

Charles Aring: A Man of VISION

Neurologist Charles Dair Aring has risen to the top of his profession. It's a long way from where he started.

Charles Dair Aring hunches over his desk, one eye beneath a tangled thicket of eyebrows eerily distorted by the reading glass permanently affixed to the desktop. He bears more than just a physical resemblance to a character from a Dickens novel.

Aring earned his rather exalted status in life the hard way, having come from rough-and-tumble origins to a place as one of the most respected members of Cincinnati's medical community. The 85-year-old neurologist's name now graces some of the city's most esteemed medical institutions: the Aring Center for Neurology, the Mayfield-Aring lectures, the Aring Institute of Beech Acres (a local orphanage).

Life was not always charmed for Charles Aring. He was born on a

Charles Aring was born in Dent, Ohio, in 1904. He survived polio as a child but lost his parents, and he entered the Home at age 7. At age 15, he began serving as errand boy and office clerk for Cincinnati General Hospital. He attended the University of Cincinnati and its College of Medicine. Dr. Aring founded the UC Department of Neurology and served as its chairman for 30 years. In recognition of his demonstrated belief in the power of education, Beech Acres named its new divorce-education program in his honor. The Aring Institute became a comprehensive education and support resource, serving over 6,000 divorcing families. The first director of the Aring Institute, Jim Mason, is seen below with staff member Joyce Virge celebrating the opening of the Aring Institute.

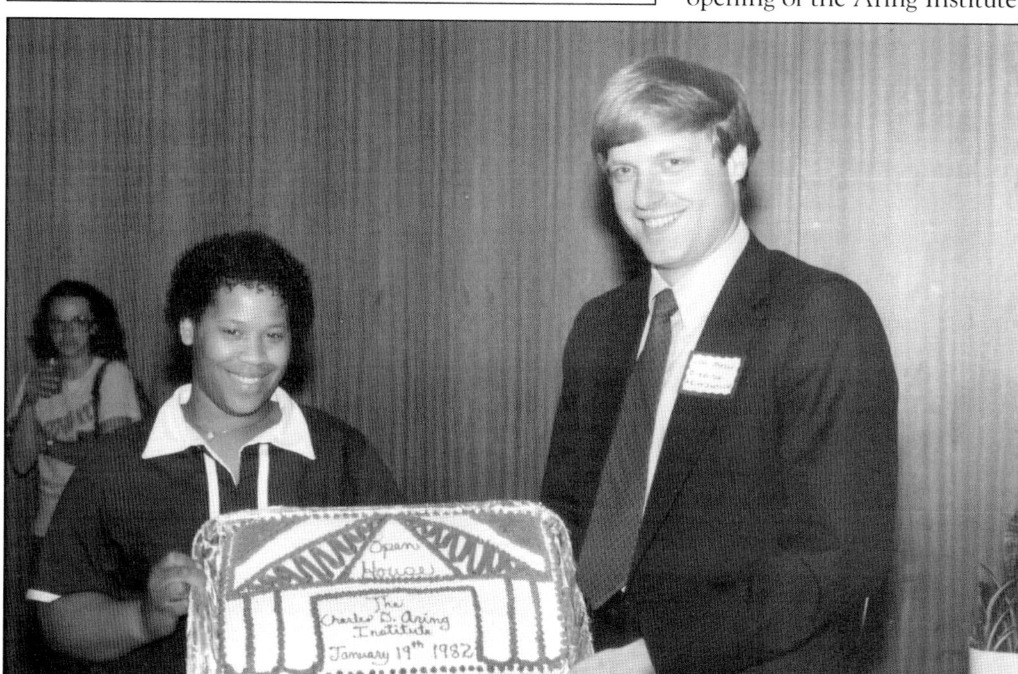

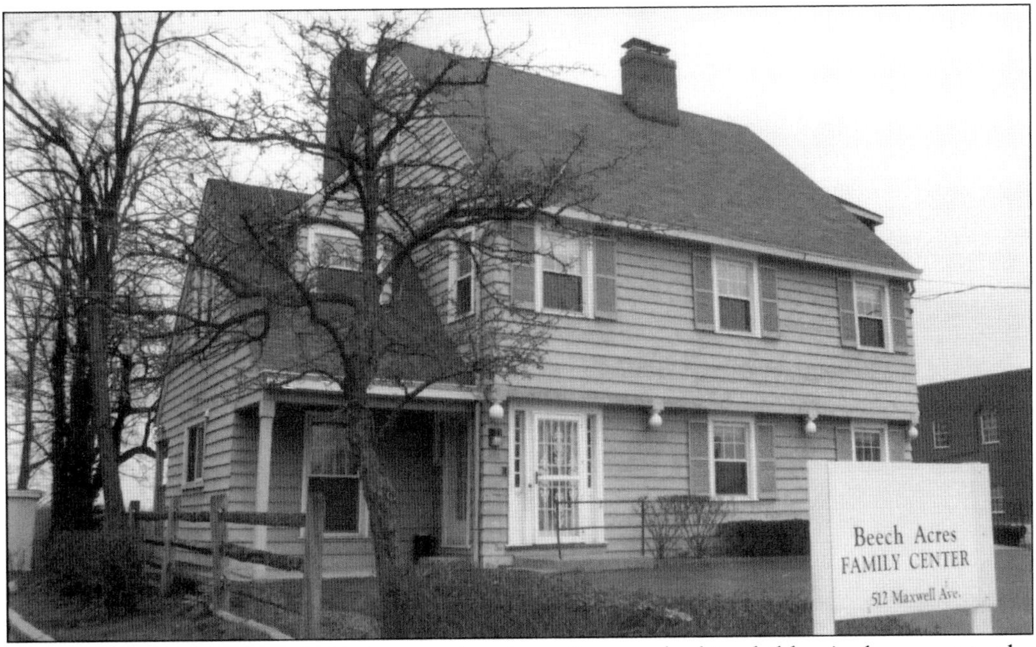

The rising tide of modern child abuse and neglect often resulted in children's placement in the orphanage. Beech Acres established the Cincinnati Family Center in 1984 to help prevent child abuse and neglect by providing a safe place for at-risk families (children and their parents) to come for respite, counseling, parenting education, and support. Thousands of families received lifesaving services each year in this converted Corryville home, fully funded by the generosity of Beech Acres' donors.

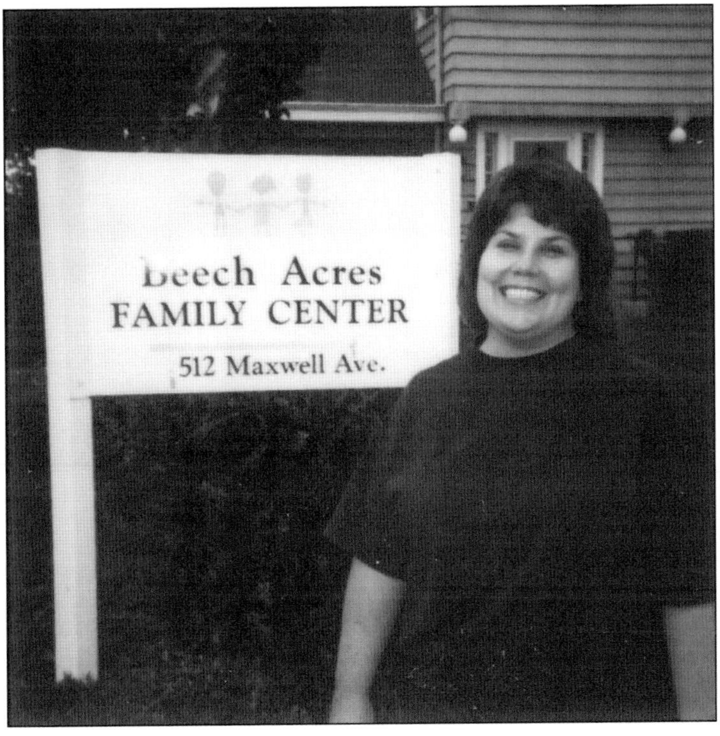

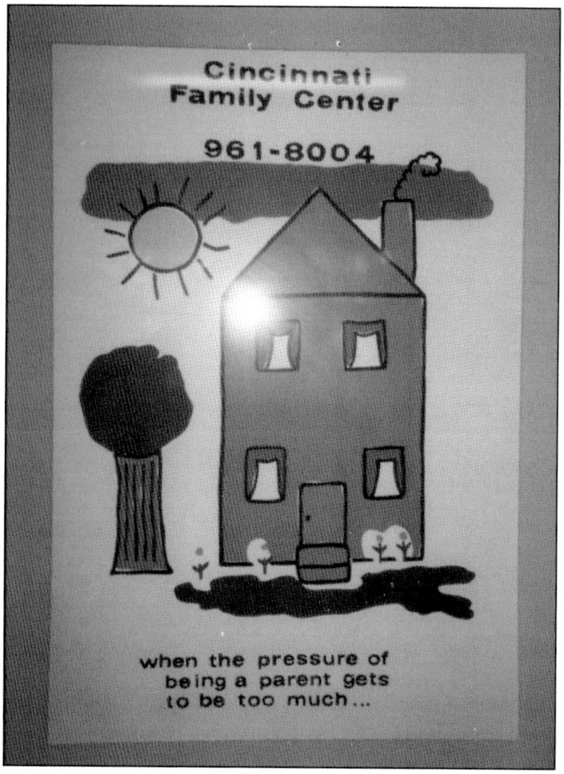

With a goal of preserving the children of at-risk families, the Beech Acres' Cincinnati Family Center opened to address the prevention of child abuse and neglect. Parents were able to find support for their own issues, and their children were provided with other support and activities. Play areas for the children were provided outside the family center. Posters advertised the Cincinnati Family Center to local churches and businesses.

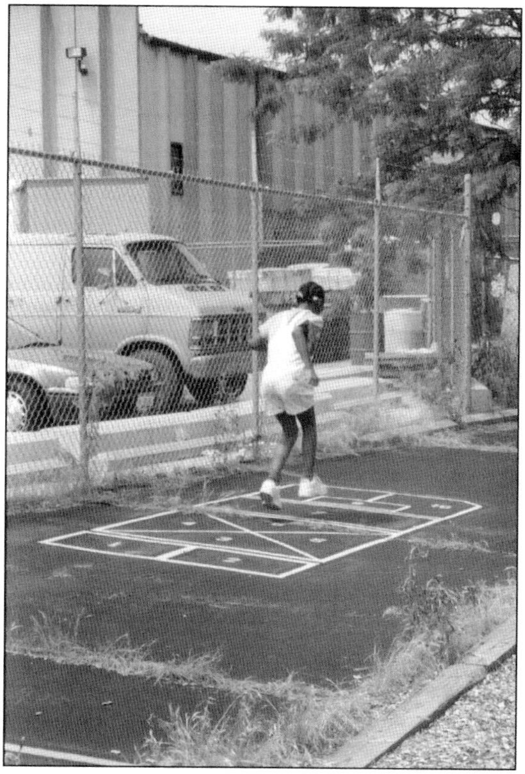

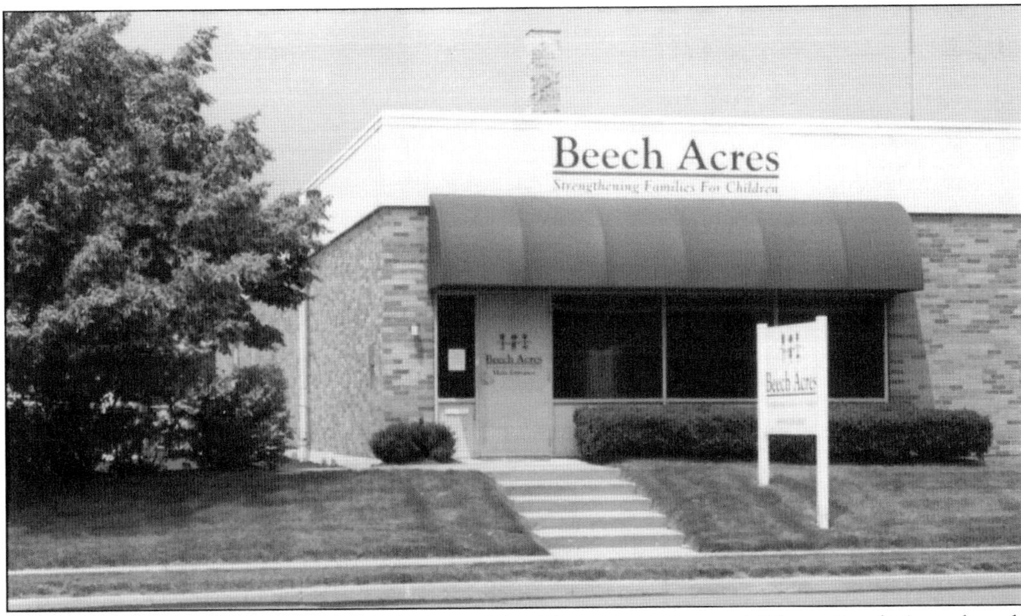

In an effort to meet the growing need for mental-health services among children, Beech Acres bought a for-profit company in 1998 and converted it to not-for-profit to provide partial hospitalization and outpatient counseling to children at risk of expulsion from Cincinnati Public Schools. Located on Dalton Street in the West End, the program drew students from a broad range of communities on the west side of Cincinnati. The program was transitioned to school-based services during the parenting center era in order to teach children and their parents the skills needed to succeed in their neighborhood schools.

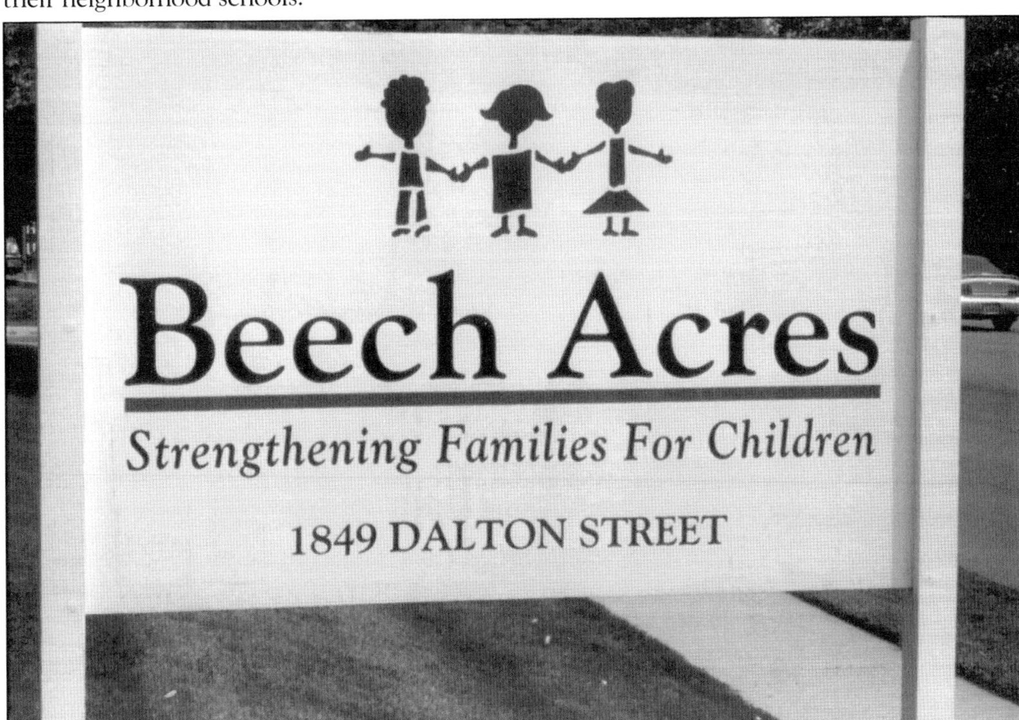

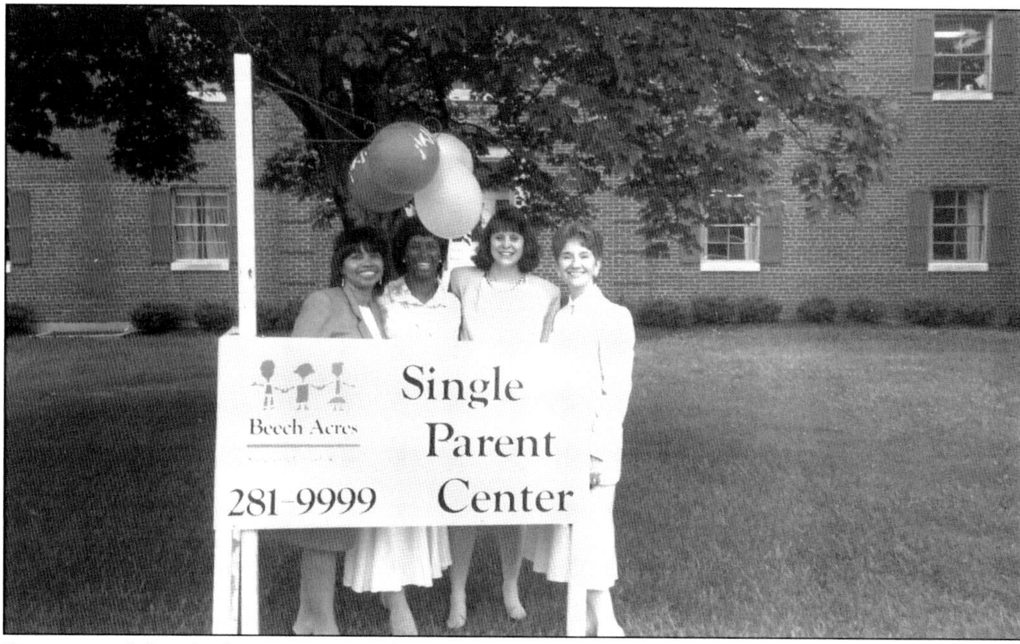

Divorce and family disruption was the second-leading cause (behind child abuse) of children's placement in the Home. The Single Parent Center was established in 1988 to support, educate, connect, and advocate for the rapidly growing number of parents rearing children alone. Barbara Fitch (below) had compassion and a vision for what single parents needed on behalf of their children. She joined the Beech Acres Board of Directors to help see her vision of the Single Parent Center become reality. Thanks to a three-year New Directions grant from the United Way, the center opened in the Walnut Hills/Avondale area. Support groups were created all over the city. The program continued long after the grant ended because of the generosity of Beech Acres' donors. Its services were eventually integrated into the larger Beech Acres Parenting Center continuum.

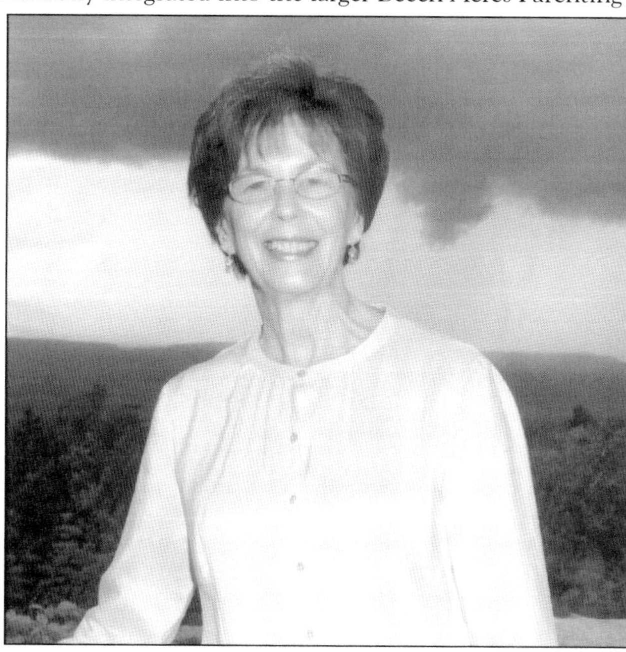

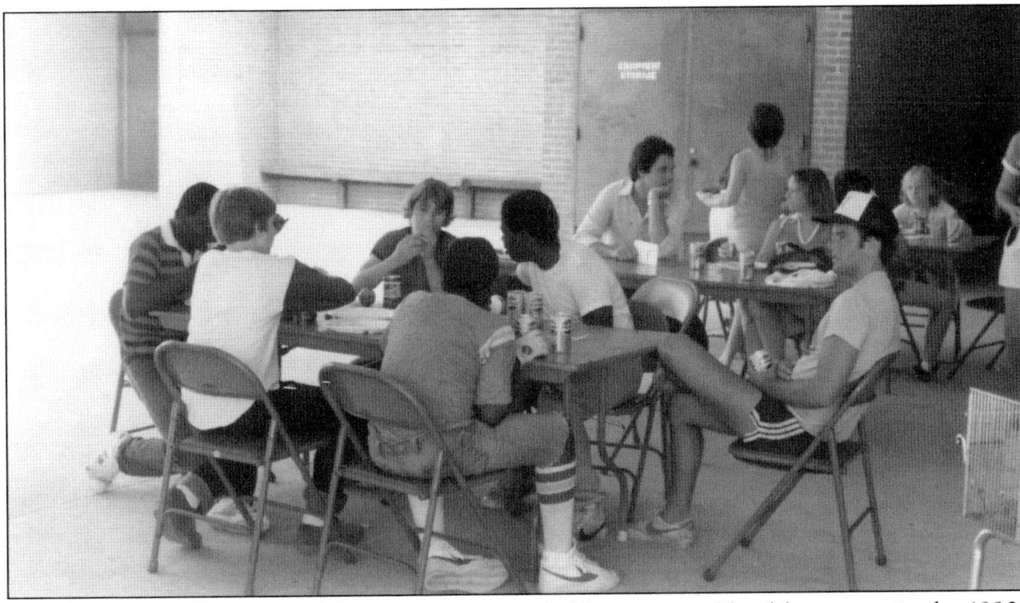

In response to the rising need for more intensive children's mental-health services in the 1990s, Beech Acres became licensed by the Ohio Department of Mental Health to deliver outpatient counseling, partial hospitalization/day treatment, medical somatic services, and community psychiatric support services. In partnership with Talbert House and Cincinnati Public Schools, the Ujima program was created in 1995. The Ujima program was designed to "wrap" customized services around each child and family, enabling them to achieve treatment goals and return successfully to the public school classroom. This included individual counseling, team building, and nonviolent conflict resolution. *Ujima* is a Swahili word meaning "collective work and responsibility."

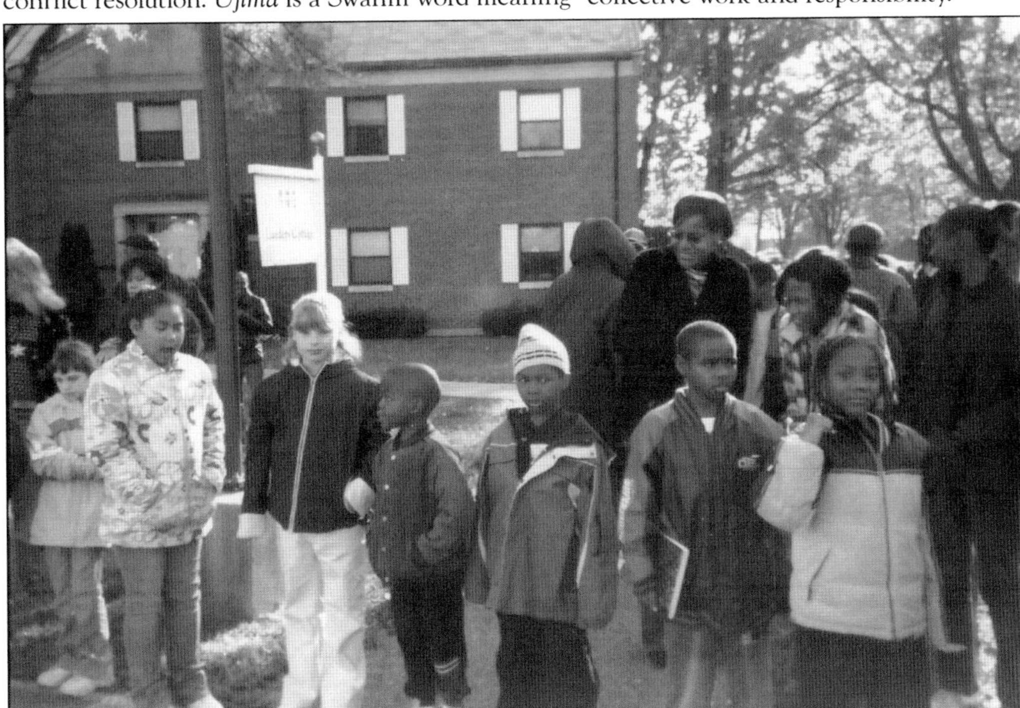

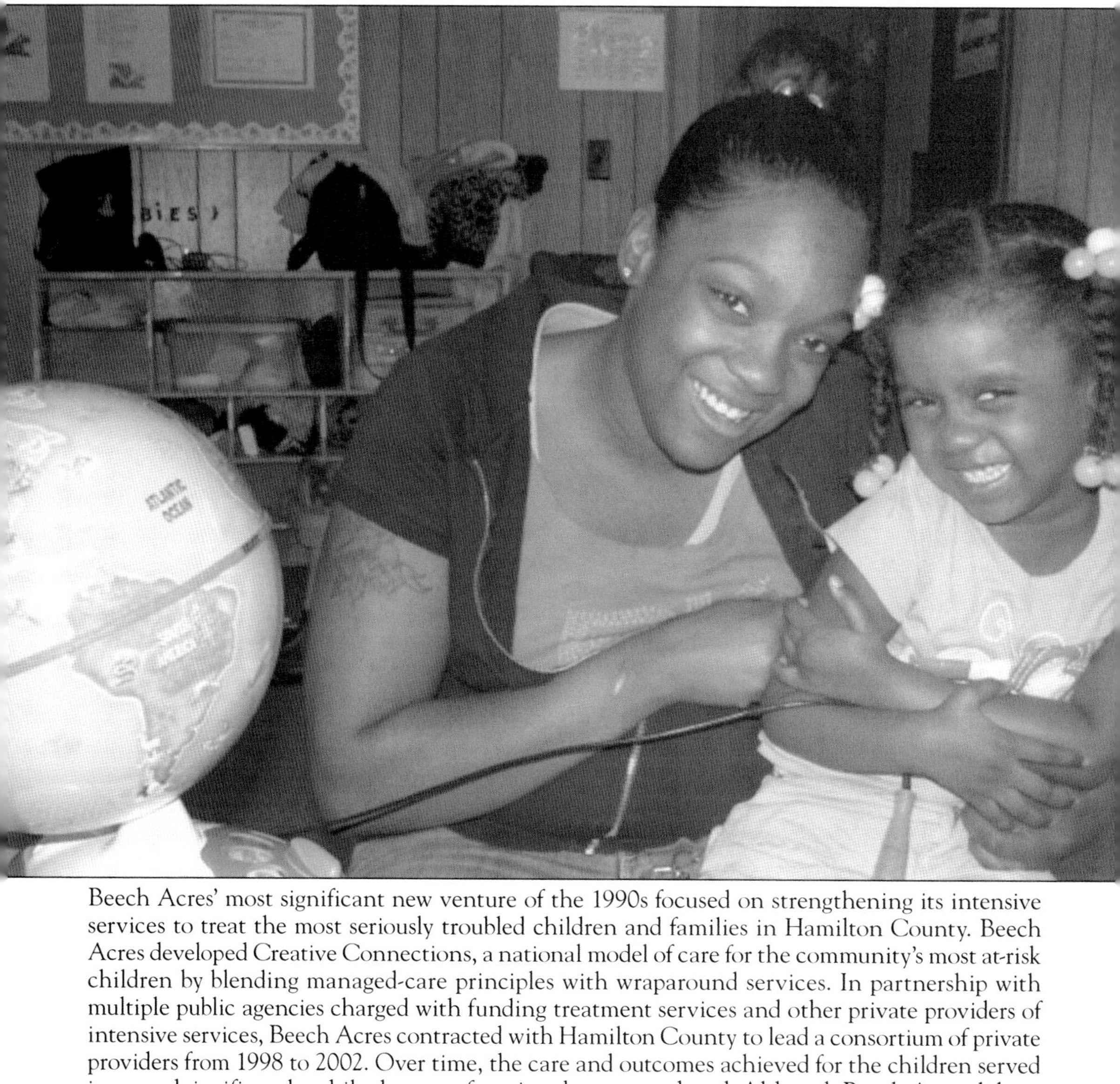

Beech Acres' most significant new venture of the 1990s focused on strengthening its intensive services to treat the most seriously troubled children and families in Hamilton County. Beech Acres developed Creative Connections, a national model of care for the community's most at-risk children by blending managed-care principles with wraparound services. In partnership with multiple public agencies charged with funding treatment services and other private providers of intensive services, Beech Acres contracted with Hamilton County to lead a consortium of private providers from 1998 to 2002. Over time, the care and outcomes achieved for the children served improved significantly, while the cost of serving them was reduced. Although Beech Acres did not renew its contract in 2002, the agency strengthened its belief in the power of parent involvement in the lives of the community's most vulnerable children.

Seven

The Parenting Center Era

Helping children grow to become capable, caring, contributing, and connected adults has been Beech Acres Parenting Center's steadfast focus since its establishment. Beech Acres has always supported the needs of children specific to their times. During the cholera epidemic in 1849, they needed an orphanage. Today, they need a parenting center.

Over the years, the board and staff learned a lot about children and their development. Generations of experience taught that *the* critical ingredient to a child's ability to thrive is the full engagement of a competent parent or dedicated adult. Whether this is a birth parent or other dedicated adult serving that role, such as a foster parent, adoptive parent, grandparent, or guardian, the relationship with a positive parenting adult is critical to every child's success.

With a mission of "Strengthening Families for Children," the parenting center was designed to support today's parents in the most challenging and important job of their lives—raising children today so they will thrive tomorrow. As a parenting center, they believe that working with children, parents, caregivers, and educators together is proactive, strengthens relationships, and helps promote sustainable learning and growth.

Intentional, strength-based parenting is Beech Acres Parenting Center's approach. Embedded into every program, it promotes clarity of vision, mindfulness, and interactions that build on each family's unique strengths. It teaches parents how to shift from being reactive to proactive.

The parenting center offers services in homes, schools, and in the community to strengthen parenting and relationship capabilities. By 2006, the strength of these programs enabled the adjustment of its name to Beech Acres Parenting Center. Modern programs include Parent Peer Support, Mediation, Parent-Child Interaction Therapy, Community Psychiatric Supportive Treatment, School-Based Services, Every Child Succeeds, Parent Coaching, Relationship Consultation, Foster Care, Family Restoration, and Parenting Education.

Success often boils down to good people doing great work together. Exceptional board leadership came from chairs Ellie Berghausen (2001–2003), David Hathaway (2003–2005), John Bloomstrom (2005–2007), Tom Cassady (2007–2009), Barry Morris (2009–2011), and Priscilla Ungers (2011–present). Their vision and ability to live the organization's values are exemplary.

Staff creativity came from all levels of the organization; formally led by Jim Mason, Diane Jordan-Grizzard, Ruthann Zins, Pam McKie, Christine Hall, Chandra Mathews-Smith, Rick Sorg, Jay Lescoe, Betty Young, and Joe Cresci, M.D., its child psychiatrist for nearly 40 years. Many others, too numerous to mention here, contributed mightily. The following pages represent a small fraction of the people and programs contributing to the modern Beech Acres Parenting Center.

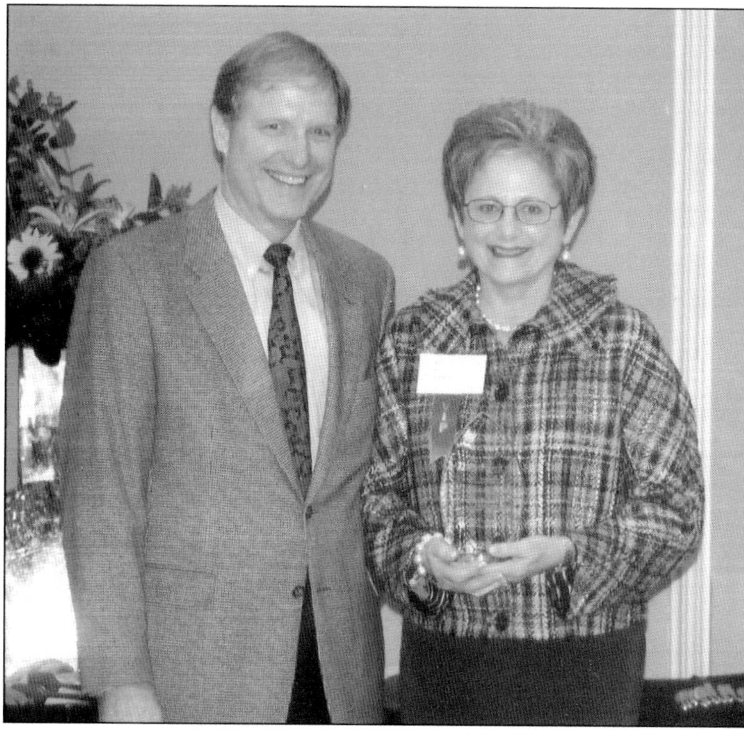

Linda Smith was Beech Acres' first female board president (1989–1990). In 1999, she co-founded For the Love of Kids® parenting conference with staff member Roseann Hassey and Procter & Gamble executive Bob Wehling to celebrate Beech Acres' 150th anniversary. Here, Jim Mason honors her at the 10th conference. The all-day conference featured multiple national, regional, and local parenting experts who provided insights, tips, and resources on topics parents ranked as most important.

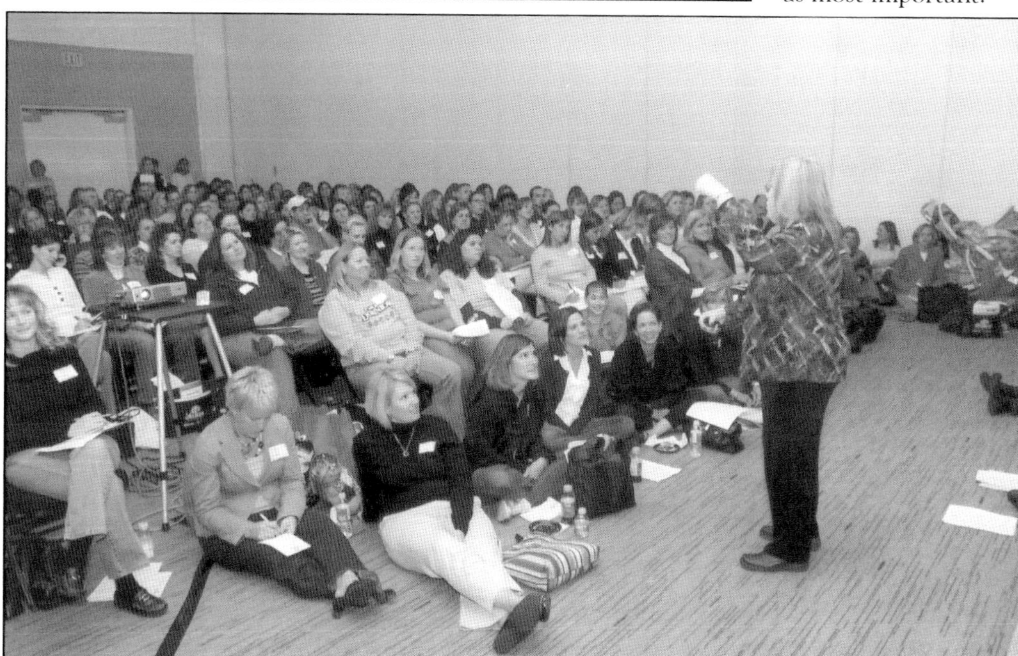

Jane Bluestein, PhD, discusses discipline with parents at a For the Love of Kids® seminar. She joins dozens of well-respected parenting experts, such as Madelyn Swift, Dr. William Sears, and Rosalind Wiseman, as a Beech Acres' favorite. Speakers enjoy Beech Acres' events because Greater Cincinnati parents are passionate and engaged. Beech Acres now provides multiple seminars throughout the year and monthly workshops in schools, businesses, and other organizations.

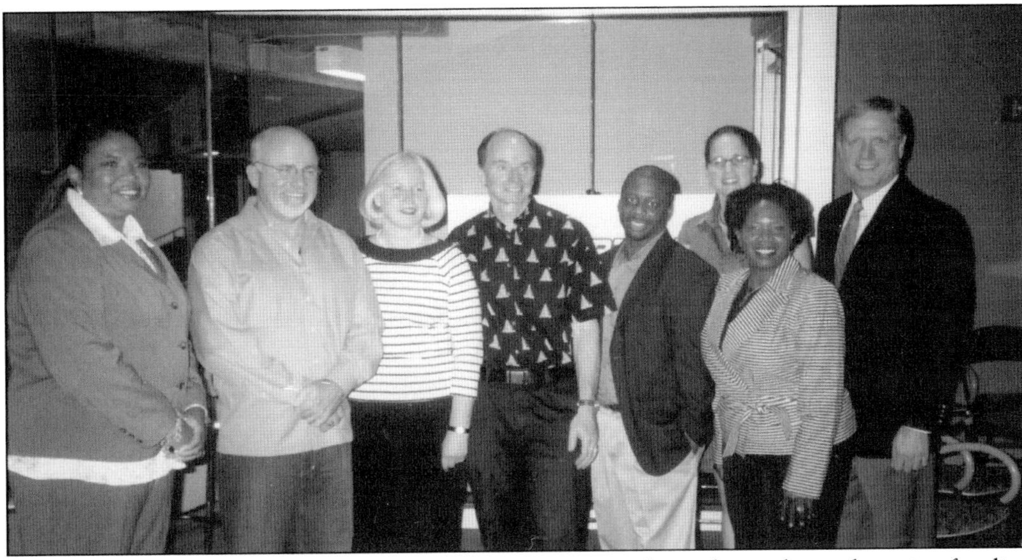

As a parenting center with a naturally preventive approach, traditional social service funding sources like government reimbursements can be challenging to attract. Strong relationships with community partners is the only way the parenting center is able to reach today's families and serve them in relevant ways. Above, Stephanie Dumas, Dave Ramsey, and Gloria and Rodger Henn partner with staff member Nate Lett, COO Diane Jordan-Grizzard, and CEO Jim Mason to spread the word about Beech Acres' Healthy Marriages and Relationships program. Below, Beech Acres' family mediators Marie Hill and Sharon James stand with Judge Michael Voris, Deborah Cadwallader, Jim Mason, and managing business director Pam McKie to celebrate the success of Beech Acres' innovative programs conducted in partnership with the Clermont County Courts. These include Mediation, Relationship Consultation, Back on Track, Helping Children Cope with Divorce, and the award-winning Access and Visitation program.

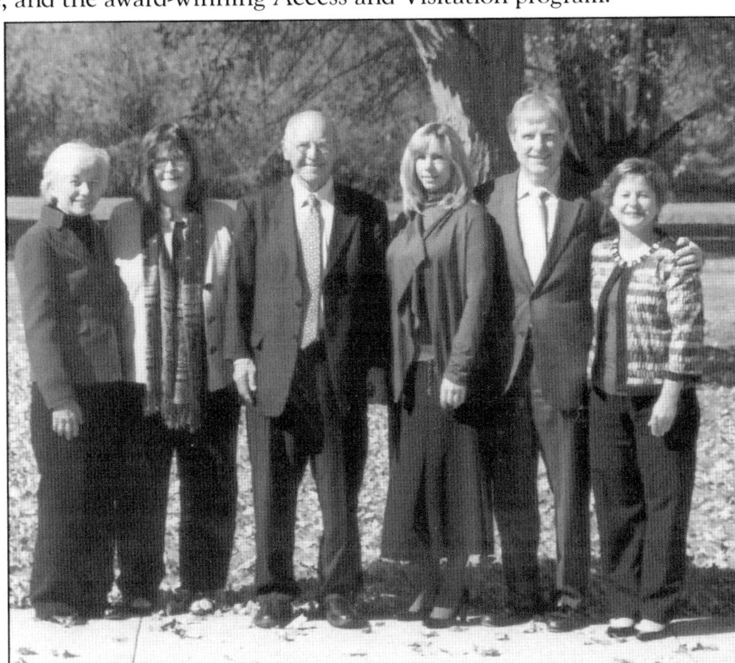

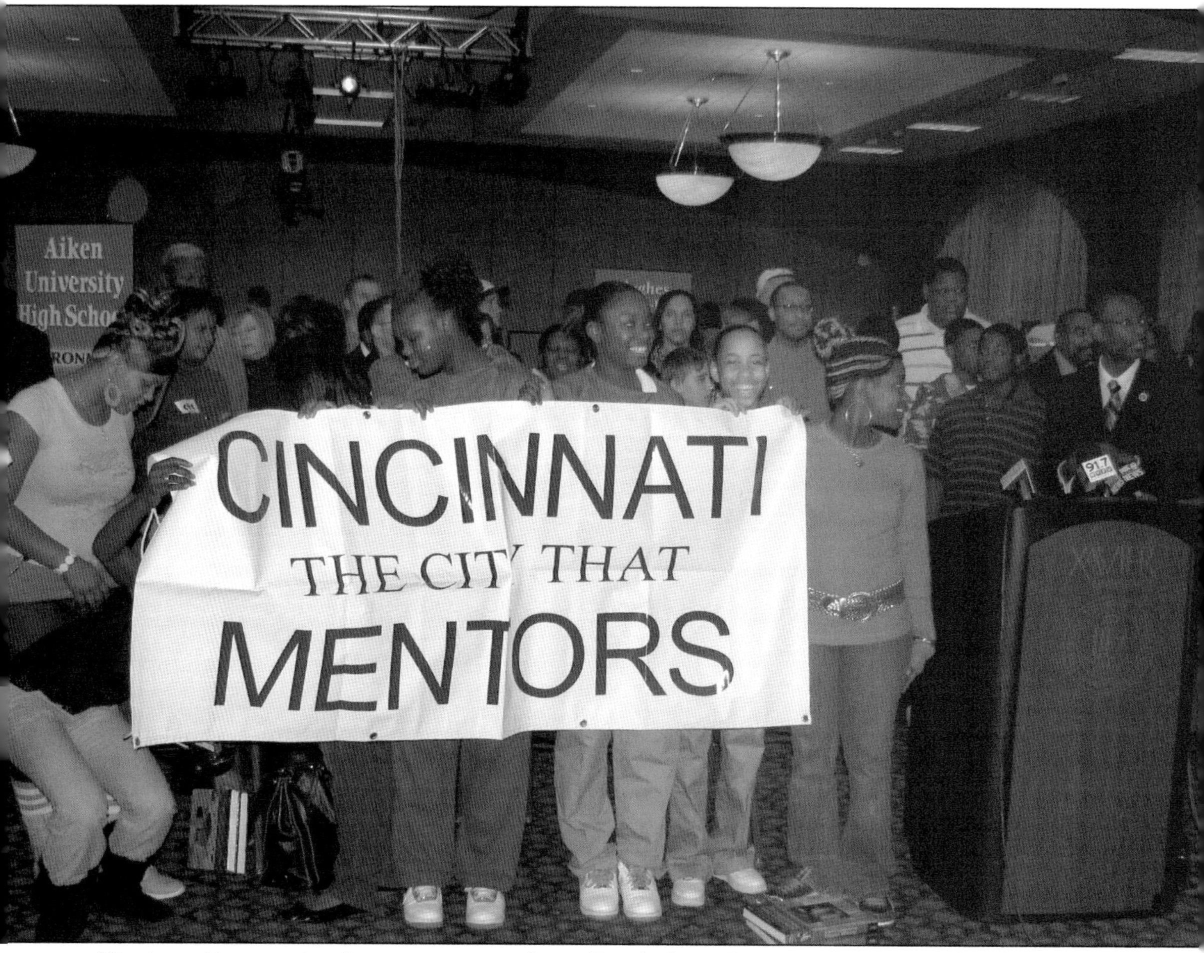

Cincinnati is committed to mentoring and so is Beech Acres Parenting Center. In this photograph, Beech Acres' Therapeutic Mentors, who aid children with behavioral, emotional, or developmental needs, participate in a citywide mentoring event. Unique to Beech Acres among providers of mentoring services is its significant investment in parent-to-parent mentoring. Family Peer Support (funded by the Hamilton County Mental Health and Recovery Services Board) connects parents who have firsthand experience navigating schools and behavioral health systems with families whose children are experiencing problems that threaten their success in school. Intensive Family Reunification (funded by Hamilton County Job and Family Services) supports the successful reunification of foster children back into their homes. Foster parents mentor birth parents or kin to help increase life and parenting skills and to build a new relationship with their children. Power in Parenting® mentors help struggling parents from their own communities.

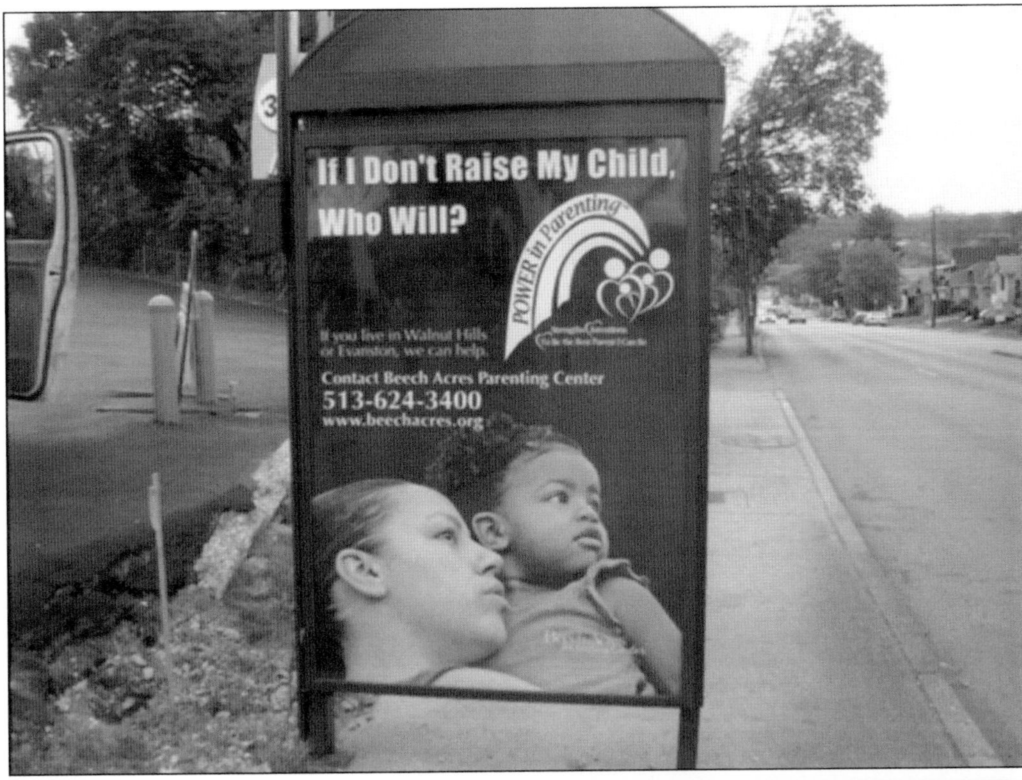

Another parent-to-parent mentoring program is Power in Parenting®. Mentors live in the same communities as the high-risk families they serve and have firsthand understanding of the issues they face. A component of Power in Parenting, funded by the United Way, focuses on preparing children for kindergarten. Some parents focus on increasing self-sufficiency, job readiness, and life skills by partnering volunteer mentors from middle-class families with low-income families working to achieve self-sufficiency. Parent Peer Mentoring can be very effective, because it reduces stigma and provides an opportunity for building strong personal connections within groups of everyday parents. Several private foundations and individuals have invested significantly in its success, most notably the Alpaugh Foundation and "Pat" Landen. At right, Jim Mason (holding cup) recognizes Peter Alpaugh (whose belief in the power of parenting is second to none) for his family's steadfast support.

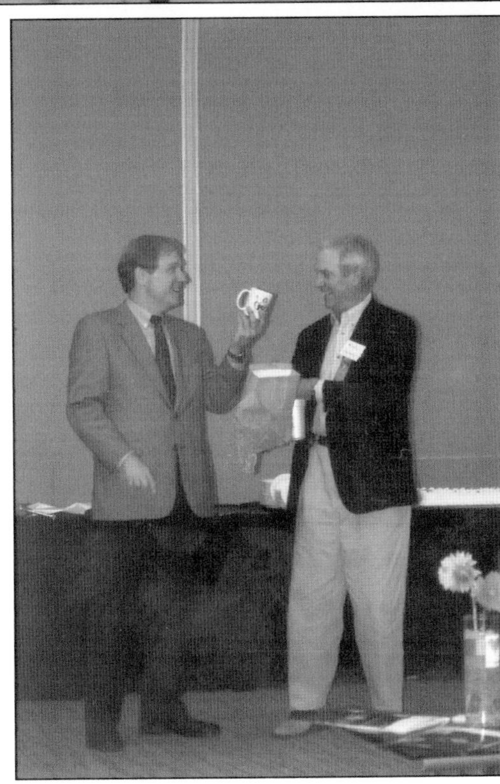

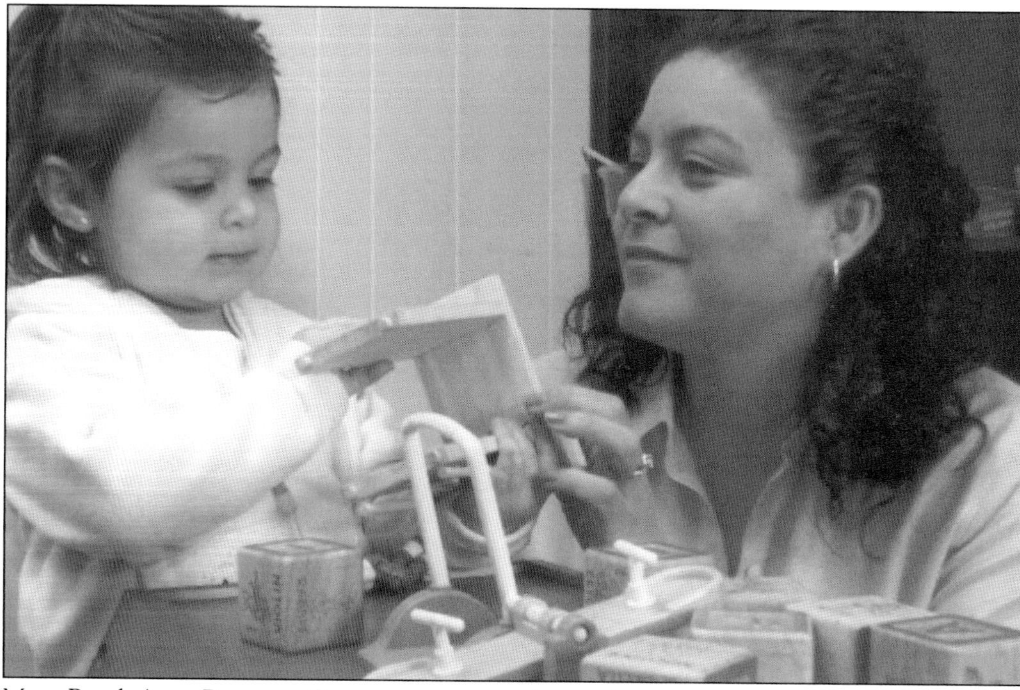

Many Beech Acres Parenting Center programs are designed to intervene early in a child's life before major disruptions have occurred when warning signs may be present. Parent-Child Interaction Therapy (PCIT) teaches caregivers specific behavior-management techniques as they play with their child to improve relationships and increase positive behaviors. Caregivers are coached in specific play therapy and discipline skills by a therapist through an earpiece while the therapist observes the caregiver and child. The program teaches parents how to connect with, and direct, their children in positive and effective ways. In 2009, Beech Acres Parenting Center's PCIT was featured in the national PBS documentary *Cry for Help* to show how some parents are starting early and intentionally building a strength-based relationship with their children from an early age.

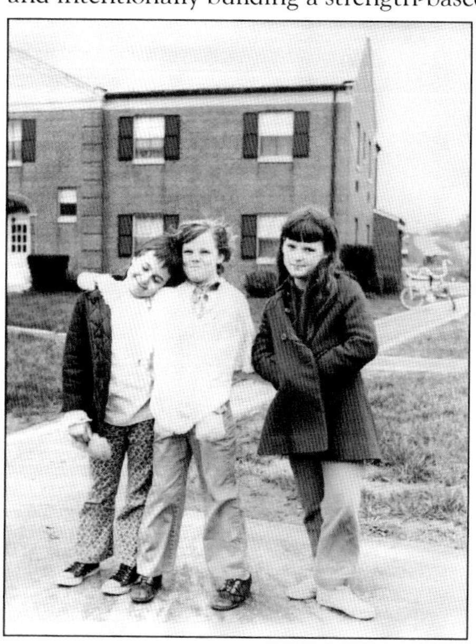

Helping Children Cope with Divorce was created to prevent children from getting caught between their parents during the typical divorce process. This three-hour seminar, mandated by both Clermont and Hamilton County Courts of Domestic Relations, helps divorcing parents understand the emotional and psychological effects of divorce on themselves and their children. It teaches common-sense tools for keeping children out of the middle and providing as much stability as possible during what is one of the most difficult transitions of their young lives.

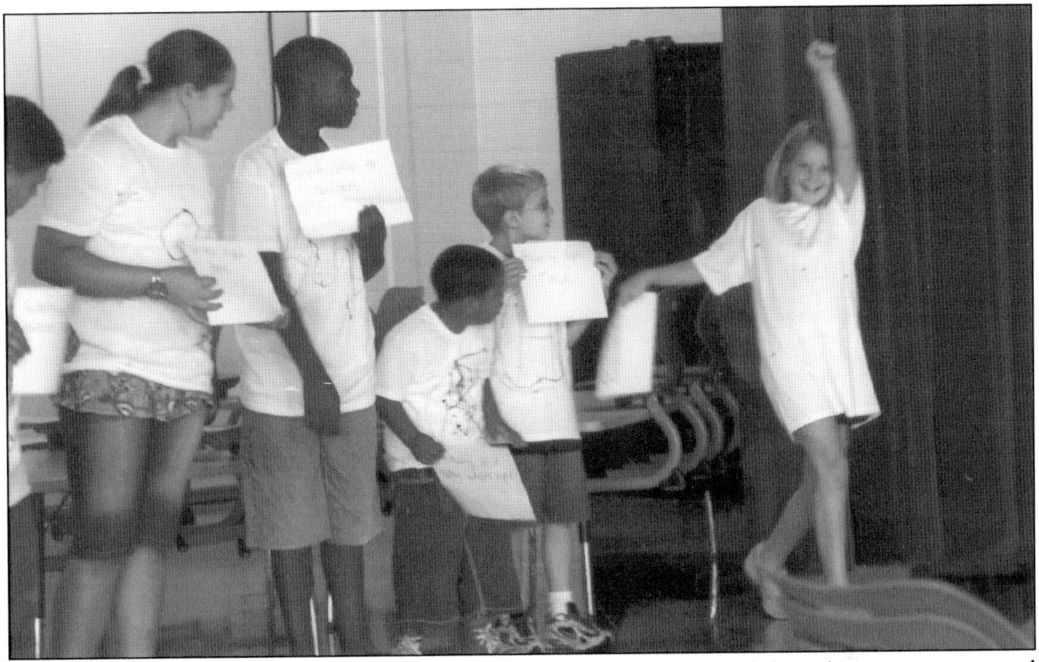

Beech Acres Parenting Center builds partnerships with schools, faith-based organizations, and other community resources to ensure the success of children in school and the community. Its comprehensive menu of school-based services includes counseling, crisis support, diagnostic assessment, mediation, parenting education and engagement, peer mentoring, prevention/group services, professional development for teachers and staff, psychiatric assessment, and therapeutic mentoring for children. The focus is always to build the skills and attitudes children need to enhance their school performance while assisting their parents and school personnel to become helpful resources to their children. Beech Acres provides its full continuum of services in several schools where agency staff members are located to serve as a connection between the school, community resources, and the parent/family. In other schools, specific components are selected. Parent engagement is a critical element for all Beech Acres programs.

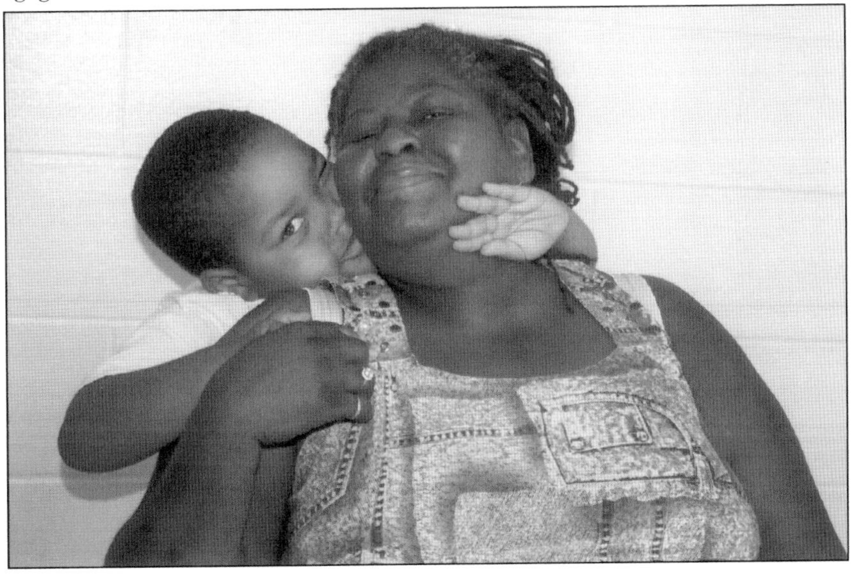

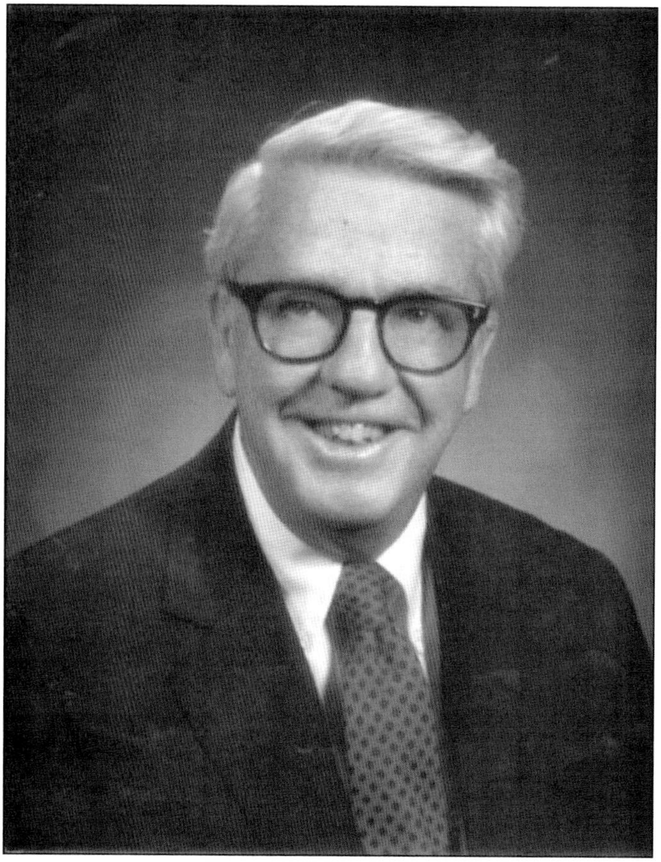

The list of leaders and contributors of talent, time, and treasure to Beech Acres' success is so long it would require a book of its own to ensure proper acknowledgement. Humbly, a few are mentioned here as examples of hundreds of others. Former member of the board of directors, the late Robert C. Schiff Sr. (left) and his wife, Adele, passed their legacy of investing in Beech Acres innovative services to their sons, Bob, Jr. and Jim, and their families. Chandra Mathews-Smith and Jim Mason (below) honored several supporters on National Philanthropy Day. Pictured in attendance are, from left to right, Mathews-Smith, Mason, Les and Priscilla Ungers (vice chair, board of directors), Mary and Don Dufek, and Peter Alpaugh; Dr. Arthur Nadler and Marianne Rowe were also honored but not shown here.

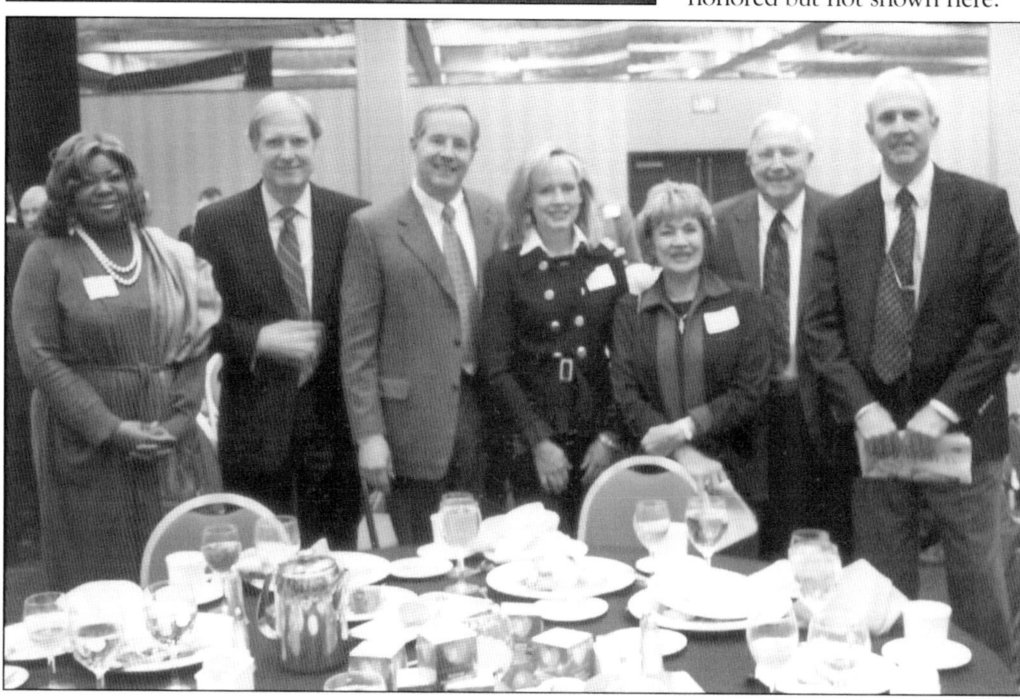

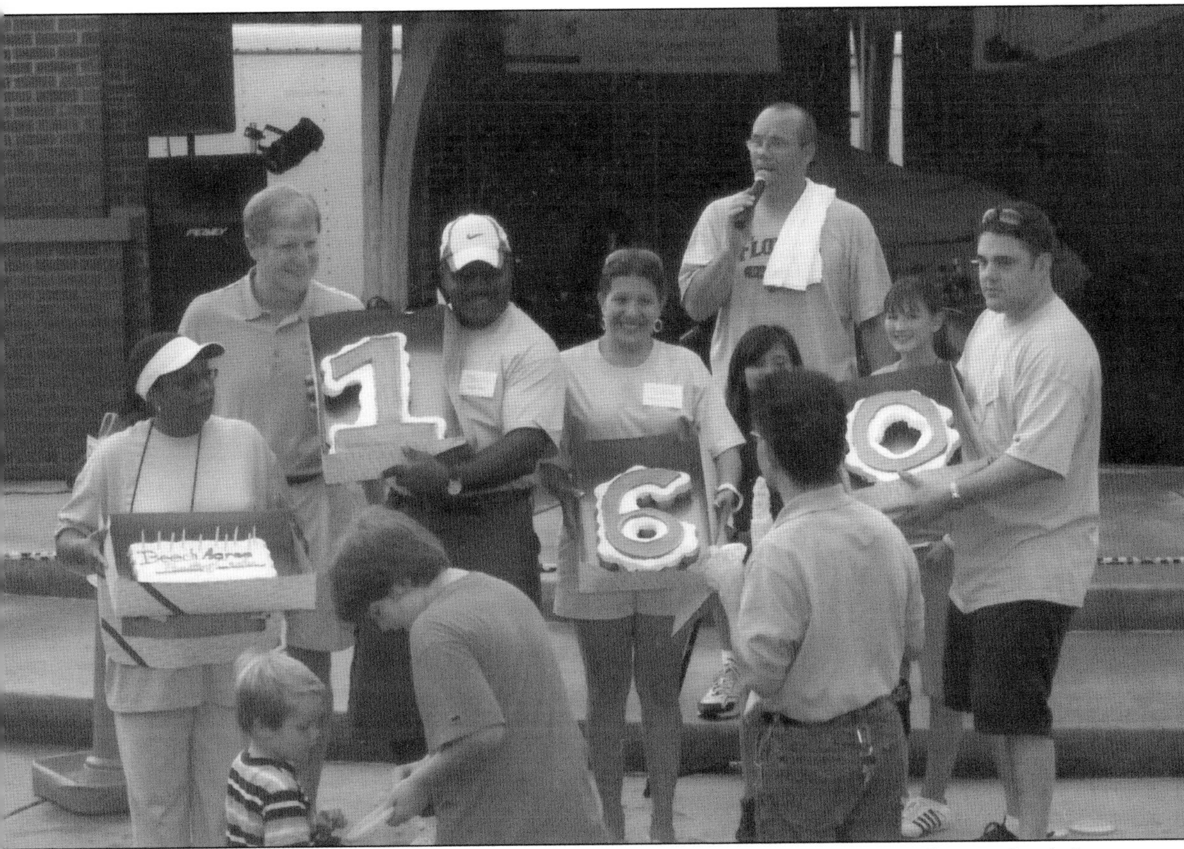

One hundred sixty years young and still growing! The organization's recent milestone birthday party provided a fitting opportunity to reflect upon its rich heritage and imagine its future legacy. Staff members Betty Young, Jim Mason, Robert Bell, Natasha Rezaian, and Mathew Rood serve 160 cupcakes to children during the party. Beech Acres Parenting Center draws strength and wisdom from its enduring core purpose—preparing children to become capable, caring, contributing, connected adults. It maintains its relevance today by valuing high-quality services, innovation, and continuous learning. Because of the depth of the community's support and realization that helping children thrive today ensures a hopeful future for everyone tomorrow, Beech Acres Parenting Center eagerly anticipates another 160 years in pursuit of its mission of "Strengthening Families for Children"!

Consistent with our mission to preserve history on a local level, this book was printed in South Carolina on American-made paper and manufactured entirely in the United States. Products carrying the accredited Forest Stewardship Council (FSC) label are printed on 100 percent FSC-certified paper.

MADE IN THE USA